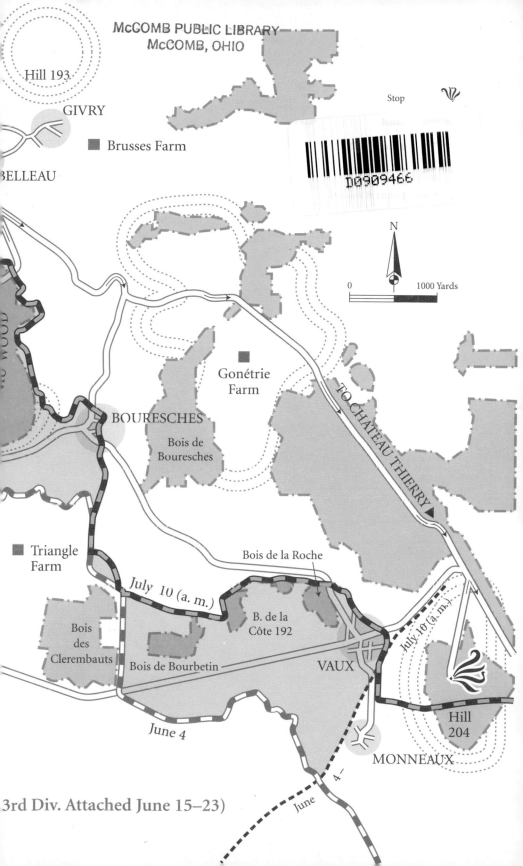

Hill 193

GIVRY

Brusses Farm

BELLEAU

Stop

N

0   1000 Yards

Gonétrie
Farm

BOURESCHES

Bois de
Bouresches

TO CHATEAU THIERRY

Triangle
Farm

Bois de la Roche

July 10 (a. m.)

July 10 (a. m.)

Bois
des
Clerembauts

B. de la
Côte 192

Bois de Bourbetin

VAUX

Hill
204

June 4

MONNEAUX

June 4

3rd Div. Attached June 15–23)

Alan Axelrod

Best-selling author of *Patton on Leadership*

Miracle at Belleau Wood

The Birth of the Modern U.S. Marine Corps

THE LYONS PRESS

Guilford, Connecticut

An imprint of The Globe Pequot Press

The Lyons Press is an imprint of The Globe Pequot Press.

10 9 8 7 6 5 4 3 2 1

Printed in the United States of America

ISBN: 978-1-59921-025-4

Library of Congress Cataloging-in-Publication data is available on file.

For Anita and Ian

▪ Contents ▪

▪ Introduction ▪

A Patch of Woods

*And, waking or sleeping, I can still see before me the dark threat
of Belleau Wood, as full of menace as a tiger's foot, dangerous as a
live wire, poisonous with gas, bristling with machine guns, alive
with snipers, scornfully beckoning us to come on and be slain,
waiting for us like a dragon in its den. Our brains told us to fear it,
but our wills heard but one command, to clean it out, and I can
still see before my very eyes those waves in the poppy-spattered
wheat-field as the steady lines of our Marines went in.*[1]

—Colonel Albertus W. Catlin, U.S. Marine Corps, 6th Marine Regiment

By spring 1918 the world was nearly used to being a world at war. After
four years, it had grown accustomed to the killing machine, almost as if
it were a fixture of nature, like a thunderstorm that rarely let up or an earth-
quake that would not cease upheaval. But none of it was ever really natural,
of course. It was a machine, a filthy, muddy, bloody machine of vast extent.
Its western front stretched in a network of trenches from the English Channel in the north some six hundred miles south to the border of Switzerland.
Into these ditches were fed the young men of Europe and Europe's
colonies—and, more recently, of America as well—65,038,810 in all, of
which 8,020,780 emerged as corpses.

Four years of boots, bombs, shells, and rain had churned much of
Belgium and France into a glutinous mud indistinguishable from the

mud-dun uniforms of the young warriors who contended for this ugly ground. By 1918, with the United States in the struggle, the Great War (as it was then called) had become truly a *world* war, and it was now increasingly difficult to find a place on the planet untouched by the conflagration. Yet, in France, on the western front, no more than two score miles east of Paris, at the very seam of the inferno, there was such a place, even in the spring of 1918. It was called the Bois de Belleau, Belleau Wood.

Nearby, the village of Belleau, along with other towns and villages and farms, had been scarred by the combat that had swirled around them, but the woods—an ancient hunting preserve, the domain of a wealthy Parisian sportsman whose château lay just within it—was virtually untouched. It had not been purposely preserved but was somehow overlooked by the forces of destruction. Amid the chaos it was, in fact, a profoundly peaceful place, darkly green with old-growth trees, its paths overgrown, its underbrush wild, a place of lichen and mushrooms, of soil almost intoxicating with the rich, loamy fragrance of fertility. The boundaries of Belleau Wood were difficult to discern, since its shape was organic, reminding some of a kidney and others of a seahorse. In extent, the place was little more than a mile north to south, and at its widest, east to west, perhaps a thousand yards across—about half the size of New York City's Central Park.

Not that Belleau Wood was any manicured park. It was, rather, a concentration of thick woods rising over a heavy blanket of undergrowth. On its perimeter were fields chest-high with winter wheat, the kind of crop that shines in the sun as if some caring, patient hand had polished each stalk individually. Those glistening fields separated the southern end of the woods from the villages of Lucy-le-Bocage to the west and Bouresches to the east.

It was an ancient forest, mostly innocent of the ax; for wild as it was, Belleau Wood had never been a source of lumber or firewood but a place of recreation and pleasure, a place of sport, the domain of the Saturday hunt, civilized, none too strenuous, gentlemen shooters bagging some birds, some game, all to be prepared in the château scullery that very evening and enjoyed, among weekend guests from Paris, with several bottles of very fine wine from the master's cellars. It was, then, a tiny forest of very old growth, split by streams, gullies, and ravines, and punctuated by boulders the size of (as the Americans would say) railroad boxcars. Small game and game birds abounded in this place, a place known before the war chiefly to the privileged few who were guests of the château, and during the war, a place neglected.

Shortly before the spring of 1918, cool, dark Belleau Wood, named for the clear, icy spring nearby, had been the quiet heart of what seasoned commanders called a "quiet sector," a corner of the war reasonably close to the fight but in which little had happened and even less was expected to happen. By the time the U.S. Marines arrived at the end of May 1918, however, tranquil Belleau Wood had been transformed into a "dark threat . . . as full of menace as a tiger's foot, dangerous as a live wire, poisonous with gas, bristling with machine guns, alive with snipers,"[2] a dragon's den, beckoning entry, promising death. It was as if the lovely woods had fallen under a curse. And so, like much of the world beyond it, it had.

There had been a time when soldiers did not hug the earth in mud-dun uniforms but paraded in bright cloth and gleaming brass, a time when statesmen were full of big plans and rational words. Of those statesmen, Germany's famed Iron Chancellor, Otto von Bismarck, was the most important. In 1871, he forged from a collection of petty states a unified Germany in the wake of Prussia's quick victory over France in the Franco-Prussian War. This new Germany would be fueled on coal from the Alsace-Lorraine, the territory France had given up as a condition of its ignominious surrender. Bismarck understood that Germany's territorial acquisition would create a lasting enmity with France, and so he played all Europe like a chessboard, acting to isolate France from any potential allies by binding Russia and Austria-Hungary to the strong, new Germany. France and Russia played their own games, however, and by the end of the nineteenth century, formed an alliance against Germany and Austria-Hungary. Up to the beginning of the twentieth century, Britain managed to remain outside the entangling web of European alliances and enmities, maintaining a policy of what its statesmen termed "splendid isolation." But early in the new century the British made agreements with France and Russia, so that before the first decade of the twentieth century was over, what started as ill will between Germany and France metastasized into the division of all the major European powers. Germany and the Hapsburg empire of Austria-Hungary were on one side, and France, Russia, and Britain on the other—with Italy more or less oscillating between.

Although armed to the teeth and divided against itself, Europe remained deceptively peaceful as the new century's single-digit years gave way to double digits—peaceful everywhere except in a part of the continent few western Europeans gave much thought to. The Balkan Peninsula was chronically wracked by violence, as its tiny nations and would-be nations sought freedom from Hapsburg domination even as they craved ethnic identification with Russia, which eagerly offered itself as the defender of all who proclaimed themselves Slavs. Even as he put together the alliances and counteralliances he hoped would ensure German domination of a stable Europe, Bismarck had predicted the very detonation that threatened to shatter all he was then building. "If a general war begins," he remarked, "it will be because of some damn fool thing in the Balkans."

That "thing" was the assassination on June 28, 1914, of the heir apparent to the Hapsburg throne, Archduke Franz Ferdinand, and his wife, the Grand Duchess Sophie, when they visited Sarajevo, capital of Bosnia and Herzegovina, a Balkan realm unhappily languishing as a province of Austria-Hungary.[3]

The assassin, a tubercular student named Gavrilo Princip, had been armed, coached, and prompted to act by the Black Hand, a Serbian secret society dedicated to the overthrow of the Austro-Hungarian Empire. Now, the Black Hand was by no means an agency of the Serbian government, and had men of goodwill in the Hapsburg government chosen to look upon the assassination as the crime of a desperate youth, the tragedy might not have reached beyond June 28. But Count Leopold von Berchtold, Austria-Hungary's foreign minister, was not a man of goodwill. By accusing Serbia of having killed the heir apparent, Berchtold saw an opportunity to crush Bosnian nationalism and the pan-Slavic movement.

Far from wanting to avert war, Berchtold was motivated to provoke one—short and sharp, just a little war to bloody Serbia's nose and thereby deliver to the other nations and would-be nations of the Balkans a lesson they would not forget.

But no flame, no matter how small, can burn harmlessly in a room packed with explosives. In the Europe Bismarck had created, there could be no such thing as a short, sharp, local war. Nations great and small were bound by treaties and covenants public and secret. Start a war with one country, and others would detonate in turn until the whole of Europe exploded. Even as he called for the mobilization of the Austro-Hungarian army, Berchtold dispatched a message to the German government, asking if Austria-Hungary could count on its support. On July 5, Kaiser Wilhelm II invited the Hapsburg ambassador to lunch in Berlin. Germany, he pledged, would stand behind Austria-Hungary, even if this meant war with Russia—which, the Kaiser knew, was bound to defend Serbia. Those privy to the exchange thought it was merely an impulsive promise. In any case, the Kaiser could afford to be expansive. Like everyone else, he was confident that Serbia would comply with whatever Austria-Hungary demanded, and the matter would end there.

At six o'clock on the evening of July 23, Berchtold made ten demands of Belgrade, including a demand that Austrian officials be given free rein to root out and punish all sources of anti-Austrian agitation and propaganda within Serbia. In the meantime, the government of Czar Nicholas II promised Serbia's premier, Nicholas Pashich, that Russia would "do everything" to help Serbia defend itself. Armed with this pledge, on July 25 Pashich delivered his response to Berchtold's ultimatum. Serbia would comply unconditionally with nine of the demands, but could not allow Austrian military and judicial officials to operate independently within their sovereign country. Berchtold proclaimed this a cause for war, and Austrian Emperor Franz Josef signed the declaration against Serbia on July 28. Russia responded by ordering a partial mobilization of forces near the Austrian border. Germany's chancellor, Theobald von Bethmann-Hollweg, urgently telegraphed Berchtold: "Serbia has in fact met the Austrian demands in so wide-sweeping a manner that if the Austro-Hungarian government adopted a wholly uncompromising attitude, a gradual revulsion of public opinion against it in all of Europe would have to be reckoned with." Berchtold made no reply.

Even as he tried to make the unreasonable Berchtold see reason, Bethmann-Hollweg warned Russia that its partial mobilization was a cause for war, and the German navy was put on a war footing in the North Sea. This caused Winston Churchill, at the time Great Britain's First Sea Lord, to mobilize the British Grand Fleet on July 29—the very day on which Austrian gunboats commenced the shelling of Serbia's capital, Belgrade, thereby beginning the war. On the next day, Nicholas II ordered the full mobilization of Russia's armed forces, prompting Helmuth von Moltke, chief of staff of the German army, to pick up a telephone and instruct Field Marshal Franz Conrad von Hötzendorff, chief of staff of the Austro-Hungarian army, to "Mobilize at once against Russia."

Moltke was a military commander, not a head of state, and yet it was on his unquestioned orders, barked over a telephone line, that the war was first fatally expanded. Austria-Hungary shifted from its Plan B, the scenario for a local war against Serbia—the only war it really wanted—to its Plan R, a blueprint for a general war against Serbia and Russia. As for Germany, it was governed by a plan first drawn up at the start of the century by Count Alfred von Schlieffen, which had been repeatedly refined and modified, but, in a strange lapse of imagination, did not include a scenario in which Russia played no part; the plan therefore committed Germany to war against France *and* Russia. Moreover, Moltke and everyone else in the German government and military assumed that every other major government operated from the same set of assumptions: that war necessarily meant a general war, all encompassing. Therefore, Germany issued an ultimatum to Russia, demanding that it call off its general mobilization. To France, Germany threatened war if it made any move to mobilize. While Russia rejected the German ultimatum flatly, France replied more coyly that it would consult its "own interests." The German government took both replies as a motive for its own general mobilization, which was ordered on August 1. On that day, the German army began to execute the Schlieffen Plan.

The Schlieffen Plan was predicated on the assumption that the French, whose military was more modern and more efficiently led, would mobilize more quickly than the Russians, who, though numerous, were poorly equipped and poorly led. Schlieffen calculated that Russia would take at least six weeks to mobilize effectively; therefore, his plan called for a quick offensive war against France and a simultaneous defensive war against Russia. France would be invaded at lightning speed and with overwhelming force while a smaller army would fend off a Russian invasion of eastern Prussia. It was critically important that France be neutralized within weeks, so that forces could be transferred from the western front to the eastern before Russia fully mobilized. With France out of the picture, Germany could convert its eastern defense into an offensive operation. Knock out the French, and the Russians would be defeated.

Schlieffen did not propose a direct frontal assault on France—a straightforward east-to-west march across the border—but instead laid down what he called a "great wheel," a wide, turning movement up through Flanders Plain, northeast of French territory. From there, the German armies would swoop down on France, hitting the French left flank and also hooking around from behind. Five major German armies would sweep wide from Alsace-Lorraine all the way west to the English Channel. Schlieffen instructed field commanders to "let the sleeve of the last man on the right brush the English Channel."

To execute the great wheel, the German army needed to march through neutral Belgium. On August 2, the German government demanded free passage through that country. Even before King Albert could refuse, German divisions began advancing through Flanders. At three o'clock on the afternoon of August 3, Britain's prime minister, Sir Edward Grey, addressed Parliament on the nation's solemn treaty obligation to protect Belgian neutrality: "If . . . we run away from these obligations of honor and interest as regards the Belgian Treaty . . . I do not believe for a moment that, at the end of this war . . . we should be able . . . to prevent the whole of the West of Europe opposite us from falling under the domination of a single power . . . and we should, I believe, sacrifice our respect and good name and reputation before the world." That evening, Germany declared war on France, and as day slipped into twilight and twilight into night, Grey took a friend aside. "The lamps are going out all over Europe," he said. "We shall not see them lit again in our lifetime." At dawn, having already invaded Belgium, Germany declared war on Belgium, and England, coming to Belgium's aid, joined all those other European powers, great and small, in what would be an all-consuming war.

Germany's Kaiser Wilhelm II did not share Grey's foreboding. As his armies started west that August, he promised: "You will be home before the leaves have fallen from the trees." And it soon appeared that he would make good on that pledge. Following the Schlieffen Plan, the German army stormed through France, throttling it, reaching by the end of August the very outskirts of Paris. Victory—victory before the leaves had fallen from the trees—was in sight. But, on August 29, the French commander in chief, Joseph "Papa" Joffre, ordered his Fifth Army to attack the flank of General Alexander von Kluck's First Army. This forced General Karl von Bülow to bring elements of his Second Army to Kluck's aid, thereby interrupting Bülow's hitherto relentless advance. With his army stalled, it now became Bülow's turn to seek aid from Kluck. The requirement of the Schlieffen Plan was for the right wing of the German army to sweep wide to complete the encirclement of the French forces. In response to Bülow's plea, Kluck departed from the plan by turning his entire First Army, which constituted the right wing of the German invasion (the wing containing the man whose sleeve was supposed to brush the English Channel), so that it suddenly headed southeast. Up to this point, the French had suffered one defeat after another, and Kluck's object was to strike at what he believed was the exposed left flank of all that remained of the French army.

Joffre understood what was happening. He understood that his French army, which for the past month had been rolled over and mauled by the German invaders, was now in possession of a great gift. The entire German right wing would now move east of Paris instead of west, the direction by which it would have encircled the city, strangling France into surrender. Accordingly, Joffre gave General Joseph Simon Gallieni, commander of the garrison of Paris, the whole of the Sixth Army with which to make a stand against Kluck.

Determined not to let what he thought was the all-but-beaten French army escape him, Kluck drove his First Army far in advance of the Second, unaware of the buildup in and around Paris of the French Sixth Army and therefore also unaware that he was leaving Bülow's Second Army exposed to attack *from* Paris. When Moltke explicitly ordered Kluck to protect the Second Army's flank, Kluck decided to obey what he took as the intention of the order without actually altering the direction of his advance. Therefore, instead of rushing directly to the aid of the Second Army, he continued to drive southward, against what he mistakenly thought was all that was left of the French army. This, Kluck believed, would not only prevent the escape of the Frenchmen, but would also drive them away from the Second Army.

So Kluck departed even further from the Schlieffen Plan, marching across the Marne River, not only leaving the Second Army vulnerable, but exposing his own right flank just east of Paris—right where the French Sixth Army had massed. The immediate result was the First Battle of the Marne, which stopped the German advance. The far greater consequence was the multiplication of a month of war into four years of war, a war—on the western front—fought along opposing lines of trenches that writhed rather than moved, each convulsion a few yards east or a few yards west then back again, fueled by unimaginable torrents of blood.

By the time the First Battle of the Marne began, eleven major powers were already at war. Italy would join the Allies in 1915, bringing the total to twelve, but the United States, buffered by an ocean and blissfully free from entangling treaties, stood aloof, watching the terrible madness of Europe with a combined sense of moral superiority and relief.[4]

The overwhelming majority of Americans wanted no part of the "European War," and in 1916 they would reelect their president, Woodrow Wilson, largely on his campaign slogan: *He kept us out of war.* Not that the United States in 1914—or 1916—could have contributed in any significant, direct military way to that war. In 1914, the French army consisted of 4.5

million men; the German army, 5.7 million; the Russian army, 5.3 million. The English, it is true, had a professional army of just 160,000 men, but it soon raised by conscription far more—and it had the largest navy in the world. In 1916, the U.S. Army numbered about 133,000, a force smaller than the army of Montenegro, a force so small that General Peyton C. March called it "scarcely enough to form a police force for emergencies within the territorial limits of the United States." When trouble broke out on the U.S.-Mexican border during this year, seventy thousand National Guardsmen were federalized, bringing the strength of the active U.S. Army to a bit over two hundred thousand. In addition, perhaps one hundred thirty thousand reservists—National Guard and regular army—were on hand. The U.S. Navy was better prepared. In 1916, it had sixty-seven thousand officers and sailors to man three hundred ships and one hundred thirty shore stations.

The Department of the Navy also controlled another force, miniscule even by comparison with the puny army. It consisted of the officers and men of the U.S. Marines. In 1916, there were about ten thousand of them. The Marine Corps had been around since the American Revolution, but it had nearly been ordered out of existence in 1908 and 1909 by President Theodore Roosevelt. The reason? It was almost too small to bother with in the event of a major war.

In a conflict involving millions of fighting men, of what possible consequence could ten thousand troops be? That was largely a theoretical question in 1916, when America's prospects of joining the European War seemed most remote. President Wilson compared the United States to a man "too proud to fight," but that didn't mean the nation had nothing to do with the war. As a neutral, America had the right—and, indeed, the legal responsibility—to trade with both sides impartially. There was very good money to be made supplying weapons, other goods, and general finance to the combatants. But impartial neutrality became increasingly difficult to maintain. The actions of the Central Powers, as Germany and its allies were called, were morally repugnant. Germany's declarations of war on France and Russia, entirely unprovoked, seemed impossible to justify, and its violation of

Belgian neutrality was brutal—its very real brutality magnified by skillful British propaganda. More and more, the flow of trade and finance from the United States to the European belligerents turned away from the Central Powers and toward the Allies (as France, Britain, Italy, and Russia were called). Moral revulsion played a role in this shift, but, even more, it was the product of a collective business decision among U.S. manufacturers and financial institutions. High demand, an ample supply of gold, favorable shipping, and the realities of geography made dealing with the Allies far more reliable and profitable than doing business with Germany and the other Central Powers. Moreover, American financial and business interests were coming to believe that the Allies would win, which made them a far better credit risk than the Central Powers. By 1917, American firms had done some $2 billion in business with the Allies, and U.S. banks had made $2.5 billion in loans to them. In contrast, U.S. banks had loaned by this time no more than $45 million to Germany. Politically, the United States might be neutral; economically, it had already taken sides. As for Wilson, he came increasingly to believe that if the United States—in the person of himself—wanted a leading voice in shaping the postwar world, it would have to earn that voice with an American commitment to the war.

For Wilson, going to war on the side of the Allies came to seem both an economic and an ideological imperative. Selling this to the American people would not be easy, however. The nation's large German-American community was pro-German, of course, raised significant charitable funds for the homeland, and even agitated for U.S. entry into the war on the side of the Kaiser. The even larger Irish-American community was also willing to side with any nation that fought the hated English. And to most other Americans—those who didn't run a bank, a steel mill, or a munitions plant—it made little difference who won this "Great War," just as long as America stayed out of it.

Public opinion notwithstanding, U.S.-German diplomatic relations steadily deteriorated. The first major challenge to Wilson's neutrality policy came on May 7, 1915, when a German U-boat torpedoed, without warning, the British liner *Lusitania*, killing 1,198 passengers, including 124 Americans.

Wilson responded with a stern note of diplomatic protest. War hawks, such as Theodore Roosevelt, condemned the response as weak, whereas pacifists, most prominently Wilson's secretary of state, Williams Jennings Bryan, criticized the note as blatantly provocative, and after Wilson wrote a second one, Bryan resigned in protest from the cabinet. In August, another British liner, *Arabic*, was sunk, also with loss of American lives. For a time after this, unrestricted submarine warfare was suspended, but on January 9, 1917, Kaiser Wilhelm II ordered the resumption of unrestricted submarine warfare effective February 1. Three days later, a U.S. warship, the *Housatonic*, was torpedoed, prompting President Wilson to sever diplomatic relations with Germany. Very shortly after this, British intelligence authorities turned over to Wilson a telegram they had intercepted between Germany's foreign minister, Alfred Zimmermann, and the German ambassador to Mexico. Transmitted on January 16, 1917, the "Zimmermann Note," as it was called, authorized the ambassador to propose a German-Mexican alliance to Mexican president Venustiano Carranza. In return for a Mexican declaration of war against the United States, Mexico would receive Germany's support in a military campaign to recover its "lost territory in Texas, New Mexico, and Arizona." It was an implausible, not to say harebrained proposal, but it was quite enough to stir patriotic outrage among the American public and to move Wilson to ask Congress for a declaration of war on April 2, 1917.

What was Woodrow Wilson thinking when he delivered his thirty-two-minute War Message to Congress? With its puny army, America was far from being prepared to go to war, and even mobilizing at the fastest conceivable speed, it would be months, maybe years, before the nation's military could make a strategically meaningful contribution to the Allied war effort.

Some recent historians believe that President Wilson hoped he would never actually have to send troops to Europe. He gambled (they say) that the mere threat of entering the war would be sufficient to end the war—especially at so desperate a stage of the conflict, when both Allies and Central Powers were beyond exhaustion. But instead of backing down,

Germany responded to the entry of the United States with dramatically heightened aggression. Knowing that it was one thing to declare war and quite another actually to mobilize for war, Erich Ludendorff, Germany's top general, decided to mount a new series of all-out offensives intended to destroy the British army and to conquer the French capital—in other words, to end the war—before the Americans could arrive in sufficient numbers to have any impact on the fighting. What this meant was that the U.S. Army and a handful of marines would find themselves marching into the most prodigious slaughter in a war that had been nothing but prodigious slaughter. And in the middle of it all was a formerly idyllic patch of forest called Belleau Wood.

▪ 1 ▪

Bellhops and Stevedores

Teddy Roosevelt was not the first American president to try to get rid of the Marine Corps, but he may have been the most determined. His Executive Order 969, issued on November 12, 1908, defined the duties of the marines, which included garrisoning navy yards and naval stations, providing mobile defense of naval bases and naval stations beyond the continental limits of the United States, manning naval shore defenses, garrisoning the Panama Canal Zone, and furnishing "such garrisons and expeditionary forces for duties beyond the seas as may be necessary in time of peace."[1]

At first glance, this hardly seems like an attempt to phase out the Corps, but the key duty that had been eliminated from this list was that of ship's guards. From the Corps' inception as the Continental Marines in 1775, this had been its defining mission. It was a mission that made sense in the age of sail when warring vessels typically fought at very close quarters and attempts to board one another were made at critical points in any battle. Seagoing soldiers—marines—were required both in boarding parties and to repel enemy boarders. In addition, marines served to enforce military-style discipline on often unruly ship's crews—they were a shipboard police force—and trained in artillery, they also assisted in manning a ship's guns. (This is why the marine equivalent of the army sergeant first class is still called today a gunnery sergeant—or "gunny" for short.)

As cops, marines were never popular aboard ship. American sailors felt about them much the same way as British sailors felt about the Royal Marines. The origin of the old expression "Tell it to the Marines!" is not, as many Americans believe, a dare to try to get a cock-and-bull story past a group of tough men who will brook no nonsense, but was an expression used by eighteenth-century Royal Navy sailors who considered the marines gullible landlubbers capable of believing anything told to them about ships and matters of the sea. Indeed, British seamen called an empty bottle, after all the rum had been drained out of it, a "marine," because it was simply useless. Yet American marines were never exclusively a boarding party and seagoing police force. Almost from the beginning, the marine contingents carried on American ships were used in amphibious operations, going ashore, under cover of the mother vessel's looming guns, to carry out often quite daring small-force operations. Strangely enough, this did not result in the universal perception of the marines as a supremely nimble and versatile force but tended to blur the identity of the Corps. Were these men to be used on ships or on shore?

The Continental Marines—never more than about four hundred men—were disbanded in 1783 at the end of the American Revolution, and a new U.S. Marine Corps was not approved by Congress until 1798, during an undeclared naval war with France. Once again, marines were assigned as a contingent of U.S. warship crews, their duties to keep order aboard ship, to help man guns, and to serve as boarding and landing parties. The "Franco-American Quasi War" (as the conflict is often called) ended in 1800, but the next marine mission was not long in coming. During the late eighteenth and early nineteenth centuries, U.S. commercial shipping, like that of other "Christian" nations, was preyed upon by the Barbary pirates, state-sanctioned seaborne raiders operating along the coast of North Africa, especially out of Tripoli. In 1805, marines landed "on the shores of Tripoli," attacking the port of Tripoli and capturing Derna.

During the War of 1812, marines once again served mainly aboard navy ships, but they earned distinction on land as part of the defense of Washington at the disastrous Battle of Bladensburg (Maryland) in 1813. Whereas U.S. Army and militia forces disintegrated here before the British advance on the nation's capital, a contingent of marines and sailors held their ground until finally flanked and overwhelmed by vastly superior numbers. Marines were also at the core of Andrew Jackson's splendid victory at the Battle of New Orleans on January 8, 1815.

After the War of 1812, the marines assisted in the grim duty of "removing" the Seminole Indians from Florida and Georgia during the Second Seminole War of 1835–1842. This was followed by action in the United States-Mexican War (1846–1848), in which the marines served aboard ships and were also attached to army general Winfield Scott's command in 1847. Marines seized Mexican seaports on both the Gulf and Pacific coasts before joining Scott's advance at Pueblo, Mexico. The marine role in the invasion of Mexico City is commemorated in the passage of the "Marine Corps Hymn" that refers to the "halls of Montezuma."

Marines fought in the earliest action associated with the Civil War when, on October 18, 1859, under the command of U.S. Army Colonel Robert E. Lee, a marine company fought a three-minute battle to recover the federal arsenal at Harpers Ferry, Virginia (present-day West Virginia), which had been taken over by the militant abolitionist John Brown and a handful of followers. Once the Civil War itself broke out, marines served mainly at sea, but a marine battalion did fight at the First Battle of Bull Run (July 21, 1861) and participated in various amphibious operations thereafter.

In the years following the Civil War, small contingents of marines landed in Egypt, Colombia, Mexico, China, Cuba, Formosa, Uruguay, Argentina, Chile, Haiti, Alaska, Nicaragua, Japan, Samoa, and Panama to defend local American interests. The largest marine operation prior to the Spanish-American War was in Korea in 1871 against the Salee River pirates. During what was dubbed a "weekend war," marines captured 481 guns, 50 Korean battle flags, and neutralized the important Han River forts. Two marines were awarded the Medal of Honor, the first time this decoration was presented to members of the service.

By the outbreak of the Spanish-American War in 1898, the marines had a reputation as a first-response utility force and enjoyed enthusiastic congressional support that was out of proportion to its diminutive size: fewer than three thousand men. As it happened, a marine, Private William Anthony, assigned as orderly to Captain Charles D. Sigsbee, skipper of the *Maine*, became the first hero of the Spanish-American War when he rescued Sigsbee after the explosion of the battleship in Havana Harbor. Subsequently, a contingent of marines attached to the navy squadron commanded by Commodore George Dewey in Manila Bay was put ashore to secure the Cavite Navy Yard. They accomplished their mission, then held Cavite for three months until the arrival of the U.S. Army. The marines were not only the first Americans to fight in the Philippines, they were also the first Americans to land in Cuba. On June 10, 1898, a marine battalion hit the beach at Guantanamo Bay, capturing an advance base for the U.S. fleet. Four days later, marines won the Battle of Cuzco Well.

After the war, marines fought in the Philippine Insurrection and the Boxer Rebellion. They fought elsewhere in China and also in Nicaragua, Panama, the Dominican Republic, Cuba, Mexico (when President Woodrow Wilson ordered an invasion at Veracruz in 1914), and in Haiti.

Whenever the country needed a small, tough, amphibious, highly mobile force, the marines were there. Yet, when they were not needed, they were neglected, even spurned. Before Theodore Roosevelt moved to abolish the Corps in 1908—to absorb it into the U.S. Army—President Andrew Jackson recommended to Congress in 1829 that the marines be incorporated either into the artillery or infantry. In 1831, the secretary of the navy recommended that the marines be assigned either to the army or the navy—or dissolved altogether. In 1834, Congress formally made the Corps part of the navy, but reserved for the president the option to place it under U.S. Army control if the president deemed it necessary. After the Civil War, in June 1866, the congressional Committee on Naval Affairs debated disbanding the Corps on the grounds that it largely duplicated the functions of the army. The committee voted against disbanding the Marine Corps, but neither the navy nor the Corps itself did anything to address the very real problems that plagued the organization in the years after the Civil War. While it was undeniable that small units of marines had taken on tough assignments and had handled them boldly and heroically, the Marine Corps high command was, by the final quarter of the nineteenth century, nearly senescent. Without pensions, there was no incentive for superannuated officers to retire. A growing proportion of the marines' senior command was simply too old ever to take the field. As for new blood, recruitment had also become a problem. The Corps had few standards, and a majority of junior officers received commissions through their political connections rather than on any military merits. For many officers, especially those serving at marine headquarters in Washington, DC, service was more a social activity than a military commitment.

The army-navy military establishment resented the political influence the diminutive Corps enjoyed, and in the 1880s, the navy began a new attack on the marines—this one from the point of view of naval progress. With the passing of the age of sail, naval officers argued that marines were no longer necessary aboard ship. The advanced professionalism of naval officers and sailors made the policing role of the marines unnecessary. The nature of naval combat, in which ships no longer tangled at close quarters but fought with long-range guns, made boarding parties for the most part obsolete. Even the role of marines as gunners and assistant gunners was called into question. Naval officers argued that the presence of marine gunners actually detracted from the training and experience of sailors assigned to gun crews. Increasingly, the navy called for an end to shipboard marine service.

At the very time that the attack on the continued existence of the marines had been renewed, Secretary of the Navy Benjamin F. Tracy appointed a Board of Organization, Tactics, and Drill (immediately dubbed the Greer Board, after its chairman, Commodore James A. Greer) to address shipboard organization and landing parties, including the shipboard role of the marines. Among other things, the board recommended thorough professionalization of the marines and standardization of the training of marine officers. The Appropriations Act of 1882 required future U.S. Marine officers to be drawn from graduates of the U.S. Naval Academy. This coincided with the retirement of some die-hard officers, which made way for the promotion of the academy men. In 1891, the Corps' new commandant, Lieutenant Colonel Charles Heywood, secured authorization from the Department of the Navy for the creation of a School of Application, which would give junior marine officers specialized training in infantry tactics and other fields. This was a step forward for the service, but simultaneously a step back—for Heywood included in his curriculum training in the servicing of secondary guns on the new battleships. He believed that this would maintain the marines' traditional shipboard role. What it did, however, was to ensure that the identity of the Corps would remain ambiguous, caught between a land mission not always distinguishable from that of the army and a seagoing mission the navy just did not want.

Heywood retired as commandant in 1903, having taken important steps to increase the professionalism of the U.S. Marines, but having also reinforced the ambiguous identity of the Corps and the discontent concerning it felt by both the army and the navy. President Roosevelt consulted with the army's Major General Leonard Wood on the status of the marines. Both men agreed that, for the good of the army and the navy, the Corps should be absorbed into the army. On October 16, 1908, when Rear Admiral J. E. Pillsbury, chief of the navy's Bureau of Navigation, formally requested that the secretary of the navy withdraw the marines as ship's guards, Roosevelt issued his executive order. Most in Washington saw the order as a prelude to the dissolution of the Corps. President Roosevelt remarked to one of his military aides that he did not "hesitate to say that [the marines] should be absorbed into the army and no vestige of their organization should be allowed to remain. They cannot get along with the navy, and as a separate command with the army the conditions would be intolerable."[2]

With the Corps nearing the brink of extinction, the senior command of the marines suddenly realized the urgency of carving out a unique mission for the service. Even the navy pulled back from its criticism. True, naval officers no longer wanted marine ship's guards, but they wanted even less for the U.S. Marines to be eaten up by a rival service. Both the marines and the navy began to realize that U.S. victory in the Spanish-American War of 1898 had created a new naval mission—the defense of what amounted to an overseas empire, something never before contemplated in American history—and this, in turn, created a potentially new mission for the U.S. Marine Corps. The navy now had a number of overseas bases and coaling stations. It did not want to depend on the U.S. Army for the defense of those bases but wanted instead a navy-controlled, navy-dedicated land force to garrison these far-flung outposts. In 1901, the General Board, a nine-officer committee created in 1900 to make recommendations on naval policy, suggested that the Corps create "a military organization of sufficient strength in numbers and efficiency, to enable the Navy to meet all demands upon it . . . without dependence on the cooperation of the Army."[3] This would be the U.S. Marines' "Advanced Base Force," a role that, for the first time in its long, colorful, but chronically precarious history, would give the Corps a unique and indispensable identity. Astoundingly, for the next decade, through two commandants—Heywood and George F. Elliott—the marines did little to develop the Advanced Base Force. Indeed, although the 1908 Executive Order 969 provided the necessary wake-up call, Congress, not the Corps itself, secured a reprieve by forcing the repeal of the executive order and bringing about the restoration of all the marines' old missions, including that of ship's guards and gun duty. The reprieve motivated William P. Biddle, who became commandant in 1911, to accelerate development of the Advanced Base Force. By April 1917, when the United States declared war on Germany, the U.S. Marine Corps had a unique mission and identity.

Yet when the nation entered the Great War, this mission and this identity were not, in and of themselves, sufficient to allow the Marine Corps to claim, for the first time in its history, a major role in a major conflict. True, the Advanced Base Force concept provided a rationale for using the marines as a special land force, but that was only a start. The hard fact was that General

John J. Pershing, commander in chief of the American Expeditionary Force (AEF), an army man through and through, was not enthusiastic about welcoming large numbers of marines into the war. By 1917, the marines had an unofficial motto to place alongside the official "Semper Fidelis." It was "First to Fight." Yet General Pershing seemed determined to prevent the marines from living up to that motto. The first marine contingent to be shipped to France was the 5th Regiment, which comprised three infantry battalions, each with more than one thousand officers and enlisted marines. The regiment was attached to the army's 1st Division, the first major U.S. unit to reach France. The 1st Division was complete as an army unit. The attached 5th Regiment of marines was, in military parlance, "excess." The United States had never sent a vast army overseas before and had severely underestimated the need for logistical troops to support combat soldiers. Accordingly, when the "excess" troops arrived in the form of U.S. Marines, Pershing put them to work as laborers and security forces—essentially stevedores and military police. Pershing was not obliged to justify these assignments, but he nevertheless explained that he had perfect confidence in the marines and that he admired their soldierly appearance and training; however, his most urgent need was for support personnel, and the 5th Regiment had come along at just the right time.

Mostly assigned to logistics, few marines were released to train with the rest of the 1st Division during the summer and fall of 1917. Instead, they unloaded ships and loaded trucks, they policed the camps, and they patrolled the bistros and other local hangouts popular with doughboys. They were treated as longshoreman and cops. Army and navy personnel sometimes derided marines as "bellhops"—because of their fancy dress blues and white caps—bellhops, they said, "assigned to carry the admiral's luggage." Now, newly arrived in France, many marines began to feel that this slur was all too accurate. A marine assigned as a sentry remarked to General Pershing's press officer that this lackluster duty was good training for civilian life. After the war, he said, "I can wear a striped waistcoat and brass buttons and open cab doors in front of a New York hotel." Some new lyrics began to circulate to "The Marine Corps Hymn":

So here we are at St. Nazaire
Our guns have rusty bores,
We are working side by side with Huns
And nigger stevedores.
But if the Army and the Navy
Ever gaze on Heaven's scenes
They will find the roads are graded
By United States Marines.[4]

George Barnett, who had become the twelfth commandant of the U.S. Marine Corps in 1914, did not for a moment accept that the marines' assignment as bellhops and stevedores was the product of necessity. He believed that Pershing and the War Department deliberately conspired to keep the marines from ever seeing combat, and he intended to ensure that his men would be put into the fight.

Major General George Barnett was a Wisconsin native, born in 1859, who graduated from the U.S. Naval Academy in 1881. Plucked by the marines on July 1, 1883, he received a second lieutenant's commission. As he worked his way up through the officer ranks, Barnett served on many ships and in various shore stations. During the Spanish-American War, he was assigned to the USS *San Francisco* and the USS *New Orleans*. He saw action in the capture of Santiago, Cuba, then, in 1902, commanded a marine battalion aboard the USS *Panther*, serving in Panama. He commanded another battalion in the Philippines, served as fleet marine officer of the Asiatic Fleet, and in 1905 was attached to the Cuban Army of Pacification. He took command of the marine detachment of the American legation in Beijing, China, in 1907, then returned to Cuba, serving there from 1908 to 1911.

On February 25, 1914, Barnett was appointed major general commandant of the Marine Corps, and he saw the war as an opportunity to expand the marines significantly. It was not that he was a personally ambitious man, but his ambition for the Corps was boundless. Shortly after the outbreak of hostilities in Europe, when almost all of America was congratulating itself on blissful neutrality, Barnett sent a contingent of marine officers to observe the fighting. They returned with their reports in 1915, and Barnett wasted no time in assigning his chief of staff, Colonel John A. Lejeune, to analyze all that had been observed. How had the war affected tactics and military technology? Barnett and his staff sorted through the lessons of trench warfare on an unprecedented scale and on the revolution in warfare wrought by trucks, heavy artillery, aircraft, and, above all, by the machine gun. Barnett was determined that his marines would learn the lessons of modern war.

After the Kaiser ordered the resumption of unrestricted submarine warfare effective February 1, 1917, and following President Wilson's severance of diplomatic relations with Germany on the third, after a U-boat sank the USS *Housatonic*, the preparedness movement, which had been ongoing—unofficially—for nearly two years, got into full swing. Whereas the sinking of the RMS *Lusitania* in 1915 had prompted a stern diplomatic note from President Wilson, it moved U.S. Army Chief of Staff Leonard Wood to establish at Plattsburg, New York, the first of what were popularly described as "businessmen's military training camps." By the summer of 1916, forty thousand men had been put through basic training in these camps as part of what was called the Plattsburg Movement. The training was officially "unofficial," even though it was conducted by officers and noncommissioned officers of the regular U.S. Army and was supported by government-funded advertising. Moreover, while the war raged in Europe, the United States conducted its own—far more modest—military adventure in the pursuit of the Mexican social bandit and revolutionary Francisco "Pancho" Villa during 1916 through early 1917. The so-called "Punitive Expedition" Wilson authorized against Villa moved Congress to augment the puny American military by passing the National Defense Act of 1916, which funded the enlargement of the regular army, created a federal National Guard (up to this time organized on the state level, like a militia), and, through the related Naval Appropriations Act of 1916, expanded the navy. This expansion included an authorized increase in marine ranks to 17,400 enlisted men. Acting on this authorization, Barnett ordered the Corps' New York-based Recruiting Publicity Bureau to produce and publish posters, pamphlets, and "news" stories promoting the marines and portraying the U.S. Marine Corps as the service arm pledged to be the First to Fight. Recruiting sergeants were assigned substantial quotas, with the object of building up to the 17,400-man authorized strength as quickly as possible. At the beginning of 1917, Barnett was fully poised to make the most of the preparedness movement and to see to the rapid wartime expansion of the U.S. Marines.

By March 1917, President Wilson and his cabinet were persuaded that U.S. entry into the war was inevitable. On March 26, Wilson ordered the navy to increase strength from 68,700 officers and sailors to 87,000. This entailed an increase of 7,000 marines beyond the 17,400-man authorization. In contrast to the War Department—which controlled the army and which seemed stunned into paralysis on the eve of war—both the navy department and the Marine Corps recruiters responded to the situation with gusto. As matters stood at the end of March 1917, the marines were slated to serve the fleet in their traditional capacity as ship's guards and security forces as well as in their more recently developed role manning advanced bases. Even with the nation's almost certain prospect of entering the European war, the marines' principal responsibility was likely to remain the patrol of the Caribbean. There was no guarantee—indeed, no real likelihood—that marines would be sent to Europe as a land force to fight "the Hun." Nevertheless, recruiters ratcheted up their drive by selling the First to Fight motto and by signing up recruits for "wartime service only." This not only implied service in *the* war, it also limited the commitment of recruits. At this point, the army and the National Guard could not enlist men "for the duration," but were able to offer only fixed terms of service. Most patriotic young men wanted to fight for their country, not make the military a career for a set number of years.

On the verge of war, the marines discovered that they already enjoyed an overwhelmingly positive public reputation for gallantry and ardor in combat. When President Wilson signed into law the Selective Service Act of 1917 on May 18, marine recruiters found they had an even stronger incentive to offer: *voluntary* service in an elite military organization. From the very beginning of the conflict, therefore, the marines had no difficulty attracting men, and the Corps could therefore afford to be highly selective. Of 239,274 who applied during the course of the war, just 60,189 were accepted as marines. In contrast to the Marine Corps of the nineteenth century, the selection process was based entirely on merit. Leadership was emphasized, and officer material was sought wherever it could be found. This meant instituting a vast democratization of commissioning policies. The demands of war, of course, necessitated going beyond Annapolis graduates, and officers were commissioned from among new recruits, from veteran enlisted marines, from military schools, from colleges and universities, and from the Plattsburg program.

The boost in manpower authorization was part of the naval appropriation, but Barnett meant to ensure that the marine expansion would not be entirely in the navy's service. As mentioned in the previous chapter, a growing number of historians have come to believe that President Wilson entered the war in the hope—if not the belief—that the mere threat of American intervention might bring about an end to the war. When this failed to happen, the Wilson administration delayed sending troops to France. There was a natural reluctance to commit America's youth to the cauldron of the western front, but, more important, there was a conviction among the military that to send U.S. forces into combat piecemeal would be tantamount to slaughtering them. The army general staff wanted to build up a force of millions before sending them into battle. Understandably, however, the French and British, who were reeling—and even faltering—under the punishment of General Ludendorff's massive offensives, clamored for immediate reinforcement. At length, President Wilson prevailed on the general staff to send a symbolic force right away, an army division under General Pershing.

Between organizing the 1st Division and cobbling together the massive machinery of conscription and mobilization, the War Department was overwhelmed. Barnett waded into the confusion to sell his marines as part of the 1st Division. He persuaded Secretary of the Navy Josephus Daniels and Chief of Naval Operations William S. Benson to back his campaign to include in the very first contingent a marine regiment, with a second regiment to follow—thereby incorporating into the 1st Division an entire marine brigade: about six thousand men. Barnett knew that Pershing would resist, even refuse, but by presenting his appeal directly to the War Department—and with the backing of Daniels and Benson—Barnett maneuvered around Pershing, who was not even consulted. At this point, Secretary of War Newton D. Baker and army Chief of Staff Tasker H. Bliss were willing to agree to anything that promised to get the 1st Division put together and on its way to France. Baker and Bliss promised to supply weapons and equipment equivalent to that furnished to army troops. The navy agreed to provide transport vessels. In return, Barnett was asked to commit not only two marine regiments, but a pool of replacements as well. Informed of the fait accompli, Pershing put the best face on it, promising to give the marines equal treatment with the army. Baker, however, could not have pleased him when he declared that the marine brigade would definitely be committed to combat.

Animated by Baker's pledge and choosing to ignore Pershing's likely resistance, Barnett sent his first contingent—the 5th Regiment, veterans drawn chiefly from duty in the Caribbean—and began preparing the second contingent, the 6th Regiment, at the new marine base in Quantico, Virginia.

The 5th Regiment was commanded by Colonel Charles A. Doyen, a thirty-four-year veteran of the Corps. He was a New Hampshire man, dignified and reserved, a graduate of Annapolis, class of 1881. In France, he would assume command of the 4th Marine Brigade, which was composed of the 5th and 6th Regiments as well as the 6th Machine Gun Battalion. At fifty-eight, he drove brigade training overseas with the zeal of a much younger man. It broke his health, and he was sent home. This would prove a blow to the marines—as marines—because, although command of the 5th Regiment was taken over by Colonel Wendell Neville, a relatively young marine officer, command of the entire 4th Brigade was assigned to a U.S. Army brigadier—Pershing's former chief of staff, no less—James G. Harbord. No career army man liked being assigned to staff duty, in command of a desk, and Harbord had badgered his chief to permit him the test of combat. When the 4th Marine Brigade suddenly became leaderless, Pershing gave it to his insistent chief of staff. "You are to have charge of the finest body of troops in France," Pershing told him in what must have been a hard admission for an army man. He continued: "If they fail to live up to that reputation, I shall know whom to blame."[5]

At Quantico, command of the 6th Marine Regiment was assigned to Colonel Albertus W. Catlin. Born in Gowanda, New York, in 1868, Catlin graduated from the Naval Academy in 1890 and commanded the ship's guards on the battleship USS *Maine* when it exploded in Havana Harbor in 1898, triggering the Spanish-American War. Catlin commanded marines aboard the USS *St. Louis* during that war and led the first contingent of marines to land on Cuba in 1906. As a marine major in command of a battalion, Catlin earned a Medal of Honor for "courage and skill in leading his men through the action of April 22, 1914, in the invasion and occupation of Vera Cruz, Mexico."[6] A vigorous, hands-on commander, Catlin plunged into the course at the Army War College on the eve of U.S. entry into the Great War and graduated in May 1917.

Colonel Catlin wasn't the only Medal of Honor winner in the first two marine regiments. Gunnery Sergeant Dan Daly had been decorated with *two* Medals of Honor—one of only two marines (the other was the legendary Smedley Butler) who received the nation's highest military honor twice. Daly, who had been born in Glen Cove, New York, in 1873, joined the Corps in January 1899, hoping to get in on the action against Spain in Cuba. The Spanish-American War was over before he left training, however, but Daly did see action in China in the Boxer Rebellion of 1900, earning his first Medal of Honor for making a one-man stand against repeated Boxer attacks, not only holding his position but inflicting some two hundred casualties. Fifteen years later, he earned a second Medal of Honor for action against the Cacos, Haitian bandits. On the night of October 24, 1915, he and thirty-four fellow marines were ambushed by some four hundred Cacos. Daly and the men he led managed to fight through the ambush, enter a nearby fort, and defeat the bandits.

And there were other hardened marine veterans in the 5th Regiment, bound immediately for France, and in the 6th training at Quantico. It was a brand-new facility on the Potomac, crude and raw. Barracks buildings were primitive, and the unpaved paths connecting them were muddy with red clay. In a 1968 memoir, Major General Robert Blake recalled how he felt when he received a commendation as the first commander of the Quantico base; he believed that he really merited a court-martial, because conditions there were so grim. If anything, however, muddy Quantico may have been a most appropriate overseas depot for marines about to serve in the mud and misery of trench-scarred France. In any case, Quantico must have seemed like paradise to the new marines, fresh from their basic training at Parris Island, South Carolina. As Catlin later wrote of his regiment, "It was an aggregation as new and untried as any regiment of the National Army, but what stuff we had in it!" All officers from the rank of captain and higher were "old-time Marines," as were about fifty of the noncoms. The others, from junior officers down to privates, "were new men." Yet if "we had had time and opportunity to pick our men individually from the whole of the United States I doubt whether we should have done much better. They were as fine a bunch of upstanding American athletes as you would care to meet, and they had brains as well as brawn. Sixty per cent of the entire regiment—mark this—sixty per cent of them were college men"—in an era in which very few men attended college. "Of our young lieutenants a large number were college athletes. There was Lagore of Yale; Bastien of Minnesota, an All-America end; Moore and Murphy of Princeton; Maynard of the University of Washington; Overton, the Yale runner, who was killed in the offensive last summer, and a dozen others who won fame on the gridiron, track, and diamond while the United States was yet at peace. When you read of what these men did in Belleau Wood and Bouresches, remember who they were, and perhaps their exploits will seem less unbelievable." Catlin felt that education gave his marines an edge sharp enough to achieve victory. "The Turk will fight like a fiend; the Moro's trade is slaying; it was Fuzzy Wuzzy who broke a British square; the Boche will move in mass formation into the face of death like a ferry-boat entering its slip; but when the final show-down comes, when the last ounce of strength and nerve is called for, when mind and hand must act like lightning together, I will take my chances with an educated man, a free-born American with a trained mind."[7]

At Parris Island, marine drill sergeants did their utmost to get these "new men" on the road to becoming "old-time Marines." Quantico had been leased by the marines in April 1917, and Parris Island, originally the Naval Station at Port Royal, South Carolina, was only a little older, having been acquired by the Corps in September 1915 to replace the old recruit depot at Norfolk, Virginia. Within the brief span of two years, however, "PI" had already acquired a near mythological status within the Marine Corps. It was a world unto itself. The early classes of recruits had to be transported to the island by navy tug or motor launch because there was no road or causeway. Originally, basic training was a fourteen-week course. During the war, it was compressed into just eight hellish weeks. PI was ugly and uncomfortable, a sandy island exposed to the wind and overgrown with dwarfish scrub pine. Presiding over this realm were the drill instructors, "DIs," who, during this period, wore dress blues, just like the uniforms in the recruiting posters. What was not advertised was how they swore mightily, drilled their charges mercilessly, and meted out corporal punishment liberally. "The first day I was at camp," one recruit wrote to his mother, "I was afraid I was going to die. The next two weeks my sole fear was that I wasn't going to die. And after that I knew I'd never die because I'd become so hard that nothing could kill me."[8]

Discipline and physical conditioning were principal objectives of the training, which was crude by modern standards, dedicated exclusively to platoon-level and individual skills. Nevertheless, it was far more demanding than army basic training, and it included extensive work on marksmanship. Three of the recruit's eight weeks at PI were dedicated to it. Drill instructors ensured that every recruit knew his Springfield .03 intimately—could field-strip and reassemble it blindfolded—and the marksmanship instructors made sure that each fledgling marine knew how to fire it such that every round counted. This was a major difference between army and marine training. Soldiers were taught how to care for and fire their weapons, but little attention was devoted to marksmanship. The goal of army firearms training was to learn how to pour as much fire on the enemy as quickly as possible, "wasting" little time on careful aim. The assumption was that each soldier would be part of a relatively large combat unit, which would deliver massed fire. All that was important was to point the weapon toward the enemy and keep shooting. The marines, however, emphasized small units and the individual marine. They rarely had enough men in one place and at one time to mass fire. Every shot, therefore, had to be put on the target.

By the time a recruit had been through Parris Island and had received additional training at Quantico, he was a honed razor, an instrument eager to be used. He was not a man to be squandered on a labor detail or guard duty. Commandant Barnett made that clear to any newspaper reporter who would listen. He had been promised by the secretary of war himself that the marines would see action, and he would not let up on Pershing and the general staff until his troops were relieved of bellhop and stevedore assignments and sent to the front.

The whole of the 6th Regiment did not land in France until February 1918. By this time, the 5th Regiment had been reassigned from the U.S. Army 1st Division to the newly formed U.S. Army 2nd Division. The 6th Regiment joined it there to form what Barnett successfully sought to call the 4th Brigade (U.S. Marines). Since the regiments were already collectively designated as the 4th Infantry Brigade, General Pershing saw no harm in a minor alteration of the name. But for Barnett and his marines, the new designation made all the difference. It identified this unit, attached though it was to the army, as a *marine* unit. The distinction would soon have a profound and unforeseen effect beyond the members of the brigade. General Pershing was a stickler for security of intelligence. He did not want the enemy to learn anything about the American order of battle and so, early in 1918, he ordered American Expeditionary Force (AEF) censors to ensure that war correspondents did not identify AEF units by number; however, he did allow the marines to be identified by name as, simply, the "marine brigade." Thus, in newspaper stories, the vast army component of the AEF remained collectively anonymous, whereas the marine brigade was always singled out by name. Pershing, reluctant to accept the marines to begin with and then reluctant to commit them to combat, had issued an order that, in the eyes of the public, helped to create the marines' soon-to-be legendary status.

Marine identity did not flow alone from Commandant Barnett or as an unintended consequence of Pershing's censorship order. It was, first and foremost, a product of each individual marine. The first contingent took its distinctive forest-green field uniforms to France, but when these wore out—and they soon wore out—they were replaced from army supplies with the olive drab uniforms of the doughboy. Marines removed their dull bronze U.S. Marine Corps buttons from the threadbare original uniforms and sewed them onto the new army issue. The eagle, anchor, and globe were displayed on army overseas caps; on British-modeled, washbasin, army-issue helmets; and above the breast pockets of army-issue blouses. Nor did the marines have to depend on buttons and insignia salvaged from worn-out U.S. Marine Corps-issue clothing. Somebody—there is no record of who—shipped to the brigade an ample stash of Marine Corps insignia. There were soon plenty of eagle-anchor-globes to go around.

Barnett understood that getting his marines fully into the war was more than a matter of unit identification, uniforms, and bronze buttons. It was difficult to maintain heightened esprit in cold, rainy Saint-Nazaire and Bordeaux when, intensively trained to kill the Hun, a marine was doing dockside labor or serving on shore patrol, then sleeping on straw-strewn floors in unheated, improvised barracks. Barnett believed his best chance was to get his brigade in place—after all, two full regiments could not be sidelined forever—and then to keep adding to it. With Congress, Barnett proved highly persuasive. "There are today on the firing lines of France no better trained, no braver, no more effective force than our own Marines now serving there," the Subcommittee for Investigation of Conduct and Administration of Naval Affairs reported, "and we hope their numbers may soon be increased."[9] Yet Congress would not press for this augmented marine presence without the request of the War Department—and the War Department would not make such a request unless General Pershing asked for it.

Pershing did no such thing.

In the end, Barnett found his greatest ally not in Baker and not in Pershing, but in Germany's generalissimo, Erich Ludendorff. The intensity and tempo of Ludendorff's all-out offensives were shocking, even by the battle-numbed standards of this "Great War." In March 1918, the U.S. Army general staff decided it was imperative to accept another marine brigade. Accordingly, Barnett quickly asked Congress to raise the size of the Corps to sixty-two thousand men. Congress responded with an authorization for a U.S. Marine Corps of seventy-five thousand men. This was a victory for the Corps—if two marine regiments could not be ignored, so much less could four—but Barnett decided to press for the incorporation of a full marine division into the AEF. This would allow the marines a substantial degree of independence from the army, because, whereas the brigades were essentially infantry rifle units, a full division would have to include artillery and other specialized marines. It would be a complete force, entirely self-contained and capable of independent operation.

In May 1918, Barnett sent John A. Lejeune, now a brigadier general, and Major Earl H. Ellis to France to make the case for a division to General Pershing in person. Hopes were high, but Pershing could not be moved. He would commit marines to combat. He would ensure that marines—not army personnel—were to fill all replacement slots in the 4th Brigade. He would even allow, when necessary and appropriate, marine officers to command some army units. But the introduction of an entire marine division would invite the meddling of the navy department in the AEF, and that he would not allow.

Whether as a division, a brigade, a regiment, or even a company, the marines would nevertheless earn their place in the war. The Allies were in desperate straits early in 1918. The Bolshevik Revolution had taken Russia out of the war, releasing masses of German troops for service on the western front. Ludendorff had 194 divisions to hurl against the British and French even as the Americans struggled to deploy enough men to do more than simply die. General Pershing did not want the marines, but he would need them just the same—and soon.

· 2 ·

"A Quiet Sector"

Having volunteered to be the First to Fight and toughened by training at Parris Island and Quantico, the marines were intensely frustrated by their consignment to labor and guard duty. Yet their frustration did not come from zeal and pride alone. As they worked on a loading dock or patrolled a village street, all marines were aware of the crisis swirling about them. The war had reached a critical point—and the British and French had reached the point of exhaustion.

World War I had begun with Germany on the offensive. Shortly after the Schlieffen Plan had been compromised and then abandoned altogether, however, the German army converted to a defensive strategy. Already dug in deep within French territory, it could afford to compel the British and French to batter themselves against formidable German defenses. Usually defenders are at a disadvantage because wars are typically won offensively rather than defensively. Yet, having failed to consummate their opening offensive, German military planners consoled themselves with the realization that, in this war, all the advantages lay with the defenders. It was a question of technology. The technology of defense—from heavy artillery to the machine gun to the trench itself—was far in advance of the technology of attack (though the British hoped to close the gap with an innovation they called the "tank"). The machine gun in particular had the effect of multi-plying a defender's forces. A two-man machine-gun crew, if well dug in, could defeat scores, even hundreds of attackers. The only effective defense against the machine gun was the trench—and that was precisely the point, because offensive attack required leaving the trench.

So, for nearly four years on the western front, after the collapse of the Schlieffen Plan, the Germans made a defensive stand, seeking to wear down the Allies. And so they did—but, in the process, they were wearing them-selves down as well. Germany had transformed a war of attack into a war of attrition, in which both sides bled and melted away. Nevertheless, the Ger-man generalissimo, Erich Ludendorff, sensed that the British and French were wearing away at a marginally faster rate than the Germans and would therefore suffer defeat—provided that America stayed out of the war. Once America entered the war, Ludendorff realized that the balance of attrition was about to change. He decided, therefore, to convert from a defensive to an offensive strategy in the hope of defeating the flagging British and French before the Americans could arrive in sufficient numbers to make a significant military impact.

With the fall of the czar, Russia was now out of the war, and Ludendorff accordingly shifted large numbers of troops from the east. Since his army had been accustomed to nearly four years of defensive war, he knew that he could not simply pour his soldiers into the attack on the western front, so he began a crash training program intended to convert defensive troops into attackers. The very best of his trainees he assigned to special shock-troop units. These especially aggressive forces would lead the assaults.

The Ludendorff offensives are often termed "desperate." In fact, they were the products of careful analysis. Throughout the war, both the British and French had launched any number of go-for-broke, all-or-nothing offen-sive pushes. Each had failed to be decisive. Ludendorff did not intend to make a mindless attack and hope for the best. He pondered the Allied situ-ation and concluded that the British and French were often at cross purposes. Whereas the British were always concerned to maintain lines of communication with the English Channel ports—and home—the French were obsessed with the protection of Paris. This told him two things: first, Paris was so important to the French national identity that, if it was captured, France would almost certainly be knocked out of the war; second, divergence of purpose made the Allies vulnerable to a divide-and-conquer approach. Instead of attempting to destroy the Allies, Ludendorff would drive a wedge between the British and French by threatening Paris and attacking the British. With Paris threatened, the French (he believed) would not give the British the level of reinforcement required to prevent their annihilation. With the British out of the war, however, France would have no choice but to negotiate a favorable peace.

Ludendorff's first offensive was launched along the Somme River, beginning on March 21, 1918, days before the United States declared war. From north to south, the German 17th, 2nd, and 18th armies attacked the British on their right flank along a sixty-mile front from Arras to La Fère. Ludendorff began with an artillery attack that included poison gas, then employed what the Allies called "Hutier tactics" to break through the British lines. The name came from German General Oscar von Hutier, who, in September 1917, had led his Eighth Army on the eastern front against the key Baltic Sea port of Riga (today in Latvia) and its associated fortress. In this attack, Hutier implemented a radically innovative—and quite horrific—approach. He did not begin with a long "artillery preparation"—as prolonged artillery bombardment was called—reasoning that, destructive though such a preparation was, it also gave the defenders time to prepare for the onslaught that followed. Moreover, lengthy artillery bombardment so cratered no-man's-land (the territory between the opposing trench lines) that the advance of the attackers was inevitably slowed by the difficult terrain. Therefore, Hutier began with a brief but intensive bombardment that was immediately followed by an infantry advance. Instead of directing the artillery fire at the enemy's front lines—to soften them up for the attack—Hutier aimed at the rear. This prevented the front lines from being reinforced from the rear. As the advance was about to begin, Hutier masked the attackers and the positions they advanced from with smoke and the concentrated use of poison gas. These brutal measures helped to maintain the element of surprise until the last possible moment.

To make his attack, Hutier used light, rapid infantry units—shock troops called *Sturmbataillon* (storm battalions)—whose mission was to penetrate the enemy lines rapidly at various weak points, ensuring that the rest of the attacking force that followed would always have the ability to maneuver. Shock troops fought to attain local superiority at various places along the front while artillery support was adroitly shifted from fire directed against enemy artillery positions to fire that directly supported the infantry advance. The Germans had a name for this carefully choreographed use of artillery. They called it the *Feuerwalz* (fire waltz).

The effect of Hutier tactics when properly executed was stunning. In the case of the Battle of Riga, the Russian Twelfth Army crumbled and, panic stricken, ran from the field.

Initially, Ludendorff was thrilled with the effect of the Somme offensive. As he had predicted, France's Marshal Henri Philippe Pétain was more anxious to protect Paris than he was to reinforce the British line. He sent some reinforcements, but refused to transfer major forces. This provoked a protest from General Sir Henry Wilson, British chief of staff, who called for the appointment of "Foch or some other French general who will fight" to take over supreme command from Pétain.

This was an outcome even Ludendorff had failed to anticipate. The Allied Supreme War Council did not remove the conservative, cautious, even plodding Pétain from overall command of the French army, but it appointed Ferdinand Foch commander in chief of the Allied forces in France. Foch's sector had fallen under heavy attack at the beginning of the war in August 1914, and although he was forced to fall back with heavy losses, he never allowed defeat to be turned into a rout. Similarly, at the First Battle of the Marne, during September 5–10, 1914, Foch sent a characteristic message to General Joseph Joffre, then in overall command of French forces: "My center is giving way, my right is falling back, situation excellent, I attack." Foch was a daring commander, of whom Pershing, when he arrived, heartily approved. He was not the kind of foe Ludendorff wanted to face—

especially after his Somme offensive petered out on April 5, 1918, when Foch, shifting French reserves, checked the German advance at Montdidier. The offensive had done a lot of damage, creating a forty-mile salient—or bulge—into the Allied lines, and it had inflicted some 240,000 Allied casualties, including the taking of 70,000 prisoners of war (POWs). Yet it had not destroyed the British army, and it had cost the Germans as many losses as it had caused the Allies. Worst of all, Ludendorff's heaviest casualties were among his elite shock troops.

The Allies were mauled and even disheartened by the Somme offensive and its forty-mile breakthrough. But it imparted a valuable lesson, prompting them to create a truly unified command for the first time in the war. Whereas Ludendorff had intended to split the British from the French, he had ended up compelling them to unite—along with the Americans, when they began showing up in large numbers.

Ludendorff did not confine the Somme offensive to an attack on the enemy army. To intensify the threat against Paris—and to demoralize the French—he made use of a new "wonder weapon" dubbed the "Paris gun." There were, in fact, at least seven—perhaps more—of these artillery pieces, huge weapons with 117-foot-long barrels capable of firing fifteen-inch projectiles more than seventy miles. This put the French capital well within range, even when the big guns were safely behind German front lines. Fired during the offensive, the Paris guns inflicted 876 casualties among Parisians, yet this experiment in "total war"—war targeting civilians as well as military combatants—produced no significant effect on the outcome.

Despite the cost of the Somme offensive, Ludendorff remained determined to do what he could to break the Allies before the Americans could enter the war in force. Therefore, on April 9, 1918, he launched a new offensive against the British at the Lys River, which forms part of the Belgian-French border. Still relying on the French obsession with Paris, Ludendorff directed the attack against what he knew to be Britain's chief concern. He threatened the English Channel ports.

As with the Somme offensive, the Lys offensive began with Hutier tactics, which proved devastating. A Portuguese division fighting under British control in the sector was annihilated, opening a yawning gap that threatened the British flanks. Under any circumstances, a flank attack is dangerous. In trench warfare, it could be especially catastrophic, capable of simply "rolling up" a defender. In this case, within three hours of the first onslaught, the German Sixth Army reached the open country *behind* the British rear lines. The defenders were caving in everywhere.

By April 12, the British had been pushed far back. British General Douglas Haig begged Foch for reinforcements. As Ludendorff had predicted, Foch replied that he had none to give. Yet Ludendorff had not foreseen what Foch would *say* to Haig. Ludendorff believed that the French unwillingness to reinforce the British would drive a wedge between the Allies. Instead, Foch communicated to Haig—with utter sincerity—that he had total confidence in the tenacity of the British fighting man. This prompted Haig to issue "General Order of the Day, April 11, 1918," which became celebrated in the history of the Great War as the "Backs to the Wall" order:

TO ALL RANKS OF THE BRITISH ARMY IN FRANCE AND FLANDERS

Three weeks ago to-day the enemy began his terrific attacks against us on a fifty-mile front. His objects are to separate us from the French, to take the Channel Ports and destroy the British Army.

In spite of throwing already 106 Divisions into the battle and enduring the most reckless sacrifice of human life, he has as yet made little progress towards his goals.

We owe this to the determined fighting and self-sacrifice of our troops. Words fail me to express the admiration which I feel for the splendid resistance offered by all ranks of our Army under the most trying circumstances.

Many amongst us now are tired. To those I would say that Victory will belong to the side which holds out the longest. The French Army is moving rapidly and in great force to our support.

There is no other course open to us but to fight it out. Every position must be held to the last man: there must be no retirement. With our backs to the wall and believing in the justice of our cause each one of us must fight on to the end. The safety of our homes and the Freedom of mankind alike depend upon the conduct of each one of us at this critical moment.[1]

Words successfully substituted for reinforcements. Haig's army held then began to push back. By April 29, Ludendorff was forced to break off his second offensive. British losses in the Lys offensive were 239,000, including 28,000 dead. The Germans, who had come so close to a major victory with this offensive, lost 348,300, including some 50,000 dead.

For the first time in the war, American forces played a combat role in resisting the Lys offensive. On April 20, two companies of the U.S. Army's 26th Division came under heavy attack near Seicheprey along what was called the Saint-Mihiel salient. This was a bulge of the German lines southeast of Verdun that had been formed early in the war, during the fall of 1914. Throughout the war, all attempts to "reduce"—or push back—the salient had failed, and this outcropping of German strength seriously interfered with French rail communications between Paris and the eastern sectors of the front. Now, along this salient, some twenty-eight hundred German regulars spearheaded by six hundred shock troops rolled over the American companies, taking many prisoners and wounding or killing 669 others. German losses were inconsequential.

The green Americans had fought bravely, but the disappointing results were disquieting to Pershing and the other Allied commanders. It is little wonder that a third offensive—which the Allies surely anticipated—was a source of much anxiety. For the marines, the prospect excited anticipation: a chance not only to engage the enemy, but to achieve what the army had been unable to. Yet the inevitability of a new offensive also left many marines wondering: would they be left on the sidelines again?

Both the army and marine units of the 2nd Division had been trained in the United States, of course, but it was clear that they needed more training close to the front lines in France. This began in earnest during January 1918, as the division assembled in the rugged Vosges region of northeastern

France. Headquarters of the 6th Marine Regiment was established in the town of Blevaincourt, northeast of the 5th Regiment; however, regimental units were dispersed to billets in various surrounding farming villages. Many of these made the miserable barracks of Parris Island and Quantico seem like luxury accommodations by comparison. Platoons and even smaller groups were put up in stables and haylofts, with manure heaped outside in small mountains. This fertilizer by-product of farming was sufficiently ubiquitous that the marines took to calling their little corner of the war the "Manure Sector."

Not that the marines did much more than sleep in their billets. The rest of the time was crammed with training. Despite going to a war characterized by the widespread use of poison gas, neither U.S. soldiers nor marines had left the States equipped with gas masks. For the first time, they were issued here—and not just one mask, but two, a French model and a British one. The French M2 mask was a specially coated canvas face mask containing gauze pads soaked in antigas chemicals. It was marginally effective at best. The British mask was really a hood equipped with eye lenses and connected by a hose to a small box respirator (SBR). The SBR contained a soda-lime and charcoal filter. To ensure protection, the wearer had to breathe only through the mouth, so a clip was affixed to the nose. While the British mask provided more effective protection than the French M2, it was, as marine colonel Catlin recalled in a memoir, "hot and stifling," seeming "to impede the faculties. . . . Imagine yourself fighting with a clothespin on your nose and a bag over your mouth and you may be able to get some notion of what a gas mask is like."[2] The consequences of failing to wear the mask, however, were varied, depending on the gas used, but always horrific. Chlorine, the earliest gas weapon, caused temporary blindness, burning of the lungs and throat, uncontrollable coughing, asphyxiation, and death. Phosgene, introduced during the second year of the war, was especially cruel because, unlike chlorine, which reeked repulsively, it savored of new-mown hay, tempting many a homesick farm lad to sniff the air and then breath deeply, only to find himself drowning in his own dissolving tissues as the phosgene turned to hydrochloric acid in the lungs. Then there was chlorpicrin, which was especially designed to defeat gas masks. The substance penetrated many neutralizing substances used in masks, including charcoal filters. It was not especially deadly in itself, but chlorpicrin induced nausea and vomiting. This would prompt victims to tear off their masks, exposing them to the more lethal gases that were often fired simultaneously with the substance. By the time the marines arrived in France, improvements in gas masks were generally effective against chlorpicrin, but now, a new substance called mustard gas was also being used. In low concentrations, mustard gas was barely noticeable except as an agreeable scent of lilacs in bloom. At higher concentrations, however, it caused first- and second-degree burns on whatever body part it contacted: skin, eyes, or the membranes of throat, nose, or lungs. As with chlorine, agonizing death came as victims strangled on their own disintegrating tissues. In contrast to most of the other gas weapons, mustard gas was not really a gas at all, but a finely atomized liquid that settled onto everything, collecting in dugouts, trenches, and shell holes. Hours, even days after a mustard gas attack, the battlefield remained contaminated, so that a soldier or a marine seeking refuge from machine-gun fire in a shell crater might find himself wallowing in a pool of burning liquid.

Marines as well as soldiers engaged in intensive bayonet drill, advancing against and thrusting at straw dummies suspended from poles. The French, who were in charge of training most of the incoming Americans, were especially zealous where the bayonet was concerned. The ideal attack, as they saw it, overran an enemy trench and skewered the defenders. In a war replete with new technology, ranging from gas to the machine gun to the embryonic tank, French instructors put the emphasis on this most atavistic method of slaughter, which was, in fact, most congenial to the marines.

They also introduced the Americans to the French cast-iron hand grenade. American hand grenades available when the United States entered the war in April 1917 were clumsy and unsuited to trench warfare. The army's Trench Warfare Section rushed to create a new design, which was completed by August of 1917. Contracts were quickly let for a total of sixty-eight million of the new grenades for delivery to U.S. forces overseas; however, in April 1918, production was summarily halted when AEF command condemned the new weapons. An enduring problem with hand grenades was making them safe, but the new American grenade was *too* safe, requiring five separate actions to arm the weapon. This not only led to slow fire and the hurling of many unarmed duds, but all too often the return of duds properly armed—by the enemy. Without grenades of their own, Americans used British "Mills Bombs" if they were in a British sector or the French F1 grenade in French sectors. The marines of the 5th and 6th Regiments learned to use the F1. It looked much like the failed American grenade, consisting of a hollow cast-iron body that had been deeply scored in the "pineapple" pattern to enhance fragmentation. With early F1 models, a thrower removed a safety cover then struck the cap of the grenade against a hard object to initiate the burning of the time fuse. Once initiated, the grenade had to be thrown. By the time the marines arrived, the Billant, or automatic, fuse system was being used. This was a cast white-metal fuse screwed into the head of the grenade casing and fixed in place by a lever that was secured by means of a looped safety pin. The thrower pulled the pin, which enabled the lever to move, thereby releasing a plunger that, as it withdrew, allowed a pair of hammers to fall, initiating the primer. The thrower then had five seconds to hurl the grenade before it detonated.

Once they learned how to complete the necessary arming procedure, American soldiers and marines were taught the French method of throwing the grenade. The Americans had been accustomed to launching hand grenades like baseballs. French instructors compelled their students to unlearn this method and instead adopt a stiff-arm approach, which, although awkward—and exposing the thrower to enemy fire—imparted the high trajectory that was needed not only to land the grenade in a trench or shell hole but also to provide sufficient delay so that the enemy could not hurl it back.

Other weapons unfamiliar to the Americans included the rifle-launched VB grenade and the trench mortar. The VB was fired from what the French called a *tromblon*, a cone that was fitted onto the muzzle of the

Springfield rifles U.S. forces brought with them. The grenade weighed a pound and required the user to position the butt of the rifle not against the shoulder—which would be fractured by the recoil—but on the ground. The trajectory was therefore high, if not terribly accurate.

The rifle-launched VB grenade had a range of twelve hundred yards. The Allies entered the war without an effective trench mortar, but the British rapidly created the Stokes mortar. It was simplicity in itself, consisting of nothing more than a metal tube fixed to a recoil-absorbing base plate and elevated by means of a bipod. A bomb—that is what the mortar shell was called—was dropped into the muzzle of the tube and slid down. The base of the bomb was equipped with an impact-sensitive cartridge, which was triggered by contact with a firing pin at the base of the tube. This would launch the three-inch-diameter, cast-iron projectile. A good mortar squad could fire twenty-two bombs per minute, and the French copied the Stokes example meticulously. Trench mortars, the Americans quickly learned, were essential to trench warfare. Their rate of fire and high trajectory made firing *from* trenches relatively easy and safe, and made firing into trenches both deadly and disruptive. Even those mortar rounds that failed to find their mark caused trouble. Soldiers under attack would take cover every time they heard the *plop* of a bomb being fired out of a mortar tube. This effectively disrupted return fire from a defender.

The marines who came to France were already quite familiar with the machine gun and brought with them their well-trusted Lewis guns. The American-made twenty-six-pound, air-cooled weapon had a forty-seven cartridge circular magazine and could be fired at five hundred to six hundred rounds per minute. With an effective range of two thousand feet, it had been readily adopted by the British army early in the war and was dubbed "the Belgian rattlesnake" by German forces who came up against it. The U.S. Army and the marines took it to France, but there the marines had to trade it for the French Hotchkiss and an automatic rifle known as the Chauchat. Formally designated Fusil-Mitrailleur Mle 1915 CSRG, or Gladiator, the Chauchat was the most widely manufactured automatic weapon of World War I, with some two hundred sixty thousand units turned out.

At twenty pounds, it was lighter than the Lewis gun, yet the marines who used it complained of its weight, almost certainly because its design was clumsy. Intended to be produced in vast quantities, the Chauchat was cheap and, therefore, both inaccurate and unreliable—perhaps the least reliable automatic weapon ever used by any armed forces in any modern war. The marines hated it.

But training even with the Chauchat was preferable to what the marines spent most of their time doing: drilling and marching. As one marine recalled, they were not allowed to drill in dry, tillable areas, but were forced to use swampy meadowlands, drilling "all day, usually in water halfway to our shoe tops." At least this misery made forced marches—on dry roads—more appealing, even though each marine carried "a pack weighing about forty-five pounds, consisting of two blankets, a supply of underclothes, a pair of trousers, emergency rations of hardtack and 'monkey meat' (canned corn beef), besides a heavy belt with 100 rounds of ammunition, a canteen, wire-cutters, gas mask, helmet and rifle."[3]

Neither the American army nor the marines had yet figured out what little sense it made to send men into combat encumbered with all of their bivouac gear. Doubtless, this caused much unnecessary exhaustion in the run-up to combat—and yet it also toughened the men. Major Frederic Wise was one of the marine battalion commanders celebrated for dealing out unremitting drill. To a young lieutenant, Lemuel C. Shepherd, Wise confessed that he knew his men considered him "a martinet" and that "you youngsters fuss because I insist on meticulous obedience of my orders. Some of them seem petty to you—the making up of the bunks to regulation, the correct uniform, my inspecting every rifle in the battalion. I insist on these little things because they make the big things. One of these days we'll be in combat and the only way we can win is by strict and unqualified obedience of orders."[4]

Shepherd, who later became the twentieth commandant of the U.S. Marine Corps, said that he remembered all of his life what Wise had told him. At the moment, however, he had to take the battalion commander's words on faith, just as every marine had to convince himself that the marching, the drill, the mud, the heavy packs, the orders, the regulations would all—somehow—mean something when they finally saw combat.

But when would that be?

The 2nd Division moved closer to the fight in the middle of March, when it was transferred from the rear to a "quiet sector" between Verdun east to the vicinity of the Saint-Mihiel salient, a line of about twenty miles. This was a very well-developed corner of the war with elaborate fortifications that allowed the marines and army soldiers, under French command, to rotate to forward trench lines—where there was some shooting—and then withdraw to intermediate trench lines and the rear area. Selected soldiers and marines served with the French manning machine gun and artillery positions, receiving hands-on training that would allow them later to man these installations on their own. Mostly, however, the marines, the soldiers, and the French troops observed the enemy, even as the enemy observed them.

Elsewhere, the Americans knew, the war was an inferno, a struggle between desperate masses of attackers and even more desperate masses of defenders. Here, however, it was a grim, static game of watching and being watched. Neither the American soldiers nor the marines could long bear it. Individuals provoked armed exchanges. "They climbed like cats into the highest trees," one French general complained, "and began to fire on the enemy sentries."[5] This kind of provocation in turn provoked German provocation in the form of patrols sent to reconnoiter the Americans newly arrived in the sector. On April 6, 1918, a marine patrol from the 1st Battalion of the 6th Marines was fired on by a superior German force. The exchange escalated into a full-scale artillery duel. That ended, but some days later the Germans let fly some gas shells onto the marine rear, prompting the evacuation of most of a three-hundred-man company, with the loss of forty lives. The army—9th Infantry—was targeted by German raiders on April 14. Members of the 3rd Battalion beat them back with a combination of rifle, bayonet, and hand-to-hand combat, then the sector grew quiet again, and the boredom—strange and anxious—set in.

That was among the hardest lessons of this trench war. Moments and even hours of bombardment or close combat punctuated days and even weeks of miserable tedium. Trenches were rarely dry, and sleep was hard to come by. Filth, in this quiet sector, was a more abundant product of war than death. Everyone was lousy—plagued by body lice—and trench rats were continual companions. They acquired nearly mythic proportions and were spoken of as the biggest, toughest rats ever to appear on the face of the earth.

When Charles A. Doyen, commanding the 4th Marine Brigade, was invalided back to the United States in May, his health broken by the rigors of a war he had not even begun to fight, General Pershing sent in his former chief of staff, Brigader General James G. Harbord. The marines had no say in this, but could not have been very happy. In any event, they were not transferred from the quiet sector directly into hotter combat. Instead, the entire 2nd Division was pulled out of the trenches and transported south for yet more field training.

The marines—indeed, the entire 2nd Division—were at this point in time suspended in the collective ambivalence of the Allied situation. The two Ludendorff offensives, coupled with the certainty that another was soon to come, made the British and French desperate for fresh troops. Yet British and French commanders lacked sufficient confidence in the Americans to allow American officers to train and command American forces. They demanded that Pershing turn over his men, virtually upon arrival in France, to British and French command. Pershing objected on two grounds. First, he was absolutely unwilling to relinquish the American military to control by foreign powers. Second, he was firmly convinced that turning over units piecemeal would result in nothing less than their slaughter. Pershing wanted a fully trained, fully assembled, massive American force under American command. This, he believed, was the only way to achieve a breakthrough that would end the four-year-old deadlock of the trenches. The British and French commanders countered that, by the time the American army had reached a sufficient state of training and experience to make independent command feasible, the war would be lost. As Pershing, Foch,

Pétain, and Haig bitterly argued, the 2nd Division ventured into a quiet sector, saw some minor action, then was shuttled back to the rear.

By May, the American 1st, 2nd, and 3rd Divisions were holding thirty-five miles of the four-hundred-fifty-mile-long western front. Pershing even agreed to allow the 1st Division, under Major General Robert Lee Bullard, to launch an offensive against the village of Cantigny, about sixty miles north of Paris. The offensive was scheduled for May 28. In the meantime, the 2nd Division, after completing its new round of field training, was attached to the French Fifth Army. French officers were pleasingly surprised by the quality of the division, yet they were distressed by the attitude of independence its officers manifested. For example, one of Pétain's staff officers, a Colonel Rozet, complained about a tendency "to hold aloof from French influence" and to "keep the French at arm's length." Rozet complained in particular about the 2nd Division's chief of staff, a Colonel Preston Brown, who "should not indulge the illusion that he can not profit by the counsel and example of excellent French officers who have made war for nearly four years" whereas "he [Brown] had never made war."[6]

Doubtless, there was truth in this; but it was also true that both the French and the British indulged "in the illusion" that they could not profit from the fresh perspective and vigor of the American newcomers. It is little wonder, therefore, that the work of Pershing's G-2—intelligence—section was dismissed by the French high command. A young G-2 analyst, Captain Samuel T. Hubbard, concluded from a study that collated all intelligence reports from across the entire western front that the Germans were preparing to launch a new offensive at the end of the month. The target would be the Chemin des Dames.

In the mid-eighteenth century, King Louis XV had reserved this pleasure walk—Chemin des Dames (Ladies' Way)—for the amusement of his daughters because, traversing a high ridge, it offered charming views across the Aisne River. During the Great War, these same commanding views were prized for their strategic value, and a number of battles were fought between 1916 and 1918 for possession of the ridge. The most important had taken place just a year earlier. Called the Second Battle of the Aisne, it began on April 17, 1917, when French General Robert Nivelle made a gallant and tragically foolish assault on Germans who were strongly dug into the caves of the Chemin des Dames. The first day, Nivelle lost some forty thousand men. By April 25, when the battle was over, Nivelle had lost a total of ninety-seven thousand men. It was indeed likely that a new battle would erupt here, and Pershing was sufficiently impressed by Captain Hubbard's analysis to endorse the report and give it to his liaison officer for the attention of French intelligence. The French liaison with American G-2 was also persuaded by the report and took it to high command—which promptly rejected it, not on its merits but because of "considerable doubt that the American intelligence service could be correct."[7]

The dismissal of the American analysis was all the more egregious in view of the fact that a stream of German POWs had been reporting the imminence of a major offensive between the River Oise and Reims—the Chemin des Dames sector. Moreover, despite the obvious fact that the ridge had already been contested repeatedly, the French considered the terrain of the Ladies' Way so rugged that an attack across it was seen as simply unfeasible. High command deployed just six French and four British divisions in the sector, badly understrength at that, with two of the French and one of the British divisions held off the line in reserve.

At last, on May 26, a pair of German POWs made coldly clear the scope of the offensive, revealing, moreover, that it was just about to step off—which it did, a short time after midnight on May 27. This time, Ludendorff made liberal use of artillery preparation, beginning with gas and then following up with a three-and-a-half-hour barrage by some four thousand guns. The barrage decimated the French Sixth Army sector to a depth of as much as eight miles. By dawn, French resistance on the Chemin des Dames had been swept aside, and at the end of twenty-four hours, the Aisne offensive, Ludendorff's third all-out offensive, had resulted in an advance of between twelve and twenty miles.

In the meantime, the scheduled U.S. 1st Division offensive against Cantigny went off as planned on the twenty-eighth. The Americans attacked the village on this day, pushing the Germans out. On May 29 and

May 30, the 1st Division would successfully repulse counterattacks. Neutralizing this enemy spearhead was a welcome triumph for the Americans—which helped to undo the disappointment of Seicheprey—but it was merely an island of modest victory in a raging sea of Allied defeat. Even as the Americans pushed back at Cantigny, the entire German center lunged over the Vesle, reaching the commanding high ground to the south of this river. Ludendorff was delighted—but not fully satisfied. The offensive had so far been much more successful than he had anticipated. The assault in the Chemin des Dames area by his right (northern) wing had been intended primarily to force the French to bring down their reserves from the north, thereby exposing the British to defeat in detail while his center (to the south) threatened Paris. Progress of both wings was proving so productive that Ludendorff saw an opportunity to gain more than a strategic advantage. He glimpsed decisive victory in the form of a breakthrough that would not merely threaten Paris, but actually capture it.

By May 29, the German advances both in the north, in the Chemin des Dames region, and farther south, toward the Marne and Paris, were slowing, meeting gathering resistance and having to cope with the inevitable problem of lengthening and ever-vulnerable lines of supply. Ludendorff had to decide whether to rein in the advance of his center and concentrate again on his original plan, to focus on the north, thereby forcing the French to draw down their reserves even as the British were decimated, or to exploit the slowing but still formidable advance toward the Marne. This would give the British—concentrated in the north—a reprieve, he understood, but it might well result in the capture of Paris and victory in this Great War.

Ludendorff decided to hedge his bet, sending his right (the northern edge of his advancing forces) beyond the town of Soissons while turning his center southward, to the Marne and toward the capital. By May 30, the center of the German army was bearing down on the Marne River town of Château-Thierry, scarcely thirty-nine miles northeast of Paris.

Crisis is far too mild a word for the situation the Allies now faced. Across a broad front of some twenty miles, on which progress was typically measured in yards, the Germans had advanced as much as twenty *miles*. At the far north of this new front, two entire German corps had pushed through fierce French resistance and advanced beyond Soissons toward the Forêt de Villers-Cotterêts. In the center, the vanguard of the German army, under General Richard von Conta, had reached the Marne. The left portion of von Conta's advance slowed down as a result of the arrival of the French Fifth Army near Reims, the easternmost portion of the new battle front.

By May 30, the map of the French Vosges region looked like this: the German advance was being held at Reims and west of Soissons—but it was being held as precariously as one would hold a wet bag bulging with something very heavy and very dangerous. The bulge—in military parlance, the German salient—ran all the way to the Marne, the most concentrated outcropping of German strength being a six-mile front between Château-Thierry and Dormans. This apex of the bulge was really the point of the German sword, and it was aimed at the heart of Paris.

Feeling the hot breath of the German advance on the capital, French high command nevertheless found a crumb of comfort in the fact that the bulging salient had been held. This freed up the French army to concentrate more on the westernmost portion of the German advance, which was to the north near Soissons. Foch scheduled for May 31 a French counterattack by four divisions north toward Soissons and three divisions northeast toward Fismes near the confluence of the Vesle and Ardre rivers. Although these positions were in the northern portion of the German advance—the German right—and not against the center, French high command always spoke of the counterattack in terms of arresting "the German advance on Paris." Colonel Rozet of Pétain's staff declared to Major Paul H. Clark, General Pershing's representative at the French general headquarters, "We must stop the drive for Paris. If Paris is taken, that probably means the end of the war for France." Rozet went on to explain that the "great trouble" was that the French reserves "are so far away. It takes three or four days to get our troops here. . . . If the counter-attack [at Soissons and Fismes] . . . does not halt the advance, then I think our next move must be to abandon the front Rheims to Switzerland . . . and assemble all we can thus get together and fight an open battle for Paris."[8]

From Reims to the Swiss border was a distance of two hundred and fifty miles, the entire southern portion of the western front. It is no wonder that General Pershing noted in his diary the somber atmosphere of the dinner meeting at which the French counterattack plans were discussed: "It would be difficult to imagine a more depressed group of officers. They sat through the meal scarcely speaking a word as they contemplated what was probably the most serious situation of the war."[9]

General Pétain understood that, in counterattacking the westernmost salient in the north, the French army could not afford to stop von Conta on the Marne in the south. Both advances threatened Paris, to be sure, but von Conta was closer to the capital. Pétain asked Ferdinand Foch to order the French Tenth Army south from the area of Soissons and the forest of Villers-Cotterêts to the Marne. With him would be some British-trained American divisions. The transfer from one sector to another would take time, and the small numbers of immediately available French reinforcements, Pétain pointed out to General Foch, were so "overwhelmed by [German] numbers" that they "evaporate immediately, like drops of rain on white-hot iron."[10] Turning his eyes on Pershing, Pétain crossed to a map of France on his wall. With his thumbnail, he drew a semicircle some thirty miles east of Paris. This, he said, was the French Sixth Army sector. His tension was so great that his nail dug into the wood paneling beneath the map. Could you, he asked Pershing, send American troops here, to Château-Thierry?

Although Pershing had continually resisted committing small units to battle, he knew that in this situation there was only one answer to give. It was yes.

▪ 3 ▪

Orders

O nly two American divisions, the 3rd and the 2nd, were within reach of Château-Thierry on May 30, 1918, when Pétain appealed to Pershing for help in stopping the German thrust on the Marne. The 3rd was the latest to arrive in France; in fact, it had been assembled in that country rather than shipped intact from the United States, and its commander, Major General Joseph T. Dickman, had been scrambling to get it trained. After just a month of field training in and around Châteauvillain, the 3rd Division was ordered to relieve the U.S. 26th Division, which occupied a quiet sector. This was standard procedure: training in theater—in this case, however little—followed by "blooding" in a sector where relatively little fighting was expected. While reconnoitering the area on May 28, General Dickman received new orders—to occupy a sector in the Vosges on May 31. On May 30, responding to Pétain, Pershing issued a third set of orders. The barely trained and unblooded 3rd Division would now attach itself to the beleaguered French Sixth Army southeast of Château-Thierry. That city straddled both banks of the Marne River. By the time the advance units of the 3rd Division arrived, the Germans had overcome French defenses north of the city, had entered Château-Thierry, and had dug in on the north bank of the river. The Germans brought up artillery, which commanded the bridges across the river, and the French, still holding the south bank, had ever-diminishing prospects of preventing a forced crossing of the river. Such a crossing would have made stopping the Germans short of Paris virtually impossible. No one knew this better than the Germans themselves, who, having broken through to Château-Thierry, had every reason to believe they "were going to push straight through to Paris," as marine colonel Catlin recalled. "They came," he wrote, "in ever increasing numbers, gaily goose-stepping down the roads to Château-Thierry, in columns of fours, with their rifles on their shoulders, singing. There were many on both sides who said, 'Well, the war is over.' It looked like a mere matter of marching to the Germans."[1]

The Germans paused at the northern Marne bridgeheads in Château-Thierry, forming up for the final assault across the river. What they had not reckoned on was what Catlin described as "a small but irresistible whirlwind" that blew into Château-Thierry from the southeast, "a sort of Kansas cyclone" that "hit the bewildered Boche square in the face."[2]

It was an element of the U.S. 3rd Division in the form of a platoon of the 7th Machine Gun Battalion (motorized), led by army Lieutenant John T. Bissell. The unit had been about sixty miles to the rear and was awaiting the consolidation of its parent unit, the 3rd Division, when the call came to reinforce Château-Thierry. Ordered into the breech, Bissell and his men made an all-night ride by *camion*—the generic name for French trucks—reaching the village of Montmirail, about fifteen miles southeast of Château-Thierry, on the Petit Morin River, around noon on May 31. As the Americans sat down to a quick lunch, a French officer asked them where they were headed.

Condé-en-Brie, the Americans answered, about ten miles due north.

The Frenchman responded with urgent advice to turn back. There was, he said, no stopping the Germans there. The town was already under heavy enemy bombardment.

The Americans thanked the French officer for his advice, but pointed out that orders were orders, and they soon resumed their march. Nevertheless, it could not have been comfortable for these untested troops to march with the knowledge that they were heading into hell—especially as their progress was increasingly impeded by southward-bound refugees, a thickening stream that choked the road.

At Condé, the Americans did not encounter hell so much as chaos. The disorganized French forces there had not been told to expect the arrival of these advance elements of the U.S. 3rd Division and had no idea what to do with them. At last, a French general commanding the 10th French Colonial Division took them on and planted them just south of Château-Thierry, where they immediately joined the fighting on the Marne.

Like the rest of the 3rd Division, the machine gunners had yet to face the enemy. On the morning of June 1, under fire, they set up their machine guns to cover the first crossroads just north of the main bridge over the Marne. Bissell and his men held off the Germans and covered the retreat across the bridge of the survivors of a French Senegalese division. French engineers detonated the bridge prematurely, killing advancing Germans and the Senegalese rearguard as well, and also cutting off Bissell and his platoon. Through the dark, the platoon nevertheless managed to cross a remaining railway bridge and withdraw from the town. Bissell and his machine gunners were all soldiers of the U.S. Army, of course, but their battalion commander was a marine, Major L. W. T. Waller Jr., who had been serving with the army unit for training.

As more of the 3rd Division arrived, the men were deployed along a ten-mile front from Château-Thierry east to the village of Dormans. Although the Germans would remain in possession of the northern portion of Château-Thierry until the Allied offensive of July 18–19, the 3rd Division prevented their gaining so much as a foothold through the town on the south bank of the Marne, and by June 2, with the 3rd Division firmly entrenched along with the French colonials, the sector from Château-Thierry east had been stabilized, and the German advance halted—at this point. The sector west of Château-Thierry, however, was still vulnerable. That is where the U.S. 2nd Division would come in.

The 2nd Division, to which the 4th Marine Brigade was attached, had been ordered to relieve the U.S. 1st Division, which, victorious at Cantigny, was still parrying German counterthrusts there. From the point of view of Ludendorff, the thrust through and beyond Chemin des Dames had slowed by May 29, but that is not the way the U.S. Marines saw it. While they "were in the rest area," 6th Marine commander Catlin recalled, "it was with consternation that we watched the ease with which the enemy carried the Chemin des Dames and the Aisne near fortified Soissons. Both natural and human barriers seemed to crumble before them." Like other marine officers and like General Pershing, Catlin admired the ferocious French commander Ferdinand Foch, but even Catlin now had his doubts. "Possibly Foch was for the moment outgeneralled," he speculated, only to wonder, however, if the inexorable French retreat was actually "all a part of his farsighted plan to let the enemy wear himself down by extreme efforts." Catlin, like the other marines, was hardly in a position to know what was in Foch's head. All he knew for certain was what he saw—a stream of retreating French soldiers and civilian refugees—and what he heard: how the Germans "came, sweeping everything before them, demoralizing the French army opposed to them, and heading straight for the Paris of their dreams. We realized that with a sinking of the heart; Paris realized it; everybody realized it; but what was to be done? The Metz-to-Paris road was definitely threatened, but what barrier was there to throw across their path? And we, lying in our pleasant billets, could only curse and wait."[3]

Catlin's bitter recollection notwithstanding, soldiers, marines, and officers did not just curse and wait. The 2nd Division used May 30—Decoration Day[4]—as a precious day of rest and recreation before it was slated to trudge off to Cantigny. Into this day, the men crammed as much as they could of whatever passed for rest and recreation. Some played sports, some listened to the music of regimental bands, others attended memorial services. There were even some amateur theatricals. For a few—a very few—there was time to be stolen with a new French girlfriend. Colonel Frederic Wise spent the day in the Parisian suburb of Neuilly-sur-Seine with his wife, who had arrived in France as a volunteer with a hospital unit. A few men were given leave in Paris, where the war sometimes seemed far away, but on this day, came very close. At La Madeleine, the stately neoclassical church offering a lovely view of the Place de la Concorde just down Rue Royale, Monseigneur J. N. Connolly, chaplain of the AEF, preached a memorial service to an audience of soldiers and civilians. When Connolly finished, Cardinal Léon-Adolphe Amette, archbishop of Paris, paid a brief but eloquent tribute to the American soldiers. His speech was punctuated by the detonation of shells from one of the German "Paris guns." The cardinal concluded his tribute, the soldiers and others filed out of La Madeleine, and shortly after the last of the audience left, a German shell passed between the ornate Corinthian columns of the church, shattered the head of the statue of St. Luke, and augured into the stonework behind the altar. As if anyone could long forget it, Paris was the ultimate objective of the German offensives even as it was the treasure at the heart of the French nation.

Days earlier, Brigadier General James C. Harbord, the army officer now in command of the 4th Marine Brigade, had left the brigade's first headquarters, at "Venault-les-Dames, a quaint little French village of several hundred inhabitants, not far from the Marne River and its big battlefields." Yet, to Harbord, it had seemed very far, farther than Paris, "a very attractive part of France, now in the full chilly glory of her springtime. The woods," he had recorded in his diary, "are full of strawberry blossoms, and of lilies of the valley, my wife's wedding flowers. . . . My room is redolent with lilies of the valley, bringing memories of nearly twenty years ago." He left this for the brigade's new, more forward headquarters, Bout du Bois (End of the Woods), a château in the Oise town of Montjavoult belonging to the Vicomte and Vicomtesse Villeneuve, who had been "giving a house party to relatives when the staff officer of the 2nd Division had rolled by . . . and without inquiry as to room or space had waved his hand and murmured '4th Brigade Headquarters.' Imagine one's feeling if one were a patrician whose family had owned the same land since about the year 1000, and one had invited one's father-in-law and sister, and one or two other guests, to have six American officers drop in uninvited to be billeted." Harbord thought of how his "own beloved wife would feel under the same circumstances" and asked Madame la Vicomtesse if "she would accept a concert"—for the "band of the 6th Marines is a good band." She would, she said, and "Friendly relations were soon established. The Adjutant gave the Vicomte a bag of Bull Durham for his pipe. The A.D.C.'s made themselves agreeable to the two young ladies of the family."[5]

Harbord and his staff had been most pleasantly billeted at Le Bout de Bois for a week when, on Decoration Day, as the general and his aide, Fielding Robinson, rode "through the gates into the long driveway of the chateau," having returned from a horseback ride "through the fertile fields and woods," they were met by a "sergeant . . . hurrying toward us with the news of orders to move."[6]

Elsewhere, others were getting the word. Lieutenant Shepherd—the future twentieth commandant of the U.S. Marine Corps—was bicycling to visit his French girlfriend when he was intercepted. "[I was] told to turn out my platoon for boarding *camions*. . . . All I could do was send my orderly with a note of apology to my *marianne*." In Paris, Colonel Wise's dinner was interrupted by a telephone message from his adjutant. "We've been ordered up to the front at once," he told his wife, and hopped in an ambulance from her hospital unit to get him to 4th Brigade headquarters. As for Harbord and his staff, the Villeneuves, whose château had been so abruptly commandeered, "were at the window shedding tears and waving lace handkerchiefs when we drove away in the early dawn of the 31st of May."[7]

To each man the orders reached, they seemed electric, the highly charged product of dire emergency. They had originated with General Pershing, of course, and were passed down to Major General Omar Bundy, commander of the 2nd Division, by a French staff officer, who conveyed the full force of the crisis: how, on May 27, the Germans drove across Chemin des Dames, rolling over French and British divisions alike, all the way to the Marne. Camions would take the infantry to Meaux, a Marne River town some twenty-five miles west of Château-Thierry.

Colonel Catlin, who carried into the war a Medal of Honor earned at Vera Cruz in 1914, had, like all marine officers, a special passion for the Corps. Like all officers, too, he found that passion difficult to articulate. "*Esprit de corps*," he wrote, "that is the thing . . . a difficult thing to weigh, to describe, to analyze, for it belongs to the realm of the spiritual. We only know that it exists, that it is woven into the very warp and woof of our Corps, that it is an invaluable quality for the fighting man." Unable to define it abstractly, Catlin, in a postwar memoir, told the story "of some distinguished visitors who were passing along the cots in a military hospital in France. On one of these cots lay a man, quite still, with his face buried in the pillow. Something about him caused one of the visitors to remark, 'I think this must be an American soldier.' From the depths of the pillow came a muffled voice—'Hell, no; I'm a Marine!'"[8]

Catlin saw the approach to his regiment's first encounter with "the Hun" through the lens of esprit. "When the United States declared war on Germany," he wrote, "a thrill went through the Marine Corps." As a marine, Catlin was thrilled "to be rushed over to France to take [a] stand on the Frontier of Liberty." And so he looked on the camions not as the lumbering, malodorous, painfully hard-sprung and harder-benched French troop transport trucks that they were, but as "big, powerful motor trucks" whose "canvas covers" were "like those of prairie schooners." The trucks were promised by 6:00 p.m. and then when they failed to materialize the promise was changed to 10:00 p.m., accompanied by "indefinite orders . . . to be ready to leave at any time on short notice."[9] By nine, most units were saddled up and ready to go. Rations and ammunition were issued. Sergeants inspected the troops' gear. Each company, each platoon was formed up and marched to designated embarkation points for boarding. But by ten, the camions had yet to appear. When the trucks had still not shown up at midnight, the men in most units were told to break for a meal—cold rations, for the most part—then unroll their blankets and catch what sleep they could.

It was four in the morning, May 31, when the first trucks finally arrived in convoys of fifty to seventy-five vehicles, each convoy led by a French staff officer in a staff car. Loading was slow; it was 5:30 a.m. before the trucks started, the last vehicles leaving the embarkation point at 10:00 a.m. The sun was already up by the time the lead vehicles had reached the main highway to Meaux. It had been a chilly night, and it was cold and damp at 4:00 a.m. Now, as the sun ascended, the weather became hot. The men, packed tightly along the board benches in their woolen uniforms, twenty-five marines to each truck, soon felt the heat, and they choked on a combination of exhaust and road dust, which settled on uniforms and sweaty flesh in a thick gray pancake. Most of the way, the ride was excruciatingly slow, yet rough in the extreme—a combination of bad roads, solid rubber tires, primitive suspensions, and hard benches that were little more than slats. The drivers would speed up only when they converged "on a main highway," then they "would race to get there first and avoid the other's dust." A lieutenant of the 5th Marines yelled above the groaning motor and grinding gears: "Lucky if we don't get killed before reaching the front."[10]

It was not an idle remark. The drivers were French colonial troops, mostly from French Indochina. The trucks had been running continuously for seventy-two hours, many without changing drivers. Catlin recalled that some "of them fell asleep at their wheels and several ran off the road into the ditch." Most of the time, however, the refugee stream made it impossible to travel faster than a crawl along what was for the 6th Regiment a seventy-five-mile trip. Young, old, women, children, often accompanied by scrawny livestock, the refugees were a sight that made a strong impact on most of the American soldiers and marines. "Hundreds of refugees crowded the roads," General Harbord wrote in his diary. "Men, women, children hurrying toward the rear; tired, worn, with terror in their faces. Some riding on artillery caissons or trucks. Many walking, an occasional woman wheeling a baby carriage with her baby in it. Sick people resting by the side of the road in the fields. Some driving carts piled high with their little properties including all kinds of household effects, one old woman leading two poor little goats while she trudged along the crowded driveway. Little flocks of sheep, occasionally a led cow, sometimes a crate of chickens on a cart. Everything that a frightened peasantry fleeing before a barbarian invader would be likely to think of bringing from among their little treasures was to be seen on that congested highway. I have never seen a more pathetic sight."[11] This was a war not just against armies, but people.

If Harbord saw the refugees, Catlin looked only at his marines, "fresh and eager after their night on the hard ground. We must have seemed an extraordinary spectacle to the inhabitants of the country through which we passed, the interminable caravan of motor lorries filled with merry men in khaki."[12]

It was late in the afternoon before the first trucks arrived at Meaux. From there, the soldiers and marines would be sent to their positions on the line—some by camion, some on foot. The only question was, who was going where?

Preston Brown, 2nd Division chief of staff, was driven out of Paris in a staff car, reached Meaux where he was briefed by his adjutant, then drove on to Trilport, headquarters of the French Sixth Army. Knowing that his division—some fifteen hundred men—was already beginning to arrive at Meaux, he was anxious to get them deployed to the front as quickly as possible, but the only answers he could get from the French was to concentrate them "near Meaux." Unsatisfied, Brown confronted General Denis Duchêne, commanding officer of the Sixth Army. Brown was chagrined to discover that Duchêne had no concrete plans for the defense of Château-Thierry, but he was vaguely aware that the direction of the German attack seemed now to be changing, the chief danger coming from the north, from the direction of Soissons, rather than from due east. This was his sense of the situation, a hunch at best, for the situation was terribly confused and continually changing. Nevertheless, a hunch was better than nothing. Brown studied the maps at Duchêne's headquarters and saw that north of Château-Thierry—that is, in the direction of Soissons, the new source of danger from the Germans—were three parallel streams flowing east to west. The northernmost was the Ourcq River; just to the south of it, the short, small Alland; and, to the south of the Alland, the even shorter and smaller Clignon. Rivers are, of course, natural barriers, which is why it was so important to stop the Germans before they could cross the Marne. Hold an enemy force on the far bank of a river, and you had it nailed. Stalled at a river, a moving invader became a static target. As the meandering Marne was a defensible barrier to invasion from the east, so the much smaller Ourcq, Alland, and Clignon rivers were barriers to an onslaught from the north. Brown proposed to Duchêne that the 2nd Division should not be deployed at Meaux to defend the Marne—especially given the fact that the Paris-Metz highway was jammed with refugees and retreating French troops—but should be positioned in and around the village of May-en-Multien, to the west and north of Meaux along the Meaux-Soissons highway. The left flank of the division could thereby defend this highway, blocking the German advance along it from Soissons, while the center and the right flank took up positions along the Clignon east to the village of Gandelu, to block a broader advance.

Whereas General Duchêne had been quick to dismiss the wisdom of American intelligence when it predicted the German offensive at Chemin des Dames in the first place, he now accepted Brown's analysis and proposal without so much as a question. He authorized Brown to divert the 2nd Division from Meaux and to deploy instead with the 7th French Corps on the left—the north—to defend against an attack from the direction of Soissons. This, naturally, compounded the confusion of orders and revised orders. General Harbord, commanding the 4th Marine Brigade, received his new orders about two in the afternoon. The brigade was to "go out to the northeast of Meaux and billet in four little villages west of the Ourcq River. . . . The Germans were said to be not far away and we might expect to be attacked before morning." By this time, the Meaux-Soissons road was as crowded as the Paris-Metz road had been. "Every rod of the road was covered," Harbord recorded in his diary. "All kinds of French units . . . Hundreds of refugees . . . tired, worn, with terror in their faces. . . . Meanwhile, we passed a great many French officers and men, but all going from and not towards the front. All afternoon they passed, that motley array which . . . characterizes the rear of a routed army."[13]

By the late afternoon, Harbord and other officers had reached May-en-Multien, as had Frederic Wise's battalion of 5th Marines and two battalions of the U.S. Army's 9th Infantry under Colonel Leroy Upton. Preston Brown was also present and soon received an order from General Duchêne to deploy the 2nd Division between Montigny and Gandelu to close up a gap in the French line along the Alland River while also preparing to counterattack north of that small river. The army commanders, Brigadier General E. M.

Lewis (3rd Brigade) and Leroy Upton (9th Infantry), set about finding contact with French line, which was supposed to be at Saint-Quentin. All they encountered, however, were more retreating troops—and soon learned that Saint-Quentin had fallen to the enemy.

In the meantime, Harbord made his own reconnaissance to find his own point of contact with the French line. He was intercepted by a French officer who handed him a new set of orders from General Duchêne. Harbord's marines were now told to position themselves on the right of the 3rd Brigade, facing Chezy-en-Allier, northeast of the road connecting Montigny with Gandelu. Thanks to ceaseless road congestion, getting there was not easy, and the sun had already set when Harbord arrived. After assigning aides to set up brigade headquarters and designating forward positions for his marines, Harbord and his French-speaking aide Norris Williams ventured back onto the clogged Meaux-Soissons road to get final orders. Overtaken along the way by a French division commander, Harbord—through Williams—asked him where the Germans were. The Frenchman replied that he did not know. Desperate for some idea of who was where, Harbord instructed Williams to ask him where his own command was. But he didn't know that, either. *Then where are you headed?* Harbord demanded.

Williams translated the question, but the Frenchman's response required no translation: "La soupe."[14]

Well, thought Harbord, at least he knew where *he* was going.

It was 7:40 p.m. by the time Harbord found division Chief of Staff Preston Brown, who was embroiled in an animated discussion with French officers. He turned to Harbord to tell him that Duchêne had changed his orders yet again. The 2nd Division was to march to a position *west*—not east—of the Ourcq River. Just as Harbord was getting ready to ensure that his marines were pointed toward the new location—pursuant to this third order from Duchêne—a *fourth* order arrived in Brown's hands. Suddenly, the main thrust of the German offensive had shifted back to Château-Thierry and the area just to its west. The 2nd Division was now to turn about and head for Montreuil-aux-Lions, to deploy between there and Château-Thierry.

By this time, 2nd Division troops were disembarking from camions all along the road, "mingling," Harbord wrote, "in the rabble that thronged the crowded highway." To compound the confusion, darkness had come on. "I hurried back to get the staff officers left at Bremoiselle, and finally got them and got back to the road and started back to a point where I had sent a staff officer to stop any marine units from coming further north." Harbord understood that Montreuil-aux-Lions, their new designated area of deployment, was a full day's march. "Our troops had been up nearly all night the night before, and in trucks all day. Some of them did not actually join us until twenty-four hours after their embarking in the trucks." As for Harbord himself, "I spent nearly all that night on that road in the dark trying to get units of dead-tired marines assembled, and turned in the right direction."[15]

As if to make Harbord's exhausting job even more interesting, a "German plane came along and bombed the highway." That impromptu air raid was the product of Preston Brown's indiscreet use of his staff car's headlights to illuminate a map as he briefed the division's trains officer. The bombs fell just as one young officer of Colonel Wise's marine battalion, Captain Lester Wass of the 18th Company, expressed the frustration of all the marines who had been jostling—aimlessly, it seemed—in the camions all day, then marched, then turned around. "I would like to see one German at least," he exclaimed. Lieutenant E. D. Cooke observed (in a reminiscence published in 1937) that he "couldn't have gotten his wish any quicker if he had rubbed a magic lamp. A lone airplane came scooting low over the treetops, banked swiftly and *wham! wham! wham!* laid a string of eggs right down the road where we were sitting. Wass and I dove for the ditch, but before I landed, a fragment of hot steel smacked against the seat of my pants." This elicited a stream of "heartfelt cursing," which Wass interrupted with an admonishment to "pipe down." He continued, "You'll get a wound chevron for this." Finding little comfort in that, Cooke asked, "And what do I say when people ask where I got hit?" Wass "offered several curt suggestions, all to the point, if a little crude," and as Cooke's unit "moved off down the road some kids in the first platoon broke out with a new version of the '*Parlez Vous*' song":

The lieutenant, he saw an airplane pass.

Parlez-vous?

"and went on happily to describe in detail just what happened to the lieu-tenant."[16] For marines, an air raid and a shrapnel wound could make a good joke—if they didn't kill you. Lieutenant Cooke survived his wound, his em-barrassment, and the war, eventually achieving promotion to major. Cap-tain Lester Wass would be killed at Soissons, shortly after the battle for Belleau Wood.

The last component of the 2nd Division's infantry to receive Duchêne's fourth set of orders was the 6th Marine Regiment. When Colonel Catlin reached Meaux at 8:30 p.m., the first of his convoys was heading toward May-en-Multien. At division headquarters in Meaux, Catlin was given or-ders to march north, "but those orders were changed twice during the night. About 10 o'clock a French staff officer stopped my car and told me that the troops had been shunted off. I started in a new direction and was switched again to Montreuil-aux-Lions. I was," Catlin confessed, "a lost Colonel, hunting around in the dark for his command, and hunting with an anxiety that, in this crisis, approached panic." Catlin well understood the source of this "sorry mix-up. The French were on the run, and the staff came pretty close to being up in the air. Orders were given and counter-manded in the effort to get the reinforcements to the spot where they were most needed, while a dozen spots looked equally dangerous. It must have been a terrible night for those upon whose shoulders rested the responsi-bility of saving their beloved Paris."[17]

Orders were being cut and recut not because of French indecision but because the fluid situation was deteriorating by the minute. Yet precisely because orders were in flux, precious time and energy were being squan-dered. As bad as it was to be a colonel hunting in the dark for his command, it was even worse for the marines on the road to Montreuil-aux-Lions. "Sometimes," Catlin recalled, "there was a jam . . . that delayed the advance for ten minutes, due to some break-down of the overworked motors [of the camions]. Some of our troops were badly held up, or were lost trying to find another way around." The only people who seemed to know precisely where they were going were the refugees and French soldiers fleeing the fight. "For the most part everything and everybody seemed to be hurrying away from the battle line except the Americans."[18]

When Catlin's marines finally reached Montreuil-aux-Lions, four miles behind the front, some were lucky enough to be assigned to hasty billets, where they grabbed what sleep could be had before daybreak. Most, however, "got no sleep before daylight on June 1st, the very day we went into the line. And remember that the night before they had slept on the ground with the expectation of being called at any moment." The marines had been riding in camions from nineteen to thirty hours. "Some got lost and had to hike with their sixty-pound packs. When they arrived they were grey with dust and hollow-eyed with fatigue. They looked more like miners emerging from an all-night shift than like fresh troops ready to plunge into battle." A French staff officer told Catlin that the marines would not be expected to go in until June 2, "but General Harbord had determined to waste no time. If the need was urgent, delay might be fatal." Harbord was an army man, but now he told the French, "the Marines . . . were always ready," as if he, too, had always been a marine. Catlin sensed that the "French hesitated to trust us too far in this crisis." Little wonder. "We were without tanks, gas shells, or flame projectors. We were untried in open warfare. But General Harbord begged to be allowed to tackle the job."[19]

Catlin reported that Harbord put it to the French like this: "Let us fight in our own way . . . and we'll stop them."

Harbord himself reported it differently. He had bivouacked the 5th Marines at May-en-Multien, where they shared the open field adjacent to the village with the 23rd Infantry and 2nd Engineers. At 4:30 on the morning of June 1, the 5th Marines began the march to Montreuil-aux-Lions, with the 23rd Infantry and the 2nd Engineers following. In his staff car, Harbord raced ahead of his marines to report to the commander of the French 21st Corps, General Joseph Degoutte. He reached Degoutte's headquarters near Coupru at about six.

Degoutte greeted him with grim news, beginning: "Things have been going badly with us." He told Harbord, "[The Germans had been] pressing us since the morning of the 27th and have advanced over fifty kilometers in seventy-two hours. I know that your men need rest. Let them get something to eat.... Your troops must be ready to go into the line any time after eleven if called on."[20]

In the end, it was almost certainly a little of both the Catlin and Harbord versions. Harbord did want to get his marines into the fight, but he knew they were exhausted. Degoutte did not want to trust the Americans, but he knew he had no choice, and because he had no choice, he wanted to pour the Americans into the fiery furnace—*now*—come what may.

To 2nd Division commander Omar Bundy and his chief of staff, Preston Brown, Degoutte laid out the situation he had outlined to Harbord. Château-Thierry, he said, had been taken by the Germans. This was overly pessimistic. The northern portion of the city had indeed fallen, but that part of Château-Thierry on the south bank of the Marne was still holding. Not that the situation was rosy. In their drive toward and into Château-Thierry, the Germans had taken sixty thousand prisoners, six hundred fifty guns, two thousand machine guns, and claimed many more casualties. Worse, the Germans occupied a position known as Hill 204, high ground overlooking the road to Paris and the Marne valley to the south and to the west. This position, Degoutte said, posed the greatest immediate danger, and he called for the Americans to join the French forces at the hill and, in company with them, to attack it without delay.

Bundy and Brown objected. Only the 9th Infantry of the 2nd Division was anywhere near Hill 204. They were meagerly supplied with only one hundred rifle rounds each. They had neither artillery nor machine guns, and their supply trains were far away. The rest of the division, in obedience to the latest French orders, were west and south of Montreuil-aux-Lions. Brown argued that the best use of the 9th Infantry was as a defensive line backing up the current French position, which would have to hold until the entire 2nd Division could be properly deployed.

After much acrimonious debate, Degoutte gave in, and the 9th Infantry was assigned to hold a line east of and facing Château-Thierry.

Can the Americans really hold this line? Degoutte demanded.

Brown replied: "General, these are American regulars. In a hundred and fifty years they have never been beaten. They will hold."[21]

Bundy and Brown had intended to buy the 2nd Division—and, with it, the 4th Marine Brigade—a little time, not to rest but to form up and to fight as a unified American unit rather than be fed piecemeal by the French into the meat grinder. But, while Bundy and Brown conferred with brigade commanders Harbord and Lewis at the hôtel de ville in Montreuil-aux-Lions after the conference with Degoutte, a motorcycle messenger arrived with a fresh message from the French general. A new German attack had just swallowed up La Gonterie, a farm just west of Belleau Wood, so that the enemy was gaining ground toward Bouresches, just south of the woods. "I beg that you direct your first available regiment to [the] line," the message said.

Bundy wanted to put in the 23rd Infantry, but in the ongoing confusion of changing orders, no one knew where that regiment was. So Bundy turned to Harbord: *Put in Catlin's 6th Marines*, he ordered.

· 4 ·

In This Line

To the marines trundled in camions endlessly, sleeplessly, from one muddy French village to another while a desperate battle raged just beyond their line of sight, the Allied situation must have seemed a hopeless muddle. The marines knew the British were imperiled and the French on the point of breaking; indeed, judging from the unceasing stream of horizon-blue-coated, Adrian-helmeted, grim-faced poilus flowing *away* from battle, that breaking point may well have been passed. It didn't matter. The marines were undaunted by that stream of defeat. They were ready to fight, burning to get on the line. Yet, here they were, moving back and forth—behind the lines. To them, it must have seemed as if the brass—French brass, American, British, whoever—were going to let the Germans win this war before the marines even got into the fight.

But the brass had no such intention. The fluidity of the orders came from the fluidity of the situation. On a battle map, the situation looked dark; that is, it looked very much like a German victory. But if the Allied high command could have seen the situation at the end of May and the beginning of June through German eyes, they would have been less downcast. This third offensive had so far been much more successful than the first two, yet, like those previous operations, it was beginning to flag. Rapid movement had caused the combat units to outrun logistical units. And while the German Seventh Army had pushed west of Soissons on the right (northern) flank of the offensive, it had failed to capture important objectives along the way, including Reims. This created a strangle point in the German supply line. Instead of flowing along multiple routes, communications and supplies trickled into the Soissons area through the village of Fismes. On the center and left flanks of the offensive advance (the southern portion), the Germans had reached the Marne—the very river that marked the extent of their advance on Paris back in 1914—but as of May 31 they had yet to cross the river, thanks in large part to the U.S. 3rd Division.

To an advancing army, a major river is more dangerous than any human enemy alone. It takes time and effort to cross, thereby imposing a pause in the advance, during which the defending army can mount a stout resistance or even a counterattack, either of which might pin down the attacker. Cross the river prematurely, and the attacker risks dividing its army on either side of it, thereby exposing the force to defeat in detail. Cross the river successfully, and yet another danger is created, because the crossing suddenly puts the river at the attacker's back, reducing maneuver and blocking any easy route of retreat.

So, on May 31, German corps commander General von Conta found himself bogged down on the near bank of the Marne. His frustration and anxiety may well have been equal to that of the Allied commanders. He issued orders forbidding his advancing columns to rest "in villages, on bridges or similar narrow places" lest they block the passage of supplies. He demanded "an uninterrupted frictionless traffic on roads."[1] He was further frustrated by signs that his corps was hardly behaving like a victorious army. The men were tired—tired of this offensive and tired of four years of war—and they often behaved like tired men. They reported themselves sick, or they drank themselves drunk.

The generalissimo responsible for the offensive, Erich Ludendorff, also showed signs of weariness, the exhaustion of a man trying to lift a great weight. He stopped lifting for a moment and looked for new places to get hold of his burden. Seen from a distance, the advance of the German line was a great bulge, not from the east but from the northeast bearing down toward the southwest, forming a great arc from just west of Soissons, south toward Belleau Wood, turning back toward the east along the Marne, through Château-Thierry and Dormans, then turning to the northeast through the forest of Reims to the vicinity of the town of Reims. Ludendorff decided to shift the thrust of the attack more to the west. It was this shift that resulted in General Degoutte's urgent request that the Americans "direct [their] first available regiment to [the] line." [2]

Von Conta's orders to his corps, issued at 1:30 a.m. on June 1, deployed seven divisions—five on the line, two in reserve—and ordered multiple attacks in and around Château-Thierry and the village of Jaulgonne, northeast of Château-Thierry on the Marne, with the object of forcing a crossing to the river's south bank and establishing bridgeheads at both places. Simultaneously, the German Seventh Army was to continue its attack to break Allied resistance between Soissons and Villers-Cotterêts, which was southwest of Soissons. Thus the German thrust had indeed shifted from the southwest to the west, except at Château-Thierry and Jaulgonne, which were now the southern objectives at the extreme left of the German advance. The German objective for June 2 was embodied in von Conta's order to reach the "line Gandelu-Marigny-Bouresches-Vaux," which would push the center of the advance west-southwest, beyond Belleau Wood, and ensure that the German forces would strongly hold both banks of the Marne, even as they continued the thrust toward Paris.

It was a good idea, because it concentrated the broad offensive in one direction—west—rather than spreading it thinner west, southwest, and south. This fresh purchase, with handholds closer together, promised to give Ludendorff the leverage he needed to finally move the great weight that lay before him. There was one factor that had not entered into his calculations, however. The U.S. 2nd Division was just now taking up positions along the line Gandelu-Marigny-Bouresches-Vaux.

▪ ▪ ▪

Put in Catlin's marines, General Bundy had ordered Harbord. As if he really needed the additional spur, "several gallopers arrived from French corps headquarters urging haste, that their troops were tired, had fought for six days without rest and in some cases without food, and were steadily falling back before the German advance."[3]

Catlin's 6th Regiment was "available," but that didn't mean it was all together. A number of his battalions were still on the march. Recognizing that it was time to play cowboy, Harbord drove out to start rounding up marines. He found the lead battalion just east of Montreuil, "unloading rations from some seventeen trucks in the edge of town." Harbord did not stand on ceremony, but ordered that battalion and the two behind it to march "toward the front along the main Metz-Paris highway" and "had the remainder of the rations thrown off the trucks," then "began picking up the men of the rearmost battalion and hurrying them to the front in the trucks." The trucks took the men "as far to the front as it was safe for vehicles to go, discharged their passengers, and hurried back for a second load. By the time the lead battalion got to the front, the other two battalions had marched to the turning-off place and were deploying through the fields toward the line to be occupied."[4]

The line that the marines were closing up began at the south, where the Metz to Paris highway crossed the village of Le Thiolet. The north end of the line that was then held by the U.S. Army 9th Regiment ended there. The 2nd Battalion of the 6th Marine Regiment, under Thomas Holcomb, made contact with the 9th at Le Thiolet. Less than a mile to the northwest was Triangle Farm. This was the south end of the French line in this sector. The line extended in a broad arc through the southern end of Belleau Wood through a position several hundred yards north of Les Mares Farm, about a mile due north of the village of Champillon. From Triangle Farm, the 2nd Battalion line diverged from and ran behind the French line northwestward a little more than a mile to a point between the southern boundary of Belleau Wood and the town of Lucy-le-Bocage—which the marines invariably called Lucy Birdcage. The northern end of 2nd Battalion's line made contact, between the woods and Lucy, with the 6th Regiment's 1st Battalion, under Major Maurice Shearer. The 1st Battalion's line ran northwest and then due west to a piece of high ground marked Hill 142 on the French maps. On the next day, June 2, a battalion of the 5th Marine Regiment would take up a position touching the west end of 1st Battalion's line. The 5th Regiment battalion filled the gap between Hill 142 and Les Mares Farm, about half a mile due west. From Le Mares Farm west was another French line behind the one that ran north of the farm. Thus, as of June 1–2, the U.S. Marines were backing up a disintegrating French line across a front of roughly four and a third miles, from Le Thiolet—at the Metz-Paris highway—northwest to Les Mares Farm. At the midpoint of this line was Belleau Wood.

The marines were under French divisional command, and, having deployed his marines, General Harbord hurried to Lucy-le-Bocage to meet with General Michel, commander of the French 43rd Division, whose failing line the marines had come to back up. "Lucy," Harbord noted, "was a fairly noisy town that afternoon with the windows shaking every few seconds from artillery fire, 'going' or 'arriving.'" In this war, the Americans quickly became accustomed, like the French, to thinking of the artillery barrages as so much traffic. The "going" shells were friendly, the "arriving" were not. "Sometimes they cross and the reports are often simultaneous. But when they are not one can hear the roar of the shells, and very easily distinguish between 'going' and 'arriving' by the sound. There is always a doubt expressed as to whether a man hears the shell that kills him," Harbord paused to speculate. "Generally the shell strikes and explodes before the roar of its passage through the air ceases. Whether a man hears the shell that kills him is a difficult question to settle without practical test, and then the impassable barrier deprives us of the answer."[5]

To the accompaniment of going and arriving ordnance, Michel conferred with Harbord. The Frenchman's instructions were simple: "hold the line at all hazards." Harbord later wrote, "That was the order I transmitted to the brigade." However, the "companies were hardly more than in place when a message from the same general suggested that I have a line of trench dug several hundred yards back of them, 'just in case.'" Harbord, until recently General Pershing's chief of staff, shared with the commander-in-chief of the AEF the conviction that the Allies' slavish devotion to trench warfare had led precisely to the desperate situation that now prevailed on the western front. Pershing detested the practice of digging in, feeling about it much as another of his protégés did. Captain George S. Patton Jr. had accompanied Pershing during the Punitive Expedition against Pancho Villa in 1916 and was on the general's staff when he first set foot in Paris in June 1917. Years later, in World War II, Patton would inveigh against "the trick expression, 'Dig or die,'" arguing that "wars are not won by defensive tactics," and "digging is primarily defensive." Patton believed that to dig a foxhole—or a trench—was to dig your own grave; besides, "the psychological effect" of digging in "is bad, because if [the soldier] thinks he has to dig he must think the enemy is dangerous, which he usually is not." It is thus easy to appreciate why Harbord rejected this supplement to the original command to "hold the line at all hazards." He replied to the French general, "With the orders our men had, they were prepared to die if necessary to hold the line, but if started to digging trenches they would know it could have but one purpose and that my orders were not to be taken as given. So, I said: 'We will dig no trenches to fall back to. The Marines will hold where they stand.'"[6]

By the evening of June 1, the 6th Marines were distributed along their assigned line, and the 6th Machine Gun Battalion was thinly distributed just behind the entire line. That was welcome but hardly sufficient. The 4th Machine Gun Battalion and the machine-gun companies directly attached to the two marine regiments were all experiencing serious delays. The 4th Machine Gun Battalion was being transported by train specifically to expedite its arrival; however, a collision between two refugee trains at Compans-la-Ville tied it up. The rail transport promised to the machine-gun companies, along with the regimental supply outfits and field kitchens, failed to materialize at all, so these heavily laden units were sent on an overland march. Late on the afternoon of June 1, word of this delay reached division headquarters, whose supply officer commandeered as many of the division's trucks as he could to pick up the units along the road. Those unlucky enough not to be picked up were given forced-march orders. Nevertheless, by the evening of June 1, the 5th Marines (together with the 23rd Infantry) was closing in on the assigned sector, and the marine brigade's various support units were beginning to set up behind the lines.

Harbord hastily set up his forward headquarters at Yssonge Farm in a farmhouse that had earlier been "occupied by the French troops." They had "completely looted and plundered the place. Every room was inches deep in property emptied from wardrobes and chests of drawers. All kinds of feminine apparel strewed the premises; books were torn up; triple mirrors shattered, keepsakes and personal mementoes were thrown into the yard, drawers rifled,—the German in his worst moments could have done no more damage than had been done by these patriotic Allies of ours."[7]

But Harbord's uncomfortable quarters amid the disarray of the looted farmhouse was nothing compared to the real crisis caused by the delay in the arrival of the marines' field kitchens. The men were exhausted, spent from a combination of meandering travel by crawling camion and trudging on foot. There was no danger of starvation, of course, but cold field rations were hardly sufficient fortification for men about to enter combat. Local commanders authorized foraging parties, and the surrounding farms were soon picked clean. Close to the front lines, however, there was nothing to be had—those farms having already been ransacked by French troops. Many marines choked down the French field rations they had been issued, which included biscuits that supplemented an entrée of what was officially called Madagascar beef, but universally dubbed "corned Willie" or "monkey meat." It was tinned beef that smelled bad and tasted worse.

Despite the problems of supply, Major General Omar Bundy, commanding officer of the entire 2nd Division, breathed a little more easily by the evening of June 1, knowing that his forces were generally in place along their assigned line. His respite, however, was short lived. Late that night, he received an urgent message from corps headquarters. All along the French line, from Château-Thierry north to the Ourcq River, positions were crumbling. French reserves had been expended. Bundy was forced to redeploy the 23rd Infantry, the 1st Battalion of the 5th Marines, and a portion of the

5th Machine Gun Battalion as well as a company of engineers to plug the gaps. This was necessary not just to bail out the French, but to prevent the Germans from rolling up the Americans' own left flank, which was now vulnerable. The redeployment stiffened this area, but it left the rest of the newly established American line that much thinner.

It was not an easy night. At the top levels of command, there was confusion and uncertainty. Among the lower echelons, soldiers and marines believed they were where they were told to be, but few of them knew exactly where that was. The French maps they had been given were woefully obsolete, their scale too small to be genuinely useful, and so crudely printed that they were almost impossible to read in any case. Along with the field kitchens, the supply trains, including those with extra ammunition, had been delayed. So the bewildered, hungry men were also acutely aware that they were short on ammunition. As for machine guns—absolutely essential to holding any line in this war—there were pathetically few in place. Artillery, the heaviest and therefore slowest element, was still substantially delayed.

Before the day of June 1 had ended, at the top levels of command and in the Allied corridors of government, it was being reported that Château-Thierry had fallen, and Georges Clemenceau, France's irascible premier, blamed at least part of that on the failure of the Americans to shoulder any significant part of the war. In this accusation, there was, of course, no awareness of irony—the irony that, thanks to a U.S. Marine-led U.S. Army machine-gun battalion and other elements of the U.S. 3rd Division, the Allies actually still clung to the portion of Château-Thierry on the south bank of the Marne and, although the Germans had indeed taken most of the city, they had been unable to force a crossing of the vital river it straddled. Militarily, that fact meant everything. The Americans knew it. The Germans knew it. Only the French seemed to take no comfort in the fact that the Marne was holding. Jean de Pierrefeu, one of Pétain's staff officers, later explained: "Some names have symbolic value, and Château-Thierry is one of them. Until this town was taken [French headquarters was] calm, but after that there was much uneasiness." When a French officer tried to explain to a "lawyer from Provence, who had taken up his abode at Paris" that "since the enemy had not crossed the Marne, the danger could be met," the lawyer responded dismissively: "They have reached it, and you can tell the gentlemen of the Staff that that is bad enough." Colonel Rozet, the French liaison officer, explained to Pershing's representative at French headquarters, Major Paul H. Clark, that "French morale is subject to change on short notice. It is capable of great heights and likewise of great depths." It was imperative, Rozet said, to "inspire the troops with confidence," and to do so immediately."[8]

During May 31 and June 1, the arrival of the Americans—marines among the very forefront—in the sector around Château-Thierry had at least the promise of an elevation of French morale. As Pierrefeu described it, it was their appearance that made the biggest initial impact: "At Coulommiers and Meaux they passed in interminable columns, closely packed in lorries, with their feet in the air in extraordinary attitudes, some perched on the tilt, almost all bare headed and bare chested, singing American airs at the top of their voices amid the enthusiasm of the inhabitants. The spectacle of these magnificent youths from overseas, these beardless children of twenty, radiating strength and health in their equipment, produced a great effect." Pierrefeu remarked on their contrast with the French "regiments in their faded uniforms, wasted by so many years of war," men whose "sunken eyes" burned with "a dull fire," yet who "were no more than bundles of nerves held together by a will to heroism and sacrifice." The arrival of the Americans, Pierrefeu wrote, was a "transfusion of blood." It is doubtful that he saw any irony in that image.[9]

Jaunty and boisterous by day, how must the tired and hungry Americans have felt that night of June 1, when all was confusion, when all the news from the front was so dire? As they fell asleep—if they fell asleep—did they recall the songs and enthusiasm of earlier hours? Or did they ponder the other images of the interminable camion rides and marches? How they beat against the tide of refugees and routed French soldiers—the same soldiers who had ransacked the billets donated by their countrymen, stuffing pockets with jewelry and other precious articles while downing wine from French tables and cellars. Drunk, defeated, demoralized, these ragged troops had called to the passing Americans, *Fini la guerre!*

Tired, hungry, not knowing exactly where they were—except for the single fact that mattered: they were "in the line"—flushed with eagerness to get into the fight yet flooded with images of defeat, the marines bedded down. Doubtless each man felt, each in his own way, what warriors have always felt the night before a battle was to begin. It was a mixture of anticipation, of fear, of dread, of doubt, of exhilaration, and of hope. Those positioned close enough to Belleau Wood to peer at its dim, forested mass might have seen in it an image of what tomorrow itself represented: a present tangle of the dark unknown that would, for better or worse, soon reveal itself. That was what it meant to "lay on the night of June 1st," Colonel Catlin later wrote, "in this line . . . waiting for the morrow." [10]

∎ 5 ∎

First Blood

The marines and soldiers of the U.S. 2nd Division awoke (those who had managed any sleep at all) on June 2 to many sensations—anticipation, fear, and hunger among them. Typically, at the end of a long march, there would be what one marine, Elton E. Mackin (who would not arrive at Belleau Wood until a few days later), described as the "belly-stirring tang of coffee, laced with the smell of cooking fires" and "food, more than we could eat; and water, flowing water, in a woodland stream," of which the marines would drink and drink, "and then, remembering thirst," would drink again, "lifting glowing, boyish faces from the wine of it."[1] Not now, though. So close to the front—a front elastic and ready to snap at any moment—there was neither time nor place for cooking fires and hot coffee, let alone the enjoyment of a woodland stream. The men made do with cold rations and canteen-stale water, lukewarm.

The sounds of battle were neither distant nor very near. The men were not quite in the war, but they knew the war was around them. Certainly, they were far closer to combat—whatever that would prove to be—than they were to home. Marine Private Mackin remembered what it was like, this strange morning of twilight, suspended on the cusp of battle, a period punctuated by the crack of small-arms fire, irregular explosions, the thud of artillery, the sputtered burst of machine guns. "Memory," at such a moment, "brought back the picture of an evening, far at sea, slouched on the deck of the transport, watching the day fade behind us." Now, far from the sea and farther still from home, "[We covered] our fears with bitter, quickly silenced jokes," Mackin recalled. "Men seek the quiet of their thoughts when going into battle," and yet they couldn't stop talking. Mackin remembered a conversation about "two pals," O'Donnell and McConnell, "O'Donnell always full of jokes about the Irish" and "McConnell, the serious one," who explained that he and O'Donnell had joined the marines together because they "'looked over this damned war and figured we didn't like the draft. . . . We figured to join this outfit and get a pretty suit of blues, knock off the girls, and miss the goddamn trenches. Had it figured—and here we are.' Yes, here they were, stinking somewhere in a stinking wood in France."[2]

Somewhere. That seemed always the operative word for the AEF in this war. General Pershing himself addressed all of his communications to the press and public as coming from "Somewhere in France," and soldiers and marines writing home were instructed to do the same. It was for security. Didn't want the enemy to intercept a communiqué or a letter and find out where you were. But the thing of it was, most of the time, *you* didn't know where you were, other than that it was, indeed, *somewhere in France.*

Whether it was to avoid the draft, stay out of the trenches, get a set of dress blues (no one told recruits they would have to buy these themselves with their own money and then probably never get to wear them), or be the First to Fight, the one thing the new marines did not expect when they joined up was to be perpetually confused. They might have expected to be afraid, to be exhilarated, to be wounded, and maybe even to be killed, but they did not expect to feel, so much of the time, so thoroughly and utterly lost.

But so it was that morning of June 2. Everyone was reeling from General Duchêne's tangle of orders and countermanded orders that had moved them back and forth the day and night before. Even as Catlin's men drank their tepid water and choked down their cold rations, many of their brother marines and army colleagues were still filtering in from back roads, straining to make sense of outdated French maps whose scale was too small for the kind of detailed deployment expected of them.

"Where's this here line we're supposed to hold, Sarge?" a green marine asked, pointing a dirty finger at a smudged map.

"We're gonna *make* a line, sonny."[3]

General Degoutte had no trouble reading the big maps at his headquarters. His order had been for the four American regiments to occupy a line athwart the Metz-Paris highway, just northwest of Château-Thierry. It looked perfectly clear to him, a line he could trace with the nail of his thumb. It made no difference which troops went where along this line, and so it was by random chance that the army was deployed south of the highway and the marines north of it. That put the marines—not the soldiers—up against what the generals liked to call the "bulldog salient," the leading edge of the bulge formed by the leading edge of the German advance. The enemy here was closer to Paris than the enemy was anywhere else. That fact wasn't yet apparent to the marines on the morning of June 2, but it was abundantly clear on Degoutte's map. To him, as to any high-ranking commander in a comfortable headquarters, it was really a matter of geometry. The salient was an arc, and the geometrical problem this implied was how to push it back upon its chord. Why? Because it was the business of Degoutte's headquarters, as it had been the business of military headquarters since (it seemed) armies first fought, to "bite off" a salient, transforming the enemy bulge on the map into a straight line. Of course, what appeared as arcs and lines on a map far from the front looked like men and sounded like gunfire to the soldiers and marines who were actually there.

On the western front, most of the war most of the time really did consist of lines in the form of trenches scarred into the continent from the English Channel in the north to the Swiss Alps in the south. But here what Degoutte called a line was really a collision of men, undulating, electric, one set of them moving forward, the other scattering and falling back. "No retirement will be thought of on any pretext whatever," Degoutte's order of June 2 read.[4] Yet it was like trying to catch and hold back the fragments of an explosion. The Northern Armies under the command of Crown Prince Rupprecht blasted against Degoutte's exhausted Frenchmen. The best of them retreated in good order. Many, however, just ran, throwing down packs and even rifles into the glistening winter wheat of what had been farm fields, in what had been a quiet sector. The crown prince's men would pause just long enough in their advance to pick through the wheat—studded, as everyone who was there remembered for the rest of their lives, with poppies of dazzling scarlet—to recover some treasure: extra rations, a blanket, dry socks.

The Americans were supposed to back up and bolster the French. The army's 9th Infantry Regiment was to the right (south) of the Metz-Paris highway, and Catlin's 6th Marines were to the left (north) of that highway, extending to the rise south of the village of Bussiares called Hill 142. By June 2, two battalions of Wendell Neville's 5th Marines backed up the 6th Marines. In addition, the 6th Machine Gun Battalion, under Major Edward Cole, supported the marine line, as did sixty 75 mm guns and a dozen 155 mm guns belonging to Degoutte's artillery.

While these marines backed up the French, Colonel Paul Malone, U.S. Army, led a mixed force of soldiers and marines, designated generically enough as "Detachment, AEF," to plug a four-kilometer gap in the French line at Bois de Veuilly. As Degoutte saw it, just after midnight on June 2, this was the only place in his sector where the Americans would be face-to-face with the Germans. Leading Detachment, AEF, was a battalion of the 5th Marines under Major Julius Turrill. During the night, Turrill's marines marched ten kilometers through deserted villages. They reached Les Gandons at about six in the morning and began closing off part of the gap. Within ninety minutes, an army unit, the 3rd Battalion of the 23rd Infantry, linked up with Turrill's line, extending it west to the town of Moulin-du-Rhône. More soldiers and the 1st Battalion of the 5th Marine Regiment soon came up and began making contact with the French on either flank.

Thus the gap had been closed, and Degoutte, if he had wanted to, could now fill in the line on his map. But even as Malone's units were moving up, German artillery opened upon the French line from Vaux to Gandelu. After this "artillery preparation," German troops began their advance against the line. At the extreme left (south) of the German attack, Lieutenant Colonel Rotenbücher led his 47th Regiment through Rochets Wood, probing the Metz-Paris highway just south of Vaux. To Rotenbücher's right (north), the German 398th Infantry attacked toward Belleau Wood, the village of Bouresches, and Triangle Farm. Firing from Bouresches, however, the French slowed this advance, forcing a deflection into the wheat fields south of the village. This put the advancing Germans within range of French machine guns, which took a murderous toll. The men of the 398th Infantry broke off their advance and took up positions in the woods and behind boulders.

While the 398th Regiment was pinned down, the German 237th Division advanced against the villages of Belleau and Torcy. At first, French defensive fire was withering, but the Germans wore the defenders down as the morning slipped toward noon. Simultaneously, the German 197th Division, to the right (north) of the 398th Regiment and the 237th Division, advanced toward the Clignon River.

The Germans were surprised by the intensity of fight remaining in the French units, but, in truth, the French were rapidly tiring. To Malone, it appeared that the French were at least delaying the advance, giving him time to consolidate his forces. To Major General James Harbord, commanding the 4th Marine Brigade, Malone's assessment seemed somehow overly optimistic. Turrill's marine battalion was attached to Malone's Detachment, AEF, but this did not prevent Harbord from keeping very close tabs on what he considered his property. He ordered his own reconnaissance sortie, then visited the front himself, concluding that in the northern part of his sector, between Vaurichart Wood and Hill 142, there was nothing left but a few French dragoons. The line would certainly not hold here. Without consulting Malone, Harbord ordered Turrill to extend his line to the northwest corner of Vaurichart Wood. Then he ordered Neville, commanding officer of the 5th Marines, to fill the gap between Turrill on the left (north) and the battalion of 6th Marines (under Maurice Shearer) on the right (south) with the 2nd Battalion of the 5th Marines under Frederic Wise and his own headquarters company. Neville drove up to Wise personally to order him to establish his line between Hill 142 to the northeast corner of Veuilly Wood: "The French are holding from the railroad on your front, but don't expect them to stick. If you don't hurry, the Germans will get there before you do. And when you get there, you stick! Never mind how many French come through you."[5] For good measure, Harbord ordered Catlin to release one machine-gun company and position it in Veuilly Wood to support the newly extended line. All of this accomplished, Harbord now told Malone what he had done, remarking to him that there was now an "American connection clear around from the 9th Infantry, inclusive, to the neighborhood of Prémont"—a solid line in the sector assigned to the Americans.[6]

In Malone's sector, first blood was drawn. Shortly after noon on June 2, enemy artillery shells hit Company A, 1st Marine Battalion, killing Private Charles Maggione and wounding Privates Sam Mathews and Prozet Zachio, as well as Corporal Sam Meyers. Despite these casualties, Malone was more confident than ever, reporting to headquarters that his men had two hundred twenty rounds of rifle ammunition each, that he had occupied his assigned position "without incident," that "Thus far no serious attack had been made," and that "The French line seems to be holding fairly well and I am not apprehensive."[7]

Alerted by Neville, Wise and his men could not afford to be so complacent. While the French directly in front of Malone were holding, those to the north, in Veuilly, were beginning to fall away. Near the village of Marigny—already deserted by the French—Wise's marines began digging in, using bayonets, mess kits, and even spoons. The engineers and their proper entrenching tools were still on the road.

Wise hurriedly set up his command post at the edge of Marigny, putting it without a trace of superstition smack up against the wall of the town's cemetery. The terrain here was typical of the entire region: woods interspersed with wheat fields, the fields themselves neatly separated by hedgerows. The company commanders of Wise's battalion smartly moved out to their defense objectives. Captain Lloyd Williams advanced to Hill 142 before the village of Champillon. Captain John Blanchfield took up a position straight ahead, in the direction of Les Mares Farm. The companies under Captains Lester Wass and Charlie Dunbeck ventured into Veuilly Wood.

Lieutenant E. D. Cooke, a platoon leader in Wass's company, recorded what happened just as the company turned to the right at the southern edge of Veuilly Wood: "Shells struck in the treetops and fragments glittered in the air, like a shoal of small silver fish." The Germans had opened up with their light field artillery, loosing 77-millimeter "whizbangs" and 88-millimeter "quick Dicks." "The blow was quick, sudden, destructive, and eleven of our men went down. One or two cried out in surprised pain, but four lay inert and silent."[8]

It was the first time they had received fire. And in this first time, they responded like ordinary men, not marines. "Faces turned white," Cooke recalled, "and the company showed a tendency to huddle and mill about."[9]

Captain Wass, "a regular terrier for action," was having none of it. "Get going!" he barked. "What do you think this is, a kid's game? Move out!"[10]

With that, the marines "scuttled through the woods, ducked and dodged as more shells pounded a shallow trench to [their] right, and then threw [themselves] face down in the north edge of the Bois de Veuilly."[11]

To the right of Wass's company, Dunbeck's was just getting into position when it, too, fell under fire. A Sergeant Rogers and three privates fell as the Germans opened up with "seabags"—big nine-inch shells—in addition to the smaller whizbangs. "We all took to digging fox-holes," Cooke recalled. "Each excavation was made according to the owner's individual taste, or idea of safety. Some were long and narrow, others short and deep."[12]

To the right of Dunbeck's company was the 55th Company under Captain John Blanchfield. A remarkable marine, Blanchfield was a "mustang," a marine who had risen to commissioned status from the enlisted ranks. No less remarkable was his second in command, Lieutenant Lemuel Shepherd, future commandant of the U.S. Marine Corps. Like everyone else, Blanchfield struggled to make heads or tails of the outdated, small-scale maps the French had distributed to the Americans and their own field commanders.

Finally, and in frustration, he ordered Shepherd to "take the company forward." It was, in fact, the kind of open-ended order great marines relish, and Shepherd led the company to high ground—designated Hill 183— overlooking the valley below. The lieutenant had just finished positioning the company's platoons when he received a message from a worried Blanchfield ordering him to pull back. He had pushed the 55th Company too far forward of either Dunbeck (on his left) or Williams (on his right). Since the object was to tie in with the other companies, Shepherd promptly obeyed the order, calling his men back, whereupon a white-bearded French colonel rushed up to him, begging that he not desert the battle. Shepherd doubtless reddened. He and his marines were here to stay, he assured the colonel. They were just withdrawing a few hundred yards to hold the line.[13]

There was that familiar military phrase again: *the line.* What the 55th Company did was to dig in—again, with improvised tools—just behind Les Mares Farm. There was no time even for an improvised trench. Instead, each marine excavated a foxhole, "similar to a grave but about a foot deep."[14] These new marines were learning the lesson all soldiers learn at the front: to embrace the earth as an infant embraces a mother, pressing its body as close as possible to hers.

Though commanders like General Harbord and Pershing himself detested the trench, even they would have admitted that a foot below the surface of the earth could make the difference between living and dying. Under some circumstances, an entire twelve inches was even a luxury. A few days after Shepherd and his men dug into their first position, the intrepid correspondent for the *Chicago Daily Tribune*, Floyd Gibbons, was badly wounded while covering the Battle of Belleau Wood. Prostrate, hit through the shoulder, his left eye shot out of his skull, Gibbons's first thought was that the field, which "had seemed perfectly flat" when he had advanced across it, now "impressed me as being convex and I was further impressed with the belief that I was lying on the very uppermost and most exposed curvature of it. There is no doubt that the continued stream of machine gun lead that swept the field superinduced this belief." Gibbons made a supreme effort to get "as close to the ground as a piece of paper on the top of a table." Twenty feet away from Gibbons lay a wounded marine, apparently unconscious. "His pack, 'the khaki doll,' was still strapped between his shoulders. Unconsciously he was doing that which all wounded men do—that is, to assume the position that is most comfortable. He was trying to roll over on his back." Each time he did so, the pack "would elevate his body into full view of the German gunners. Then a withering hail of lead would sweep the field. . . . As the Marine would roll over on top of his pack his chest would be exposed to the fire." Gibbons "could see the buttons fly from his tunic and one of the shoulder straps of the back pack part as the sprays of lead struck him." Gibbons did not pity the helpless marine but wished "that he would lie still, as every movement of his brought those streams of bullets closer to my head. I even considered the thickness of the box respirator"—part of the British-model gas mask system, worn over the chest, suspended from the neck—which Gibbons had used to lift his head off the ground; having earlier heard that gangrene was "caused by germs which exist in large quantities in any ground that has been under artificial cultivation for a long period," he feared that resting his head in the soil would fatally infect his wound. The respirator was about two inches thick and now, under fire, Gibbons wrote, "[I] remembered my French gas mask hanging from my shoulder and recalled immediately that it was much flatter, being hardly half an inch in thickness. . . . [I] forthwith drew up the French mask to my head, extracted the British one and rested my cheek closer to the ground on the French one. Thus, I lowered my head about an inch and a half—an inch and a half that represented worlds of satisfaction and some optimism to me."[15]

As Shepherd and his marines dug in, French troops all around his company streamed back from contact with the advancing Germans. Shepherd ordered his men to grab as many Chauchat automatic rifles from the retreating Frenchmen as they could, but when he noticed that a gap remained on his left—the 55th Company was not tied in with Dunbeck's as it should have been—he personally stopped a knot of withdrawing French chasseurs and ordered their lieutenant to get his men dug in. The Frenchman wearily complied.

By evening, Degoutte, had he the inclination, could have once again drawn across his map a continuous line of about two and a half miles representing the position of Wise's marine battalion. To be true to life, however, he'd have to use a very sharp pencil, because the line was thin as a thread. What no map could show was that these marines, rushed into place, had no substantial food. The emergency rations they had marched with were long gone. Field kitchens were still on some road "somewhere in France." They scrounged French rations, but these consisted mainly of monkey meat. At its best, it was barely edible. Up there, however, it was far from its best. The monkey meat the retreating French handed the marines had apparently been spoiled, the lot of it, before being canned, and in the words of one marine, it smelled like "a combination of coal oil and putrid mule."[16] Nor could the marines make it more palatable by charring it over a fire. Cooking fires were barred this close to the Germans. Most marines simply fasted, making do with a cigarette or a chew of Bull Durham. For ammunition, however, there was no substitute. And while Malone's men were amply supplied, the marines fronting the bulldog salient had scant ammo for their own rifles and their scrounged Chauchats. Of machine guns, they had none at all.

Hungry, short on bullets, Wise's battalion was also lonely. Degoutte could draw his pencil-thin line across two and a half scale miles of map, but that still left gaps on either side. Positioned at battalion left, Wass's company was not tied into the army's 23rd Infantry, while Williams, at battalion right, was not tied into the 6th Marines. When Wise telephoned regimental headquarters, he was promised: "They'll show up."[17] But evening descended without either unit materializing on Wise's flanks, and through the twilight the marines watched the German artillery barrage claw its way steadily south, a rolling barrage that preceded the advance of the German infantrymen; a barrage, the marines knew, that would before long rain down on them.

Viewed from the perspective of the entire U.S. 2nd Division, the situation by the late afternoon of June 2 was deceptively quiet. On the division's left (north), Malone continued methodically organizing his four battalions into a reasonably coherent defensive line. On the right (south), the U.S. Army's 9th Infantry, under Colonel Leroy Upton, busied itself digging in. By early evening, Upton requested seven ambulances to transport twenty-six men wounded by incoming artillery fire. That was to be expected. More upsetting had been the necessity of relieving a battalion commander because he could not read a map. Perhaps that commander's real crime was honesty. Almost no one could read the maps the French had furnished them.

The relative calm on either end of the 2nd Division line was belied by two things: the almost total absence of effective communication—working phones and phone lines were few, runners scarce and not nearly as fast as functioning phones would have been—and the rapidly heating situation in the middle, the sector occupied by Wise's marine battalion. South of there, Edward Cole's 6th Machine Gun Battalion, still in position behind Holcomb's 2nd Marine Battalion, came under artillery fire. Cole's command post was knocked out, and he had to relocate to the Montgivrault-le-Grande Farm, then try to reestablish communications with the battalions he was supposed to support. To make matters worse, the French 155 millimeter guns—the heavy artillery on which everyone in the middle of the American line relied for defensive support—were running dry. Communications with the rear supply areas were poor to nonexistent, so division headquarters had to scramble in order to cobble together a truck convoy to send to the rear to fetch more ammunition. In the meantime, the pace of French supporting fire would have to slow down considerably, lest the ammunition run out altogether. For every French shell that was not fired, X number of German soldiers were able to advance X number of yards closer to the thin Allied line, the line from which the weary French continued to withdraw.

At about a quarter past two in the afternoon, 4th Marine Brigade commander General Harbord was given more reason for veering from calm to alarm. He received a report from the 43rd French Division that Holcomb's 2nd Marine Battalion was "giving way a little" at Triangle Farm. Holcomb was without a working telephone, so Harbord had no choice but to send a runner with a message ordering Holcomb to "hold [his] line there at all cost." Seeking to be proactive, Harbord also dispatched a runner to Colonel Catlin, ordering him to send reinforcements from the regimental reserves. Yet even before the runners reached Holcomb and Catlin, signalmen had repaired the phone lines connecting Holcomb to brigade headquarters. Harbord relayed the French report and repeated his order to *hold the line*. Holcomb was well aware that he was speaking to a superior officer—his commanding officer, in fact—but he was also aware that Harbord was an army man, not a marine. He took pains, therefore, to reply with just the right blend of military courtesy and Semper Fi indignation. When the 2nd Battalion "ran," he told the general, "it would be in the other direction." As Harbord related to Catlin at 3:50 that afternoon, "The French now acknowledge that report as to 2d Battalion was a mistake and telephone with Holcomb says there is nothing doing in the fall back line." Clearly, Harbord had taken Holcomb's indignation to heart and almost certainly shared it. "I have asked the French General to investigate thoroughly the person who started the false report about Holcomb's Battalion, which is most annoying," he wrote to Catlin.[18]

With this distressing confusion cleared up, Harbord now fretted about his inability to determine the whereabouts of Major Maurice Shearer's marine battalion, which was supposed to be on Wise's right (southern) flank. Before this mystery could be solved, General Degoutte started rearranging the front in response to intelligence gathered from a German prisoner. The prisoner had reported that two regiments of a fresh German division were coming into position to attack the American right (the southern end of the American line). One regiment would hit the line south of the Metz-Paris highway, the other north of it. Degoutte responded by ordering the 3rd Battalion, 5th Marines, under Major Ben Berry, to assume a position behind the point at which the 3rd and 4th Brigades met. He would serve as a corps reserve in anticipation of the attack. This left General Omar Bundy, commanding officer of the U.S. 2nd Division, to replace Berry's battalion. He therefore ordered Turrill's battalion, together with a pair of machine-gun companies, to detach from Malone's line. Turrill was to advance to Pyramid Farm as Harbord's brigade reserve, and the machine-gun companies were to march to Ventelet Farm, where they would form a reserve for army Brigadier General E. M. Lewis's 3rd Infantry Brigade. While this shuffling was clogging the roads, truck convoys were collecting all the regimental machine-gun companies still marching in the rear areas, and more trucks were returning from the rear with the much-needed 155-millimeter ammunition for the depleted French artillery.

For the commanders in the field, it was a nervous, busy time. For the marines and soldiers they commanded, it was a time of intense anticipation tempered by the growing pangs of a dull but insistent hunger. For General Bundy in 2nd Division headquarters, it was all evidence of a machine operating normally—neither exceptionally well, nor poorly. His army and marine units were successfully deployed across a twelve-mile front. He felt confident that the Americans could provide effective local defense when and where they were called on to do so. Perhaps because he had been on Pershing's staff so long and was now eager to consummate his transition from desk to battlefront, Harbord, an army general commanding marines, saw the situation with greater enthusiasm than Bundy. "Our communications are in much better shape than at this time yesterday," he reported to Bundy at 6:25 in the evening of June 2. "It seems well established that the Germans have been repulsed today along our entire Division Front. Two attacks were made over in front of our lines and were stopped principally by the fire of my Machine Gun Battalion." He went on to report the result of German attacks toward the southern end of the division's line. "The French liaison officer here informs me the reports are that dead Germans pile the slopes." Yes, Harbord concluded: "There is every indication that the French morale has been greatly stiffened by the presence of our men."[19]

∎ 6 ∎

Retreat, Hell!

Unlike many other vocations, war does not begin in the morning and end in the evening. General James G. Harbord had a few leisure moments at the end of the day on June 2 to write his report to General Bundy, but, at almost precisely that time, half past six, the Germans made a new push against the French, and the French were very tired. Corps Conta a corps of Crown Prince Rupprecht's army group named for its commanding general—broke through to a new line, which ran from Vaux to Bouresches and to the village of Belleau. From here it angled west through the towns of Torcy and Bussiares to the little village of Eloup on the Clignon River. By eleven that night, Corps Conta had stabbed deeply through Belleau Wood—that small tangle of hunting preserve that would serve whoever possessed it as a natural fortress—which was south of the line described by Belleau-Torcy-Bussiares. They also laid claim to a nearby hill, Hill 126, which gave a commanding view of the ground below.

The French were tired, but they were far more determined than they had been for days to stop yielding ground. They fought back, hard, and General Joseph Degoutte accordingly ordered the postponement of the American takeover of the sector. Instead, he directed General Michel's 43rd

Division to mount a full-scale counterattack. Michel, in turn, sent a message to Harbord: "The American troops will maintain at ALL COSTS the line of support they occupy: Bois de Clerembauts-Triangle-Lucy-le-Bocage, Hill 142, north corner of Bois de Veuilly. They will not participate in the counter-attack which will be made to retake the position of the French."[1]

Bold words. But at that very moment, General von Conta, despite heavy losses suffered as a result of unexpectedly stiff French resistance, decided to sustain the momentum of the ongoing attack rather than simply hold his positions. One division was assigned to take the high ground at Marigny and at Veuilly Wood while another was to "roll up" Belleau Wood from both the north and the east. Other divisions were assigned supporting and reserve tasks. What this all meant was that, notwithstanding Michel's order that the American forces would "not participate in the counter-attack," the continuation of von Conta's attack put the German army up against the very Americans ordered merely to stand by.

Sunup of June 3 found the soldiers of the U.S. Army's 9th Infantry, who held the right (southern) portion of the American line, killing time with foraging expeditions—fresh chicken or rabbit was worlds better than monkey meat—or taking pot shots at the occasional German observation plane. Private John Hughes of Battery C, 15th Field Artillery, noted that "someone made a lucky shot as [one aviator] flew over the chateau. We could see the observer"—for these were two-seat aircraft, accommodating a pilot and an observer—"looking over the side of the plane. I thought that he was going to take a 'Brodie' [fall out of the open cockpit] but they managed to land in a field close by."[2]

North of the Metz-Paris highway, the part of the line held by the marines, there was no time for foraging or sport shooting German aviators. Major Frederic Wise's men strained their eyes to observe German artillery speeding up from the Clignon River, pulling off the road, then getting manhandled into position for firing—on *them*—even as French artillery showered the German gunners.

Mostly, however, especially north of the highway, the marines could not see the enemy. Not that there was any mistaking their proximity.

Michel's counterattacks, mainly directed just to the south of Gandelu, Bus-siares, and Torcy—near the ground the marines held—were already bog-ging down and breaking up. By midmorning, Frenchmen began stumbling in a trickle of ones, twos, and threes through the marines' lines. By the af-ternoon, the trickle had become a steady flow—though not, as yet, a tor-rent. The retreating troops fell back into re-formed lines, wearily resolved to attempt a new stand.

It was by no means an ignominious defeat. True, the French counter-attack had shattered against the continued advance of Corps Conta, but Corps Conta, in turn, had been badly blunted by its encounter with the French. A significant German advance had been made, but at a heavy cost—and the survivors did not feel so much like victors as they were wrung out and worried. Yes, the French line had broken. Yes, the Germans had repulsed a counterattack. And yet it seemed apparent that, behind the line that had given way, the French were receiving reinforcements. The fact was that, at the moment, only the apprehensive anticipation of the German commanders was stopping the German advance. Their belief that the French were rapidly building strength—not the French them-selves—sapped the momentum from Corps Conta's drive. Even though they had broken the French counterattack, the Germans slowed, precisely as if they were being pinned down in a firefight. Such is the cost of fatigue and anxiety.

The French counterattack had not achieved victory, but it did gain the next best thing: time. As they watched the German advance slow down, the American commanders redoubled their efforts to get everybody into place. There was now a precious space of time for the trucks to arrive with those shells for the depleted French 155s. There was time for the machine-gun companies, slower moving than the infantrymen, to arrive and assume their supporting positions. There was time for the arrival of engineer com-panies, which had the equipment and the willing muscle to dig far better fortifications than a foot-deep foxhole. Not least of all was the arrival of rolling kitchens with the promise of hot meals consisting of something other than monkey meat.

Yet communications—or the lack thereof—continued to be a major problem, and all the time in the world could not improve the cryptic and outdated maps the commanders carried into battle. Wise's 2nd Battalion of the 5th Marines, strung out over two and a half miles from Veuilly Wood through Les Mares Farm and to a road just north of Champillon, was squarely in the projected path of the now-slowed German advance. Yet on neither of its flanks was it connected to the rest of the American line. On the left (north), Wise should have been tied in with Malone's 23rd Infantry, and on the right (south) with Catlin's 6th Marine Regiment, but as Wendell Neville, colonel of the 5th Marine Regiment, reported to Catlin, Captain Lloyd Williams, commanding the marine company that formed Wise's right flank, had "not been able to get in touch with [the] left company" of the 1st Battalion, 6th Marines, which was commanded by Major Maurice Shearer. Without proper communications established, Neville had no choice but to send Wise "to find where [Catlin's] left is and to extend to the right if he finds that any gap exists."[3]

Neville sent his message in the morning. By early afternoon, Shearer replied directly to Wise: "Have been trying to connect with your right flank. My left flank is on [Hill] 142. Liaison man states your right rests on Champillon-Bussiares [road] about 1 kilometer north of Champillon. My line runs from [Hill] 142 southeast to Lucy [-le-Bocage], so if the above is true the vacancy is yours. I am trying to extend to reach your right. Please advise me exactly where your right is."[4] Yet a message later that afternoon from Neville to Harbord made it clear that the gap had still not been closed.

In the meantime, on the left (north), the situation was just as murky. Shortly after midnight on June 3, army Colonel Paul Malone sent a message the commander of the 2nd Battalion of the army's 23d Infantry imploring him, "Send me report at once as to situation. Has any attack developed on your front or flank? Is your communications with Marines on your right [that is, with Wise's left flank] well established? . . . investigate at once." Four hours later, Major Whiting, commanding 2nd Battalion, 23rd Infantry, replied: "No attack or demonstration on our front or flanks. . . . Telephone out of order all night . . . artillery fire in every direction." This seemed to satisfy Malone until the afternoon of June 3, when he received word of Corps Conta's strong attack on the 43rd French Division, news which was accompanied by General Michel's revised orders for the Americans to make a solid line behind him. Thus spurred, Malone ordered Whiting "to gain contact with the Marines on your right and hold the lines at all costs." But how? The first step was to "institute an immediate reconnaissance to locate left of the Marines, and insure continuous American line." Even as Malone was preparing this message for Whiting, General Harbord sent a runner to Neville: "[General Michel] desires that you send out someone to establish the whereabouts of the right of the 23rd Infantry Battalion [Whiting's command] . . . [and] to report if you are 'elbow-to-elbow' with people on the right and left of you."[5]

Elbow to elbow? That was hardly the case. And therein lay the crux of the rapidly developing crisis. For at precisely this point—directly in front of the unclosed American line—the French center was dissolving under repeated German battering.

Captain Lloyd Williams saw it happening. "All French troops on our right have fallen back, leaving a gap," he reported to Wise.[6] This report was seconded by marines in Shearer's company, to Williams's right. Acting on his own initiative, Shearer sent two of his reserve platoons forward to make contact with Williams's right and plug the gap. Catlin also sent two marine companies from the regimental reserve to help.

Movement in the American lines was both right and left—in an effort to find and to close all the gaps—and also straight ahead, to back up the crumbling French. There was movement backward as well—all on the part of the French. That earlier trickle of Frenchmen through the American lines had progressed through a steady stream to become what it was now—a raging flood.

Most of the French troops, dispirited and spent, passed through the American lines in silence, perhaps ashamed, but more than likely lost in the oblivion of "shell shock" and simple, dead-tired exhaustion. One of the French soldiers, a major of chasseurs, bumped up against Captain Lloyd Williams's second in command, a Captain Corbin. In breathless, heavily accented

English, the French major reported that his lines had been overrun by Germans, and he instructed Corbin, in turn, to withdraw his line. Corbin pretended not to understand, whereupon the major took a pad from inside his coat and wrote in English, major to captain, an order to retreat. Corbin accepted the paper, turned, and trotted back with it to Captain Williams. He glanced at the order, flashed eyes in Corbin's direction, and spat out: "Retreat, hell! We just got here."[7]

It was one of those lines, tailor made for posterity, desperate battle sometimes gives birth to: "I have not yet begun to fight," "Don't give up the ship," "You may fire when ready, Gridley," and the like. But it did not have to wait for the coming of posterity to have its effect. As one of Williams's platoon commanders later observed, the phrase "spread like wildfire through the units." In fact, it proved so effective that—after Williams was subsequently killed—Colonel Wise claimed it as his own, and at least one historian later credited it to Wendell Neville. But the documentary evidence for Williams's authorship is persuasive. At 3:10 on the morning of June 4, Williams sent a message to Wise: "The French Major gave Captain Corbin written orders to fall back—I have countermanded the order." Then, on a practical note: "Kindly see that French do not shorten their artillery range," lest the friendly fire fall on the nonretreating Americans.[8]

Williams's defiance of an order to retreat was hardly unique. It was, in fact, a standard marine response, which the company commander on Williams's right repeated when he too refused (or rather simply ignored) a French order to fall back. Williams's response was not born of bravado, but was actually a factual statement of the situation—and not just at the front before Belleau Wood, but along the entire American sector. America had declared war in April 1917, but it was only now, more than a year later, that American soldiers and marines were getting into the shooting war. During the preceding year—and more—they had trained to fight. Now they had arrived—had just gotten here—and no one, no matter how scared, wanted to turn back.

Yet it was not a question of advancing forward—a glorious Charge of the Light Brigade—either. Occasionally, in the far distance, less than a thousand yards away, a marine would catch sight of a German, and take a shot. For the most part, however, the only evidence—abundant as it was—of the enemy's imminence was the tramp of French feet away from the front. *That* and the inexorably increasing tempo of incoming German artillery fire. Although he did not arrive at Belleau Wood until June 7 as part of a unit of replacements, marine Private Elton E. Mackin learned what it was like to be on the receiving end of a rolling artillery barrage, the kind of barrage that was the obligatory overture to an attack. It came first as the bark of a "distant gun," a bark followed by a "screaming roar" then "a flash—an explosion." Next was the "spatter of falling fragments among the trees" and "somewhere near at hand, an anguished voice [crying] out in pain."[9]

> As though by signal, entire batteries took up the chorus. The clatter of a machine gun joined in, then another, as the rising tide of sound merged into a crescendo that stifled thought and, for a moment, paralyzed all motion. Shrapnel rained upon the ridge. A running figure dashed along the line, yelling for everyone to take cover. Men sought shelter behind half-finished mounds of earth and hugged the ground. Whole trees crashed down as heavy shells shook and jarred the earth. Fumes from the explosions became a blanket that crept over the forest floor like a pall.[10]

The veterans among them knew just how to read the tempo of the barrage. Before the shelling even ended, when the frequency of the incoming shells had begun to flag just a bit, the sergeant would order, *Fix bayonets!* He knew that the slackening tempo signaled that the German charge was about to begin.

Fix bayonets! Mackin—who refers to himself in third person as "Slim" in his memoir of the war—responded to the order by asking the question on everyone's lips: "Are they coming?" It was a question croaked "from a throat that seemed to choke the words in his breast." The answer came matter-of-factly: "'Yeah, when the barrage lifts, they'll come—and in numbers, Bud. Shoot low and be ready to go meet them if they get too close.'" Mackin knew what that meant. "The prospect of using a bayonet, of facing enemy bayonets in action, was his pet horror." The sergeant, as all good marine sergeants do, seemed to read his mind. "'Don't turn yellow and try to run,'" he warned. "'If you do and the Germans don't kill you, I will.'"[11]

The sergeant's warning, harsh and crude though it was, was nevertheless just what the men needed to hear. Under a barrage and knowing that its cessation would not mean relief but rather the certainty of an attack at the points of so many bayonets, the sergeant's warning gave release to all the pent-up fear of anticipation. "A flush of shame chased the scared whiteness from [Mackin's] face. . . . To be thought a coward on his first day of battle, in his first hour of action, threatened to place him beyond the regard of these men he strove so hard to copy." In a moment, fear of pain and death were displaced by a stronger emotion. "The taunt had reached him and hurt his pride. At that moment, boyhood lay forever behind, a page of life's story had turned. In back of a small mound of earth, a disciplined soldier faced the long slope ahead, determined to do his part."[12]

For at least one marine, late that afternoon of June 3, it was not enough to hunker down, waiting for the barrage to lift and the attack to start. Lemuel Shepherd—the future Corps commandant who was now a lieutenant in Captain John Blanchfield's company of Wise's battalion—had earlier in the morning stationed a dozen men in an observation post on a hill several hundred yards ahead of the line. "I don't know why I suggested it," Shepherd later recalled. "It was one of those foolish ideas without reason." But, foolish or not, Shepherd secured Blanchfield's permission to "go out and check this outpost" if only to get "a personal look at the situation." Yet even as he and his orderly started across the field, Shepherd said to himself, "we'll never make it. Shells were exploding all over the place. One fell six feet to our front, a dud. We got to the observation point about 4 p.m. The barrage was now passing to the rear. Behind it the Germans were beginning to appear. We watched them come on. A thousand yards, seven hundred, five hundred."[13]

Shepherd and the thirteen men with him had the best view of any Americans, regardless of rank, of a critical moment in the Great War, which meant a critical moment in history. The Germans they watched—a thousand, seven hundred, then five hundred yards away—were closer to Paris than any enemy soldier had been since August 1914.

Shepherd ordered his men to hold their fire and set their sights for three hundred yards.

Another marine, a machine gunner in the 6th Marine Regiment, identified only as a "Toledo boy," also occupied an advance position. The German artillery barrage, he recalled, lasted exactly an hour and consisted of "shells of every caliber from one-pounders to the big 'seabags,' or nine-inch howitzers." When it was over, "Fritz came at us with blood in his eye. I estimated them at about 500 and they were in fairly compact masses. We waited until they got close, oh, very close. In fact, we let them think they were going to have a leadpipe cinch. . . . Oh, it was too easy; just like a bunch of cattle coming to slaughter. I always thought it was rather a fearful thing to take a human life, but I felt a savage thrill of joy and I could hardly wait for the Germans to get close enough."[14]

Colonel Albertus Catlin, commanding the 6th Marine Regiment, later wrote that it "was a beautiful, clear day." From his observation post at the village of La Voie du Châtel he could watch everything.

The Germans swept down an open slope in platoon waves, across wide wheat fields bright with poppies that gleamed like splashes of blood in the afternoon sun. The French met the attack and then fell steadily back. First I saw the French coming back through the wheat, fighting as they came. Then the Germans, in two columns, steady as machines. To me as a military man it was a beautiful sight. I could not but admire the precision and steadiness of those waves of men in grey with the sun glinting on their helmets. On they came, never wavering, never faltering, apparently irresistible.[15]

As the Germans drew closer, more and more marines saw them. Catlin's "Toledo boy" machine gunner remarked, "Curiously, [the German] infantry, which had been steady up to this time, paused as though waiting for us of the 'devil's snare drums' to take up the great work."[16] Apparently judging that the German columns had paused close enough to the imagined three-hundred-yard line, the machine gunner—and his comrades—opened fire:

> Rat-tat-tat-tat full into them, and low down, oh! But it was good to jam down on the trigger, to feel her kick, to look out ahead, hand on the controlling wheel, and see the Heinies fall like wheat under the mower. They were brave enough, but they didn't stand a chance. The poor devils didn't know they were facing the Marines—Americans.
>
> That hour paid in full all the weary hours of drill and hike, all the nerve-racking minutes passed under Fritz's barrage, and avenged the staring eyes and mangled bodies of our dead buddies. There weren't many of them got back to tell the tale of the American's "cowardice."[17]

In his memoir of World War I, "*With the Help of God and a Few Marines,*" Catlin quoted from a letter one marine sent home. It is clear that despite the confusion surrounding so much of what happened between June 1 and June 3, every marine knew why he had been sent to the front: "The Boches were coming with seven-league boots when General Harbord threw a line of Americans across the front and ordered us to hold." If that weren't enough, the company commander added his own voice: "'Get the devils,' yelled Captain Blanchfield (now dead)."[18] For Catlin's letter writer, it was a matter of national pride:

> A minute later the Boches tore out of the woods, a machine gun to every ten of them. A rain of good American lead from good American riflemen met them. We saw them stop. Surprised? Why, they never dreamed of anything like it. . . . We lay in the open, digging with bayonets and firing while the Boches was [*sic*] frantically passing back word that a cog in the wheel had slipped. They still never dreamed of Americans, we later learned from prisoners."[19]

For the Toledo machine gunner, it was more of a personal than a patriotic matter: "I got your Dutchmen for you with a machine gun, lots of 'em, not over three hundred yards away, and one with a pistol for good luck. He bayoneted my Bunkie and he won't do it again. He's a good Fritz now."[20]

There was a price to pay for such patriotic vindication and personal retribution, and as the battle progressed that June of 1918, the price would climb higher and higher. As Catlin's letter writer noted parenthetically, the 55th Company's Captain John Blanchfield was "now dead." His death would come at first light on the morning of June 7—the very climax of the Battle of Belleau Wood. Private Paul Bonner would see him fall, "right on the road":

> Everybody scattered. I started to run, then I thought of Blanchfield and started back. I rushed across the road, machine gun bullets whipping the air everywhere, and I made the captain's side. He was still alive. He was twice my size, but I picked him up and carried him back. . . . Many weeks later I heard that an officer saw me carry Blanchfield away and had recommended me for the Distinguished Service Cross. Isn't it funny to get that for doing a thing at a time when I was more scared than at any time during the war.[21]

Even the vengeance exacted by the Toledo gunner would have its price. Later, on the very day he had opened up on the advancing "Dutchmen," he wrote, "[I] got mine":

> I had helped carry a wounded man back to the dressing station and was coming back up the road. I heard it (the shell) whistle and knew it was going to hit close. (You can tell by the whistle when they are going to hit.)
>
> I jumped into a hole and the shell hit it at the same time. A blinding, deafening roar, and a sensation of hurtling through space, and then oblivion—until several days ago. I have one faint recollection of bleeding terribly at the nose and ears, and the soft hands of an angel working over me, then darkness again. . . . How do I feel? Sometimes I'm all right and again I'm not. I have spells in which everything leaves me for hours at a time and I can't tell for the life of me what I did during that time. And

when I go in the sun I get dizzy and bleed at the nose and my head feels like scrambled eggs most of the time.[22]

Lemuel Shepherd also "got his," and on the very same day. Whereas the Toledo boy occupied a prepared machine-gun position, Shepherd ventured out "just over the crest of our hill," where he found "a lone tree."[23]

> I stood just in front of the tree where I could see and not be seen. About dusk the enemy began working around our hill. I gave the order to fire.
> We opened up with what we had. They countered with a machine gun. A bullet from its first blast caught me in the neck. I spun around and dropped to the ground. My first reaction was to see if I could spit. I wanted to know if the bullet had punctured my throat. I figured if I could spit I was all right. I could spit.[24]

Shepherd crawled up beside his men. "Several had been hit but the rest kept firing. They fired until dark. Just after dark we fell back to our main line, bringing our wounded with us."[25]

The marines had opened up with machine-gun fire and with rifle fire—extraordinarily accurate rifle fire, thanks to U.S. Marine Corps training, which emphasized accuracy of fire over speed. "The French told us," Catlin recalled, "that they had never seen such marksmanship practiced in the heat of battle." Colonel Catlin and his adjutant, Major Frank Evans, watched from the regimental command post at La Voie du Châtel. Evans's recollection acknowledged that the "rifle and machine gun fire [were] incessant," but the major was even more impressed by the effect of the artillery. The "shrapnel was bursting. Then the shrapnel came on the target at each shot."[26]

> It broke just over and just ahead of those [German] columns and then the next bursts sprayed over the very green in which we could see the columns moving. It seemed for all the world that the green field had burst out in patches of white daisies where those columns were doggedly

moving. And it did again and again; no barrage, but with the skill and accuracy of a cat playing with two brown mice that she could reach and mutilate at will and without any hurry. The white patches would roll away, and we could see that some of the columns were still there, slowed up, and it seemed perfect suicide from [*sic*] them to try. [27]

The major had a soldier's respect for the Germans' "pluck," but finally, "under that deadly [artillery] fire and the barrage of rifle and machine gun fire, the Boches stopped. It was too much for any men. They burrowed in or broke to the cover of the woods."[28]

From Catlin's observation post, it looked to be all over. "The German lines did not break; they were broken. The Boches fell by the scores there among the wheat and the poppies." He reported that they "came on again. They were brave men; we must grant them that. Three times they tried to reform and break through that barrage, but they had to stop at last. The United States Marines had stopped them." And when they took refuge in the woods, "mercilessly, methodically, we shelled the woods. . . . A French aviator who sailed overhead saw one entire battalion annihilated there, and signaled back 'Bravo!' to our gunners." Catlin admitted: "It was a terrible slaughter; the mere thought of such wholesale killing is enough to curdle Christian blood. But we had whipped the Hun. We had turned that part of his advance into a rout. We had tasted his blood and we had not forgotten the blood of our own who had been slain."[29]

Albertus Wright Catlin had been commissioned a second lieutenant in the Marine Corps on July 1, 1892, and saw action in the Spanish-American War and then at Vera Cruz when President Woodrow Wilson ordered the invasion of that Mexican port city in response to the "Tampico Affair," in which nine American sailors were detained at rifle point by Mexican soldiers loyal to the dictator Victoriano Huerta. As commander of the 3rd Marines at Vera Cruz, Catlin was awarded the Medal of Honor. Yet when another legendary marine, Smedley Butler, was awarded the same decoration for his actions at Vera Cruz, he tried to return it, explaining that he had done nothing to deserve it. His real motive for wanting to return the medal, his superiors knew, was that so many Medals of Honor had been awarded during what was, on balance, an inconsequential campaign—one to an army man, forty-six to navy personnel, and nine to marines—that the value of the "honor" was substantially diminished. Butler was ordered not only to keep the medal, but to wear it. There can be no doubt that Catlin was an experienced marine and a very courageous one, but his experience of war, though more extensive than that of most of the other marines at Belleau Wood, was limited in scale. To a man who had fought in Cuba and had received the Medal of Honor for his role in capturing a sleepy Mexican city, it must have seemed that the marines—*his* marines—that June 3 had won a truly decisive victory. For certainly he had never witnessed so hot a battle before.

"There is no gain in mincing matters," Catlin wrote after the war, "the French were thoroughly demoralized. And they had good reason to be. They had been fighting interminably, pounded by guns, poisoned by gas, and borne back and broken by superior numbers." But the "United States Marines," in sharp contrast to them, "stood face to face with the oncoming hordes of Attila."[30]

> Not for a moment did a sense of panic follow that realization. Not a man thought of such a thing as joining the retreating French. There arose, rather, a sort of feeling of exultation, that now at last there was men's work to be done, the work of Marines in a tight place. . . . [W]e had the whole history of the Corps behind us, and what a Marine has he holds; he kills or gets killed; he does not surrender; he does not retreat.[31]

Here Catlin spoke the language of final victory, but though he did not realize it at the time, it was a victory that had yet to be won. It is true that the marines had been instrumental in mauling the right wing of Corps Conta, an achievement that did prevent a German breakthrough, right then and there, west and toward Paris. But what the marines achieved did not force von Conta to quit. Instead, the German commander ordered his division commanders to occupy positions "suited for defense," which meant fighting for possession of a line running through Veuilly Wood, Marigny, La Voie du Châtel, Le Thiolet, and Hill 204, which would bring the Germans to a position about a kilometer west of Château-Thierry. And even as von Conta was converting from a full-out offensive to a temporary defensive strategy intended to allow him to recommence his offensive when the French and Americans had worn themselves out against his new line, the French—despite the relief and reprieve furnished by the marines—were approaching the point of collapse in the sector. When a new day dawned—June 4—it would be up to the marines not merely to shore up the disintegrating French lines, which they had done magnificently on the 3rd, but to stand up to a new German onslaught all alone.

· 7 ·

Teufelhunden

Colonel Catlin's sense of victory was premature, but the good news, by late in the day on June 3, was that the American units were finally tied in with one another, as they were supposed to be, and the two marine regimental commanders, Neville and Catlin, each had a buildup of reserves at hand. French supporting artillery was rumbling up into position. Ammunition had arrived. Food was finally plentiful. Not least of all, most of the telephones had begun working dependably.

All of these positive developments had occurred at a most opportune moment. Very early on June 4, Corps Conta renewed its attack against the marines, whose ferocity had given the Germans so rude an awakening. The renewed action would stretch over the next forty-eight hours, as the Germans hit from their left to the their right in a series of attacks, each of which was preceded by an artillery barrage and supported always by heavy machine-gun fire. Yet each of these attacks in turn would be met by Franco-American artillery and American machine-gun fire, as well as by the deadly accurate rifle work of the marines. In the course of the next two days, the U.S. Marines would earn a new name, bestowed by their enemy: Teufelhunden (Devil Dogs).

Corps Conta's drive might have broken against the marine line the day before, but the fact was that the Germans now occupied Belleau Wood as well as the nearby villages of Belleau, Bussiares, Torcy, and Bouresches. The German heavy artillery was close to the front, including 150s and *minen-werfers*, stubby 201-millimeter trench mortars, designed to lob very heavy shells at high trajectory in order to penetrate all cover, whether trench or foxhole. These heavy pieces were supplemented by the usual 77s and 88s. Much of the fire was concentrated on the rear echelon, including supply areas and likely headquarters locations. Both Catlin and Harbord had close calls when shells rained upon their command posts. War along this suddenly contested stretch of front was ceaseless and exhausting. It involved every mode of ground combat: artillery, including high explosives and gas; machine gun; rifle fire; and the bayonet. Each mode was designed to deny refuge anywhere on the battlefield. If a man retreated to the rear, he was vulnerable to artillery. If he stood up, a machine gun or sniper could cut him down. If he hugged the ground or burrowed into a foxhole, the trench mortar would find him. If he relaxed, if he failed to fight, a bayonet might well split his heart.

The Germans' overall plan in resuming the attack was to break through the marine line if possible. But the principal mission of Corps Conta was to protect the left flank of the entire German Seventh Army, which had taken up a position to the north, in the town of Soissons, from which it planned to drive southwest in a renewed sword thrust against Paris. The plan was for Corps Conta to assume new, advance defensive positions on June 7—while all the time maintaining what the German orders called an "offensive spirit."[1]

During June 4 and 5, it was this offensive spirit that was directed most intensely against the marines. The German operations did not consist of massive movements, just a series of sharp jabs, like a boxer looking for an opening. A marine in Major Thomas Holcomb's battalion of Catlin's 6th Marines related that the approach of the Germans, just appearing from out of the woods, brought him "back swiftly, on the wings of memory to a lonely walk in the woods I had taken, as a boy, when I had whistled to keep up my courage." He did not whistle now but, like his fellow marines, cursed and swore "in that choice collection of profanity that belongs to the Marines." The Germans approached his position in closed ranks of four lines. The marine "looked at them with almost a friendly interest. No particular hate or fear." Yet he was keenly aware of "a queer sensation along the spine, and the scalp seemed to itch from the tug of the hair at the roots." His fingers "bit into the rifle," but the barked order came: "Hold your fire!"[2]

As the command rang in my ears with the sharpness that enforced obedience, I seemed to be standing on Bunker Hill and hearing the command: "Wait till you see the whites of their eyes!" I think I know how those old Yanks felt that day, as the enemy drew nearer and nearer.

The next I recall is firing. Firing. Firing. My fingers were tearing greedily at more ammunition, then the instinct of the hunter restrained me.[3]

Instinct? Or was it Marine Corps training? In any case, the marine "began to fire slower, looking for [his] mark, making sure they hit."[4]

It was over, it seemed, in an instant. "The Huns now appeared to be almost on top of us and then, all of a sudden, there was nothing more to aim at. A few scattered groups with hands held up, racing for our lines and shouting 'Kamerad! Kamerad!'"[5]

Every marine who fought them that day and the day before was impressed by the impersonal, machinelike discipline of the Germans' advance—coming on "as steadily as if they were on parade," one of Major Maurice Shearer's marines recalled. That marine remembered how they had advanced three separate times in this manner, "but our fire was too accurate and too heavy for them." Each time they came on, they "fell by the scores, there among the poppies and the wheat" before they finally "broke and ran for cover." Colonel Catlin had a sneaking admiration for such discipline—as far as it went—but he saw the German soldier's mechanical obedience as finally his weakness. "They say the German soldiers fight blindly," he remarked, "with only such knowledge of their objectives as is absolutely necessary to send them forward." American commanders, in contrast, "believe in giving [their] men thorough orientation and realization of just what is expected of them and what they are up against." Catlin took pains to show his battalion commanders his map, "indicating the points to be held, and through them passed on to the men all the information available. I hold that men like ours fight none the worse for knowing just what they are fighting for."[6]

The quality Catlin articulated was a quality of American fighting men at their best. At such encounters as the Battle of Lookout Mountain in the Civil War or Omaha Beach on D-Day, June 6, 1944, this quality, a combination of initiative and courage, converted defeat into victory. Lookout Mountain, the Omaha Beach landing, and the Battle of Belleau Wood—all were examples of what military historians call "soldier's battles," encounters in which it is not the generals in their headquarters who bring victory, but the individual initiative of the frontline soldiers and their officers in the field. As Lieutenant Elmer Hess of the army's 15th Field Artillery recorded in his diary, a French colonel "begged" the major commanding a battalion of the army's 3rd Brigade to "remove his battalion across the River Marne to the hills overlooking the river on the south bank." No, Major Bailey responded, he would do no such thing. His assignment was to hold the line where he was. And that is what he intended to do. To make his point more forcefully, the French colonel explained that, except for some French cavalry, there was no infantry in front of the major's battalion. The "Germans at any moment might sweep through this sector," he warned. The French colonel "begged us to cross the river immediately as he expected to blow up the bridge which he said was our only avenue of escape." Bailey refused, the colonel gave up and left, and an hour later "[they] heard a terrific detonation [they] knew meant the destruction of the bridge over the Marne and [their] supposed last avenue of escape." In response, a Lieutenant Peabody, who was in the kitchen of the French farmhouse that served as Major Bailey's headquarters, "raised a bottle of wine and drank a health to the bridge," a toast "in which [they] all joined before the reverberations of the explosion passed away."[7] This was the spirit of American soldiers and marines throughout the Belleau sector.

June 4 and June 5 in the vicinity of Belleau Wood and its nearby villages were days of small, sharp engagements. The casualties during these forty-eight hours were about two hundred for Corps Contra and two hundred fifty for the U.S. 2nd Division. In a war that had been counting the dead and wounded in the tens of thousands—often in the space of less than forty-eight hours—these losses must have seemed almost inconsequential. Yet they belied, on the American side, remarkable acts of heroic initiative that added up to a result far in excess of what the casualty figures suggested.

By the morning of June 5, Les Mares Farm, a marine-held position northwest of Belleau Wood, fell under attack. Lieutenant Lemuel Shepherd, wounded in the neck during the initial onslaught, had refused evacuation because he did not want to leave his marines. He was in Captain John Blanchfield's command post when this latest German attack came, and he picked up the phone to call in artillery fire on his front. This done, he took hold of his orderly, a marine named Cable, and set out for the front line.

He did not like what he saw up there. A French colonial platoon had been assigned to cover the American line to the left of Les Mares Farm. The platoon was gone, having left without word, creating a gap of a few hundred yards. Shepherd and Cable lit out after the withdrawing colonials, determined to get them back into place. No sooner did they begin running than German machine guns and rifles cracked into action against them. The two men leaped into a nearby thicket of shrubbery, which would provide concealment, if not cover. In response to the German fire, the colonials turned and opened up on the Germans. Caught in the crossfire, there was nothing for Shepherd and Cable to do but grapple themselves to the ground. Despite this, Cable was soon hit in the foot. Under fire, Shepherd applied a field dressing, then helped his orderly crawl toward a dressing station. This done, he returned to the line.

It was taking heavy fire. Shepherd watched as Gunnery Sergeant Babe Tharau, making no attempt to cover himself, carefully directed fire, pointing out targets and range. Shepherd inched his way down the line, diverting fire to cover Tharau's position, an action that forced the Germans to break off the attack there. With a breathing space secured, Shepherd went back to battalion headquarters to call up reinforcements and to get his neck wound freshly dressed. After doing these things, he returned to the line again.

Elsewhere at Les Mares, Gunnery Sergeant Buford was becoming increasingly wary of German infiltration tactics. During periods of maneuver and small attacks, the Germans sometimes sent small parties to infiltrate a thinly held line. Such parties could wreak havoc far out of proportion to the number of enemy involved. Toward noon on June 5, a Corporal Dockx, positioned thirty yards in front of the marine line at Les Mares, reported seeing movement in the wheat. Buford rounded up a squad, including Dockx, and with them crawled forward through the wheat field. Sure enough, a knot of Germans was spread out around a pair of machine guns. Buford positioned snipers behind haystacks, then ordered his squad to open fire while he and two marines rushed the enemy.

The surprise was overwhelming. Most of the Germans scattered, running back through the wheat and out into an open patch. Buford calmly leveled his .45 automatic and picked off a number of the fleeing enemy that had been positioned around the machine guns. He then wheeled about to join his squad in taking out the machine-gun crews. The record does not say whether the first crew was killed or surrendered. In either case, that position was taken without marine casualty. The second crew, alerted by the initial attacks, fought back fiercely, killing Dockx and another marine before they were felled by marine bullets.

Despite the heroism of men like Shepherd, Dockx, and Buford, there is a limit even to what a marine can do at any given time. When the battalion intelligence officer, Lieutenant William Mathews, came up to Buford, who had just returned with the surviving squad members, he noticed Dockx's body in the wheat.

"Let me have a couple of your men," the lieutenant said to Buford, "so I can go out and see what's left out there."

"Oh, no, Mr. Mathews. We are all too unnerved now," the gunny replied. "We can't do it."[8]

Mathews could see the look in Buford's eyes. What he saw there told him that he should not push this assignment on him. Instead, he instructed

Buford to put two marines he knew to be crack shots, Corporal Knapp and Sergeant Britton, in concealment on top of a haystack under a shed. They would cover Mathews's advance. He was going out with only his own sergeant.

The pair crawled toward Dockx. Mathew took notice of a "beautiful Jersey cow . . . grazing peacefully only a few feet away." America in 1918 was still mostly a land of farms and farm boys, and in the midst of battle and danger, it was hard not to think thoughts of home. But for the fleeting comfort of that vision, it was a grisly patrol: "We crawled on past [a hay]stack and had not gone fifteen yards when we came upon at least a half dozen enemy corpses lying in the wheat." They crawled over the dead men "and a few yards further came upon a body lying across one of the paths in the wheat. I stopped because I could see the torso of the body rise and fall as it breathed. The upper part of the body was covered, head and all, with a German shelter half, while the lower part wore French sky blue britches and puttees." He was a man dressed for infiltration work, partially in the uniform of his enemy. Mathews called to him "in a low voice to surrender several times before he pulled the shelter half off and turning his head murmured in French, 'Merci.' We did not dare stand up straight as we would be exposed to enemy fire, and after several attempts to move the wounded man, we had to give it up, as he let out loud yells." The German's leg and thigh were severely wounded, and his ankle was broken. "He kept murmuring, 'Feldwachen,' and kept pointing with one arm. We heard a groan a little farther off and got what he meant." Mathews and his sergeant crawled "only a few feet when [they] came upon a young blond German lying on his back rolling back and forth groaning. He too was badly wounded in the thigh. He was barely conscious." Realizing that "the only way to get them in would be by stretchers," Mathews sent the sergeant to get some. The problem was that there were no stretchers to be had at this forward position. Buford sent a couple of men to get stretchers, but Mathews's own sergeant became impatient, with his lieutenant exposed in the wheat field. As Mathews wrote in his official report, the sergeant realized "the pickle I was in" and, seeing "a woven wire gate to a chicken coop, tore it off and crawled out to me dragging the gate after him." The two Americans put the Germans on this improvised stretcher and brought them in.[9]

Corps Conta had two missions during the forty-eight hours of June 4 and 5: to prepare to defend the flank of the Seventh Army, scheduled for a general advance on June 7, and to jab at the marine line in an effort to make a breakthrough. Such a breakthrough would have enabled a major push toward Paris. The marines, however, did not let the breakthrough happen. For their part, the French in this sector were thrilled with this fact. Having begun by doubting the capacity of the Americans even to support a French-fronted line, they now "praised the behavior of the American troops" and were "full of praise for the 2d U.S." Division in particular. French morale, which had been in a defeatist crisis since the end of May, was now, according to U.S. liaison officer Major Paul Clark, "very good." French officers were suddenly "very enthusiastic over the American troops. It is in some instances touching to hear their expressions of praise and gratitude over the rapid arrival of the Americans."[10]

By June 5, the German commanders in the vicinity of Belleau Wood were frustrated and alarmed by their reversal of fortune. After rolling up the French lines here at the end of May, after watching the French crumble, they had been first slowed, then stopped, and in some places pushed back. Casualties were high, especially among the men of Corps Conta. The commanders analyzed the situation. On their left (the southern part of the sector), a combination of French units and the 3rd U.S. Division—an army unit—had reclaimed the bridgehead that had been established across the Marne at Jauglonne. On the right (north), the French had not only recovered, but were holding their own and beginning to push back with counterattacks. But it was in the center that the arrest of the German drive had been the most sudden and the harshest. And this was the portion of the Allied line defended by the U.S. Marines.

Alarming, yes. Yet it was not the failure of progress that was most troubling, but the fact that the German offensive was losing its momentum, the troops simply wearing out. Years later, military historians would pin the blame on the Kaiser's generalissimo, Erich Ludendorff, who, they said, had conceived ambitions far too great for the forces available to him. His most recent offensive, like those that had come before, initially met with spectacular success, until its forward momentum was inexorably sapped the farther his troops penetrated Allied lines. Ludendorff had thrown everything he had into the opening waves of the offensive, leaving him little or nothing with which to follow through. As momentum flagged, Ludendorff's commanders hesitated, that hesitation serving further to bleed off the momentum of the advance. The more the momentum dwindled, the greater the hesitation. The greater the hesitation, the worse the diminishment of the forward momentum.

Ludendorff had intended to make a major thrust with his Seventh Army on June 7. To the north of this effort, his Eighteenth Army would also have to effect a breakthrough. That, however, required heavy artillery preparation, which, in turn, depended on the transfer of heavy artillery from the Seventh Army up to the Eighteenth Army's front. Seventh Army, however, found itself pushing against fresh U.S. forces and French troops reinvigorated by the American successes. In the face of such resistance, it was impossible to transfer the artillery. The major push, therefore, had to be delayed by two days and was rescheduled to June 9. It was a further hemorrhage of momentum.

As resources of the German offensive were stretched thinner and thinner, time was not the only element sacrificed. Crown Prince Rupprecht, commanding the entire army group on this front, was forced to concentrate all that he could on the planned northern attack. This meant abandoning—or indefinitely postponing—offensives in the south and southwest. That was a serious blow to German morale. All along, this most desperate of Ludendorff's offensives had been driven by the battle cry, "*On to Paris!*" The field commanders did not silence this cry, but the shift to the north made it unmistakably clear that the German army was no longer bound for Paris—at least not directly. That, in turn, meant that what this offensive promised—victory sudden and sure, an end to the war—was not going to happen, even if the offensive succeeded. At most, there would be a breakthrough. Maybe that would finally break the Allies, but the presence of the Americans, including the fierce Devil Dogs, made that seem less and less likely. Even if the offensive succeeded, the war, then, would go on.

As the Germans readjusted their expectations downward, the Allies ratcheted theirs up. General Joseph Degoutte received two fresh French divisions, increasing the strength of his battered 21st Corps by nearly 100 percent. One of these, the 167th, was to relieve Colonel Paul Malone's "Detachment, AEF" and was slated to assume coverage of part of the front that had been assigned to Frederic Wise's marine battalion. With American forces freed up, U.S. 2nd Division commander General Omar Bundy could deepen his defenses along the line held by the Americans. General E. M. Lewis's 3rd Brigade—U.S. Army—would hold the line from La Nouette Farm and Triangle Farm while James C. Harbord's 4th Brigade—the marines—would hold it from Triangle Farm northwestward to the road north of Champillon. Northwest of this position would be the responsibility of the French.

By the afternoon of June 5, the U.S. 2nd Division was in the midst of reorganizing its forces so that each of its four infantry regiments would hold the line with two battalions apiece, and one battalion per regiment could be held in reserve. Machine guns and artillery were finally getting to where they should be: in full supporting positions. Bundy was establishing a strong defensive position, which, he reasoned, was precisely what the French needed here.

It was an eminently reasonable assumption, given the French crisis that had abated only hours earlier. Yet Bundy had not reckoned on General Degoutte's mercurial command temperament. In the depths of despair days before—and with good reason—he was now in a mood verging on euphoria. Defense was a doctrine anathema to the French military mind, vintage 1918. Now that the front had been stabilized, it was not enough to build it up and hold it—to let Ludendorff batter his head against it—but, instead, on the afternoon of June 5, even as the U.S. 2nd Division was completing its defensive reshuffling, Degoutte ordered an offensive, a general advance to begin on the next day, June 6.

As usual, for the commander with the biggest map, it was mostly a question of geometry. Although it had been variously pushed back, the German line still snaked and bulged in salients, one of the most prominent encompassing all of Belleau Wood. Degoutte wanted an offensive that would straighten the line while seizing such strong points as Belleau Wood, which, with its dense tree growth and prominent rock outcroppings, was nothing less than a natural fortress.

The plan was for the 167th French Division to attack the heights south of the Clignon River while the marines advanced to Hill 142 and captured it, which would neutralize any flanking fire against the 167th. These actions would constitute phase one of the offensive. Next, in phase two, the U.S. 2nd Division would capture the ridge that loomed over Belleau, the village just north of Belleau Wood, and Torcy, northwest of Belleau. In the process, elements of the division were to occupy Belleau Wood itself, also capturing the German-held town of Bouresches, which was just east of Belleau Wood.

It was not a bad plan. Certainly, the objectives were worth taking—especially Belleau Wood. As long as that tangle remained in German hands, the entire Allied front in this sector would be menaced. As long as the sector was menaced, Paris was in danger. If Paris should fall, the war might well end—and not in the way the Allies wanted. Yet the suddenness of Degoutte's order, the call to shift in the space of a few hours from a hard won defensive position to mount an offensive, created a thoroughly unnecessary crisis. Bundy's men were on the move, making one set of shifts and reliefs when they were suddenly obliged to initiate another. The plan had been for the 167th French Division to relieve Wise's marines west of the area of Hill 142 and the village of Champillon. Major Benjamin Berry's 3rd Battalion of the 5th Marines would hold the line just east of Hill 142, down to the southwestern edge of Belleau Wood, running between the woods and the village of Lucy-le-Bocage just to the southwest of the woods. At this point, Berry's marines were to tie in with Thomas Holcomb's 2nd Battalion of the 6th Marines, which was assigned the line from the edge of Belleau Wood southeastward to Triangle Farm, tying in here with the 23rd Infantry of the U.S. Army's 3rd Brigade. Thus, two marine battalions would directly front Belleau Wood along its western and southwestern perimeter.

These movements were in progress when Degoutte's new orders fell upon them. The main movement, the relief of Wise's 2nd Battalion, 5th Marines, by the 167th French Division, had not even gotten under way. Indeed, all of the shifts now required by Degoutte's orders had to be carried out in darkness, on the night of June 5—and carried out by dog-tired marines using the usual grossly inadequate French maps.

This was all bad enough, but there were two other problems, critical ones. They were problems that should have doomed the offensive before it even began.

The suddenness of Degoutte's order left no time for reconnaissance. Local French intelligence reported that Belleau Wood was essentially "Boche free," but none of the Americans believed this and, for that matter, neither did Degoutte himself. Yet no one had the slightest idea of how many Germans might be occupying the woods. All of the Americans' nighttime movements were taking place in complete ignorance of the enemy's whereabouts. To compound this problem, whereas Degoutte's order had not budgeted time for reconnaissance, the Germans possessed extensive knowledge of the Allied positions. They flew observation aircraft and even lofted observation balloons freely along this sector, which was almost entirely undefended by Allied aircraft.

The second problem was almost as basic. Degoutte's order left scant time for the artillery preparation that customarily preceded an attack. The marines would be expected to venture into the unknown, against an enemy of undetermined numbers, barely diminished by some brief barrage immediately before the attack.

Given time—a day or two—a more reasonable and well-reconnoitered counterattack could have been mounted. Degoutte rationalized his urgency by saying that he feared the Germans were in the process of reinforcing their already formidable artillery, and he was anxious to strike before that could be completed. This may indeed have been the motive behind his haste. Yet it is also likely that he felt himself the victim of the Americans'

A photograph titled "First to Fight," circulated by the U.S. Marine Corps Recruiting Publicity Bureau during the period of the Belleau Wood battle. National Archives and Records Administration

Marine recruiting poster, 1918.
The Granger Collection, New York

General Henri Philippe Pétain.
The Granger Collection,
New York

General John J. Pershing (right) with Gener
Ferdinand Foch. The Granger Collectio
New Yor

George Barnett, USMC commandant at
the time of the Battle of Belleau Wood.
United States Marine Corps

Brigadier General James G. Harbord, t
U.S. Army officer General Pershing assign
to command the 4th Marine Briga
Collection of the auth

Marines embarking for France, 1917. National Archives and Records Administration

Albertus W. Catlin,
colonel in command of the
6th Marine Regiment.
United States
Marine Corps

General Jean Degoutte, the
harried French commander
of the crumbling sector
around Belleau Wood.
Collection of the author

U.S. personnel in France learn to throw hand grenades using the French "stiff-arm" method. The Granger Collection, New York

Poison gas was extensively used at Belleau Wood. Here U.S. personnel model various masks used in the war: The two masks at the left, both British designs, were worn by U.S. and British troops; the third man from the left wears a French mask, and the man on the right wears a German model. Belleau Wood marines were issued the mask on the far left as well as the French mask. The Granger Collection, New York

German soldiers in a trench along the Chemin des Dames ridge.
National Archives and Records Administration

Trench abandoned by the retreating French near Belleau Wood.
The Granger Collection, New York

First Sergeant Dan Daly, who rallied his marines to charge across a machine gun–raked wheat field with the words, "Come on, you sons of bitches! Do you want to live forever?"
United States Marine Corps

Panoramic view of Lucy-le-Bocage, location of Marine forward headquarters—a town the marines called "Lucy Birdcage." National Archives and Records Administration

French machine gunners fire from the ruins of a cathedral near Belleau Wood. National Archives and Records Administration

A marine holds a German soldier at bay during close fighting at Belleau Wood. The pencil drawing was made by Captain John W. Thomason Jr., United States Marine Corps. The Granger Collection, New York

Marines in a shallow dugout at Belleau Wood. National Archives and Records Administration

U.S. Army gun crew, Regimental HQ Co., 23rd Infantry, 2nd Division, firing a 37mm machine gun in Belleau Wood. The Granger Collection, New York

Marines advancing through a portion of Belleau Wood. National Archives and Records Administration

Panoramic view of Belleau Wood, looking toward the villages of Belleau and Torcy, Hill 193, and the German lines. National Archives and Records Administration

Panoramic view from the edge of Belleau Wood, looking toward Hill 193. The villages of Torcy and Belleau are on the left; Hill 193 and Les Brusses farm are in the center. National Archives and Records Administration

General Michael W. Hagee, commandant of the Marine Corps, salutes as "Taps" is played by a marine bugler clad in a World War I–era uniform during a 2006 wreath-laying ceremony at Belleau Wood. Note the French soldiers in attendance. United States Marine Corps

success. *They*—especially the marines—had saved his army. *They*—especially the marines—had demonstrated the aggressive spirit that was the professed doctrine of the French military during this period but that had been conspicuously absent in his own men as the first phases of Ludendorff's offensive rolled over them. Doubtless, Degoutte was most anxious to redeem his honor, not to mention that of France.

If any of the American commanders felt that they were being treated as pawns in a game of ego and national pride, they certainly did not let on. Quite the contrary, General Bundy assumed that the French commander's objective was strictly strategic. "As long as [the Germans] held [Belleau Wood], it would be an ever-present menace to our line," Bundy wrote. "General Degoutte . . . saw the importance of Belleau Wood, and was in full accord with our desire to take it as soon as possible."[11] But why didn't any of the other American commanders take issue with what was obviously an order to premature action, a major counteroffensive for which no preparation was permitted? The answer may be given in four words: *they wanted to fight.*

Wearily, then, the marines marched, shifted, and repositioned their units through the night of June 5. Catlin moved his command post from Blanche Farm, which was well west of the front line along the Metz-Paris highway, to Lucy le Bocage, just behind the line, a short distance southwest of the southwestern corner of Belleau Wood. "By this move to an apparently more dangerous location," he remarked, "it is probable that my life was saved, for a German shell reduced to a heap of ruins the room I had occupied at Blanche Farm very soon after I vacated it." Perhaps he took comfort in the irony of having found safety in proximity to the battle. Whatever he derived from that irony, however, Catlin was well aware of what he faced on the eve of the Battle of Belleau Wood. "We now stood facing the dark, sullen mystery of Belleau Wood," he later wrote, "Berry on the west and Holcomb on the south. It was a mystery, for we knew not what terrible destruction the Hun might be preparing for us within its baleful borders, nor at what moment it might be launched in all its fury against us."[12]

· 8 ·

Hill 142

Brigadier General James C. Harbord had led a career that accustomed him to doing the impossible. Like a number of the marines he commanded—Captain John Blanchfield, for instance—he was a mustang, having graduated from humble Kansas Agricultural College in 1887, joined the service as a private, and worked his way up to an officer's commission. In 1917, he was a one-star general and chief of staff to the commander in chief of the AEF. A desk man until he persuaded General Pershing to release him to field command in May 1918, he was thrilled to find himself in charge of marines, whom even Pershing conceded were "the finest body of troops in France."[1] His first few days on the front adjacent to Belleau Wood persuaded him that the marines were a lot like he was. They could do the impossible.

So it is was with high confidence that he met at three o'clock on the afternoon of June 5 in Omar Bundy's headquarters, the town hall of Montreuil-aux-Lions, with Colonel Preston Brown, the Yale man who served Bundy as chief of staff of the U.S. 2nd Division. Brown reviewed the situation, explaining that General Degoutte had received two new divisions, the French 167th on his left and the 10th Colonial on his right, and wanted

to make an immediate attack. At 3:45 a.m. on June 6, the 167th was to take
Hill 142, the high ground northwest of Belleau Wood. Julius Turrill's battalion of the 5th Marines would accompany this attack. Later that day, the
rest of the 4th Marine Brigade would capture Belleau Wood.

Brown spread out one of the available, miserable maps with which
Harbord was already all too familiar. He traced the vaguely kidney-shaped
outline of Belleau Wood, its southern lobe inclined to the southwest, not
quite touching Lucy-le-Bocage. Here, at this end of the woods, a shallow
ravine the locals called "Gobert"—and the marines dubbed "Gob Gully"—
entered the dense Belleau growth, providing both a clearing and cover that
would facilitate the attack from this southwesterly extreme. North of this
point, however, along the central and northern portions of the woods' western face, there was no cover. Here there was nothing but the ubiquitous,
poppy-studded wheat fields in which many marines and even more of the
enemy had already fallen.

Did Harbord wince when he saw this? When he saw how his marines
would be fully exposed along at least a mile and a half of the west face of
Belleau Wood? How they would be wading through the wheat in the open,
toward—toward (in the absence of reconnaissance) who knew what?

Whether or not Harbord betrayed any emotion, the French intelligence officer who had been sent to 2nd Division headquarters repeated the
local intelligence he had picked up: that Belleau Wood was either completely "Boche free" or lightly held "by a very short line across the northeast corner."[2]

Harbord had no confidence in the French intelligence assessment, but
he had boundless confidence in his marines. The plan he and Brown agreed
on, therefore, relied on improvisation in the field. The uncharitable way to
express this is that Brown and Harbord formulated hardly any plan at all,
and what little they discussed addressed only the first phase of the attack,
the role of Turrill's battalion in the taking of Hill 142.

For phase one, Brown advised attacking by infiltration rather than in
conventional waves. That was perfectly suited to the marine style, so it met
with no objection from Harbord. Brown also stressed maintaining close

liaison between the infantry and artillery. This, Harbord knew, would be essential. Degoutte's orders left no time for a substantial artillery preparation before the infantry advanced, so great care would have to be taken to ensure that French shells did not fall on the advancing marines. As for phase two of the attack, the taking of Belleau Wood—really the principal phase of the entire offensive—Harbord would deal with those plans later. He did not discuss them with Brown.

The artillery support for the attack on Hill 142 consisted of six batteries of 75s—the celebrated light field piece of the French artillery—and two batteries of heavy 155s. The weapons were French, but they would be manned by a combination of French and American troops under the command of Colonel McCloskey, an army officer. As if to make a virtue of the precipitous nature of Degoutte's orders, McCloskey was instructed that there would "not be any [artillery] preparation properly speaking, so as not to attract the attention of the enemy." McCloskey was instructed to direct raking fire from his 75s against Hill 142 and the slope above Lucy-le-Bocage as well as the hill that cradled Torcy on the south and west. Together, all of this constituted the high ground threatening the advance of the French 167th Division. Simultaneously, the 155s were to direct their fire against the roads communicating with the villages of Licy Clignon, Bussiarcs, Torcy, and Belleau. After this, McCloskey was directed to focus a "violent annihilation fire" against the attack objectives.[3]

Zero hour—the moment at which the attack was to commence—was set for 3:45 a.m. on June 6. Harbord therefore worked feverishly to cut field orders, issuing the first of these at 10:25 p.m. on June 5, just five hours prior to zero hour. That gave the marines ludicrously little lead time.

As Degoutte had instructed, Turrill's 1st Battalion, 5th Marines, would accompany the French division in the attack. Harbord further specified that Turrill would be supported by the 8th and 23rd Machine Gun Companies in addition to a company of engineers. Turrill and the supporting units were to attack "between the brook of Champillon, inclusive, Hill 142, and the brook which flows from one kilometer northeast of Champillon, inclusive." Harbord also ordered Benjamin Berry's 3rd Battalion, 5th Marines, to link up with Turrill's right and "conform to the progress" Turrill made in his attack. In other words, to improvise.[4]

Harbord's order was delivered to 5th Marine commander Colonel Wendell Neville, who then had to translate it into regimental terms in his own order. That was completed and issued at 12:35 a.m., June 6, three hours before the attack was scheduled to step off. Neville was able to clarify Harbord's order by identifying what Harbord called "brooks" as what they really were: ravines. Neville further ordered Turrill to tie in specifically with the French 116th Regiment.

Both Harbord's orders and Neville's were predicated on the assumption that all the shifting movements of the previous night had been completed as scheduled. By that time, Turrill's battalion was supposed to have relieved the battalion under Major Berton Sibley, taking its place in the woods just south of Hill 142. In fact, the combination of night, bad maps, and general exhaustion had delayed everything. Only two of Turrill's four rifle companies, the 67th under Captain Crowther and the 49th under Captain George W. Hamilton, were where they should have been. The other two, together with the 8th Machine Gun Company, were back at Les Mares Farm, awaiting their tardy French relief. The whereabouts of the battalion's other machine-gun company (the 23rd) and its engineering company (D Company, 2nd Engineers) were completely unknown.

What to do? Lieutenant Colonel Logan Feland, Wendell Neville's second in command, told Turrill that they had no choice but to assume that the missing units would show up soon. In the meantime, he instructed Turrill to summon the captains of the 67th and 49th companies to receive their marching orders.

When they arrived at the command post, Feland ordered Crowther and Hamilton to lead their companies to Sibley's position. Crowther was to deploy his men, ready for attack, on the left, Hamilton on the right. Their objective, Hill 142, was really more of a ridge than a hill, oriented north to south. The terrain sloping up to this ridge was varied and included alternating wheat fields and woods. The rise was bracketed by a pair of ravines. Feland instructed Crowther to lead his 67th Company in a northerly attack, his left flank skirting the western ravine. Simultaneously, Hamilton's 49th Company would advance alongside Crowther's right flank, attacking due north. The plan—such as it was—had been for the entire battalion to participate in the attack: four rifle companies, two machine-gun companies, and a company of engineers. At the moment, only the 67th and 49th companies were marching to the line. Turrill, Crowther, and Hamilton could only hope that the others would show up momentarily and get into place before the attack stepped off at 3:45 in the morning.

But that did not happen. Indeed, by the time the commanders blew their whistles, signaling the start of the attack, not only were the missing companies still absent, neither Crowther nor Hamilton had fused his lines with the French on the left or with Berry's 3rd Battalion on the right. Understrength as it was, the marine line also had gaps on both of its flanks. Bad as all of this was, there was no taking back the shrill of the whistle. Zero hour had arrived. Nevertheless, it was not battalion commander Turrill who gave the order for his two companies to attack. With less than half his strength at the front, he hesitated. But a number of his platoon leaders, green lieutenants all, with 3:45 burned into their minds and the whistle's call echoing in their ears, took it upon themselves to loft into the air the symbols of their command—straight wooden canes—point them forward, and call out, *Follow me!*

"Went down the front line and found some of the men over the top and about twenty-five yards out," Turrill subsequently reported. "So I gave the word to advance to the whole line"—that "whole line" being but half a line.[5]

John Thomason, a tall marine captain from Huntsville, Texas, who liked soldiering, sketching, and writing—and liked them precisely in that order—was assigned to the 1st Battalion of the 5th Marines. He was there that morning. He fought, he sketched, and he wrote:

> The platoons came out of the woods as dawn was getting gray. The light was strong when they advanced into the open wheat, now all starred with dewy poppies, red as blood. To the east the sun appeared, immensely red

and round, a handsbreadth above the horizon; a German shell burst black across the face of it, just to the left of the line. Men turned their heads to see, and many looked no more upon the sun forever. "Boys, it's a fine, clear mornin'! Guess we get chow after we get done molestin' these here Heinies, hey?"—One old non-com—was it Jerry Finnegan of the 49th?—had taken out a can of salmon, hoarded somehow against hard times. He haggled it open with his bayonet, and went forward so, eating chunks of goldfish from the point of that wicked knife. "Finnegan"—his platoon commander, a young gentleman inclined to peevishness before he'd had his morning coffee, was annoyed—"when you are quite through with your refreshments, you can—damn well fix that bayonet and get on with the war!" "Aye, aye, sir!" Finnegan was an old Haitian soldier, and had a breezy manner with very young lieutenants—"Th' lootenant want some?"—Two hours later Sergeant Jerry Finnegan lay dead across a Maxim gun with his bayonet in the body of the gunner.[6]

Finnegan's doomed nonchalance notwithstanding, Thomason recalled that it "was a beautiful deployment, lines all dressed and guiding true. Such matters were of deep concern to this outfit." Thomason remarked on the beauty of the day as well, "without a cloud, promising heat later, but now it was pleasant in the wheat, and the woods around looked blue and cool." Like some others in this sector, Thomason was impressed by the fact that the countryside was almost untouched. "Since the first Marne [in 1914] there had been no war here." That was an exaggeration, but the devastation there was much less thorough than elsewhere along the western front, and the "files [of advancing marines] found it very different from the mangled red terrain around Verdun, and much nicer to look at. 'Those poppies, now. Right pretty, ain't they?'—a tall corporal picked one and stuck it in his helmet buckle, where it blazed against his leathery cheek."[7] Shelling was light during the first twenty or thirty yards of the advance. There was time to pick a poppy.

Across the wheat field, Thomason recalled, were more woods, "and in the edge of these woods the old Boche, lots of him, infantry and machine-guns. Surely he had seen the platoons forming a few hundred yards away—it is possible that he did not believe his eyes. He let them come close before he opened fire."[8]

The German Maxim guns began spraying death by the time the front line of marines had advanced fifty yards from its initial position. Thomason saw it this way: "The platoons, assailed now by a fury of small-arms fire, narrowed their eyes and inclined their bodies forward, like men in heavy rain, and went on. Second waves reinforced the first, fourth waves the third, as prescribed."[9] And he heard it like this:

> Officers yelled "Battlesight! Fire at will"—and the leaders, making out green-gray, clumsy uniforms and round pot-helmets in the gloom of the woods, took it up with Springfields, aimed shots. Automatic riflemen brought their chaut-chauts [Chauchats] into action from the hip—a chaut-chaut is as accurate from the hip as it ever is—and wrangled furiously with their ammunition-carriers—"Come on, kid—bag o' clips!—" "Aw—I lent it to Ed to carry, last night—didn't think—" "Yeh, and Ed lent it to a fence-post when he got tired—get me some off a casualty, before I—"[10]

There was "yelling and swearing in the wheat, and the lines, much thinned got into the woods. Some grenades went off; there was screaming and a tumult, and the 'taka-taka-taka-taka' of the Maxim guns died down." The attack pushed on, "platoons much smaller, sergeants and corporals commanding many of them."[11]

The Germans, as Thomason saw it, had not expected to fight a defensive battle near Hill 142, so they were not deeply entrenched. That was lucky for the marines. But there were a great many Germans—and far fewer marines than there were supposed to be. "There was more wheat, and more woods, and obscure savage fighting among individuals in a brushy ravine. . . . Most of the front waves went down; all hands, very sensibly, flung themselves prone."[12]

Thomason recorded this exchange:

"Can't walk up to these babies—"

"No—won't be enough of us left to get on with the war—"

"Pass the word: crawl forward, keepin' touch with the man on your right! Fire where you can—"[13]

The officer who gave this order, a "big man, who had picked up a German light machine-gun somewhere, with a vague idea of using it in a pinch, or, in any case, keeping it for a souvenir, received the attention of a heavy Maxim and went down with a dozen bullets through the chest."[14]

"The American fighting man has his failings," Thomason wrote. "He is prone to many regrettable errors. But the sagacious enemy will never let him get close enough to see whom he is attacking. When he had seen the enemy, the American regular will come on in. To stop him you must kill him. And when he is properly trained and has somebody to say 'Come on!' to him, he will stand as much killing as anybody on earth."[15]

One of those men who said "Come on!" was Captain George Hamilton of the 49th Company. He wrote to a friend, "I realized that we were up against something unusual and had to run along the whole line and get each man (almost individually) on his feet to rush that wood." Once in the woods, Hamilton recalled, "things went better" as the marines engaged in tough, close combat, making such savage use of the bayonet that a number of Germans raised their hands in supplication for mercy, begging with cries of "Kamerad." However, Crowther's company, the 67th, which had been tasked to advance around the woods rather than through it, was taking the brunt of the Maxim fire. Crowther was killed, as was First Sergeant Beau Hunter. As Thomason recalled, the company dwindled. [16]

Hamilton rallied this dwindling force, reorganizing it, getting the men out of the open and into the woods, then leading them out into another field. "I have vague recollections of urging the whole line on, faster [through the woods], perhaps, than they should have gone." Hamilton hurriedly manhandled prisoners into groups, "Sending them to the rear under *one* man instead of several." He snatched an iron cross off the first officer he encountered, and he shot "wildly at several rapidly retreating Boches."[17] For unlike many other officers, Hamilton carried a rifle, not a cane.

But then they emerged from the woods again and into another wheat field full of red poppies—"and here we caught hell." Desperate to stop the stream of death, Hamilton led his men into a second woods—and, as he knew, directly into the German Maxim gun positions. They could stand and die, lie down and die, walk and die. Or they could rush into the very guns that were killing them. "It was only because we rushed the positions that we were able to take them, as there were too many guns"—no fewer than three German machine-gun companies, as it turned out—"to take in any other way."[18]

Thomason saw how his fellow marines—men of fragile flesh and bone and blood—rushed those machine-gun nests, overran them, and silenced them. They "crawled forward; the wheat was agitated, and the Boche, directing his fire by observers in tree-tops, browned the slope industriously. Men were wounded, wounded again as the lines of fire swept back and forth, and finally killed." The marines were sweating, "hot, and angry with a bleak, cold anger." Driven by this collective emotion, they "worked forward. They were there, and the Germans, and there was nothing else in the clanging world."[19]

At length, an officer risked his head above the wheat so that he could observe the progress. Perhaps it was Captain Hamilton himself. He detached a corporal with his squad. "Get far enough past that flank gun, now, close as you can, and rush it—we'll keep it busy"—meaning that the rest of the marines would draw the Maxim's fire while the corporal and his squad rushed it.[20]

In the end, it did not work out the way it had been planned. But it did work.

"Nothing sounds as mad as rifle-fire, staccato, furious—" When the corporal figured that he and his squad had gotten close enough to the machine-gun nest, he rose up from the wheat with a yell, and his quad rose up with him, yelling too. The problem—for him and his men, the tragedy—was that he had misjudged the distance. He had not advanced far enough and had failed to get past the flank of the machine-gun position. Immediately, two guns swung in the direction of the yells "and cut the squad down like a grass-hook levels a clump of weeds." The bodies of those men—eight U.S. Marines—would lie for days where they fell. "But they had done their job." For the other marines, those still crawling through the wheat, were "close enough to use the split-second interval in the firing. They got in, cursing and stabbing." To the left of these marines, another "little group of men lay in the wheat under the very muzzle of a gun that clipped the stalks around their ears and riddled their combat packs—firing high by a matter of inches and the mercy of God. A man can stand just so much of that. Life presently ceases to be desirable; the only desirable thing is to kill that gunner, kill him with your hands!"[21]

"By God, let's get him," a Corporal Greer called out.

And they got him. One fellow seized the spitting muzzle and up-ended it on the gunner; he lost a hand in the matter. Bayonets flashed in, and a rifle-butt rose and fell. The battle tore through the coppice. The machine-gunners were brave men, and many of the Prussian infantry were brave men, and they died. A few streamed back through the brush, and hunters and hunted burst in a frantic medley on the open at the crest of the hill. Impartial machine-guns, down the hill to the left, took toll of both."[22]

Thomason noted that knocking these machine gunners off Hill 142 "was the objective of the attack," and yet "distance had ceased to have any meaning, time was not, and the country was full of square patches of woods. In the valley below were more Germans, and on the next hill. Most of the officers were down, and all hands went on."[23]

In a letter to a friend, Captain Hamilton wrote, "I realized I had gone too far—that the nose of the hill I had come over was our objective." He and his men—what was left of them—were now on the road to Torcy, which lay to the east, east of Belleau Wood even. A corporal and two marines privates—all unidentified—continued even beyond where Hamilton had halted. They advanced into Torcy itself and discovered that the Germans there were getting together a counterattack. The three marines, vastly outnumbered, opened up on the enemy, and when a bullet hit one of the marines, the corporal sent him back to report that they had taken the town, but were in immediate need of reinforcements.

The report was, of course, audacious and premature. The corporal and the other marine remaining in Torcy continued the attack. From the very first house they approached, German troops poured fire on them. The two marines leaped into a hole—and continued firing from this cover. Two Germans rushed the hole. Neither the Germans nor the marines emerged again.

Hamilton understood that he was in no position to take Torcy, which was occupied by too many Germans and, in any case, was well into enemy territory. He also realized that having brought his men too far, "it was up to me to get back, reorganize, and dig in." He and his marines crawled back, taking whatever cover they could find—in Hamilton's case, a "drainage ditch filled with cold water and shiny reeds." As he crawled, machine-gun rounds grazed his back, and—even more terrify-ing—McCloskey's artillery (Hamilton said) "was dropping close (I was six hundred yards too far to the front.)"[24]

Yet Hamilton managed to get back to begin the grimly frantic business of putting both the 67th and 49th companies back into some semblance of fighting order. The companies had been devastated. Of the ten lieutenants between them, nine were dead. Entire platoons had ceased to exist, while others now consisted of a handful of marines, led by a sergeant or a corpo-ral. At that, these shattered units were isolated from one another and utterly disorganized. Nor was anyone there whom Hamilton could turn to. The French, with whom Turrill's battalion was to tie in on the left, had never materialized. Nor had Ben Berry's marines on the right flank.

As Hamilton moved from one knot of dazed marines to another, order-ing, coaxing, cajoling them to set up new defensive positions, a German ar-tillery barrage opened up. This could mean only one thing, the captain knew: *counterattack.*

It came not as a great wave, but as the very thing Gunnery Sergeant Bu-ford had earlier warned against—infiltration. The Germans approached with infinite stealth—relatively easy on a chaotic battlefield—then began tossing grenades, knowing that those whom the grenades failed to wound or kill would be stunned and vulnerable to the bayonet. A rock lofted by an exploding grenade hit Hamilton in the head, causing him to black out briefly. He was brought back to full consciousness by a keening animal howl coming from his right. Its source was the throat and lungs of Gunnery Sergeant Charles Hoffman—at forty, one of the battalion's "old hands"— who had just spotted a dozen Germans breaking through the brush not twenty feet away. Sufficient to bring the unconscious to life, Hoffman's howl alerted the entire 49th Company. He swung about, using the momentum of the swing to plunge his bayonet into the belly of the German at the point of the attack. Withdrawing the weapon, now blooded, he twisted it into the next attacker, by which time he had been joined by other marines who similarly dispatched the rest of the infiltration party, as well as others who were about to set up no fewer than five light machine-gun positions to finish off the marine company.

Such was the essence of the marine battle swirling around and, within hours, in Belleau Wood. The army, corps, division, and brigade generals drew up their plans on smudged and meaningless maps, while the marines on the ground did what the insufficiency and unreality of those plans required. They improvised. They improvised to survive. They improvised to achieve victory. And whereas a plan may be the product of many minds, combat improvisation typically depends on a single man, a Hamilton or a Hoffman, standing up when the bullets fly, howling like an animal when necessary, wielding and thrusting the most atavistic warrior weapon in the modern arsenal, the cold, sharp steel of a bayonet. As history sees it, World War I—the Great War—was a struggle of titanic forces. Viewed from ground level, these forces were neither more nor less than the sum of the mind, will, courage, and muscle of individual men, each becoming intimate with the same abyss. On Hamilton and Hoffman, the survival of the 49th Company depended. On men like these, victory itself depended.

■ ■ ■

While Hamilton and his men took, then overshot their objective, back below Hill 142 Julius Turrill observed the fourth wave of his two companies approach the perimeter of the first woods at the end of the wheat field. Just then—minutes past four in the morning—he was approached by Lieutenant Gilfillan, whose platoon was at the forefront of the units that had been stalled at Les Mares Farm. The rest of Turrill's battalion was beginning to come on line, he announced.

As he watched the fourth wave melt into the woods, Turrill wasted no time. He began sending the incoming reinforcements—who should have been part of the original attack—to the edge of the first woods. U.S. Navy corpsmen—the medics attached to marine units—worked on Hamilton's wounded, under fire, in the wheat fields along the woods' periphery. Within a short time, the rest of the 66th Company joined Gilfillan's platoon, and by 5:30, the 8th Machine Gun Company was in place, providing much-needed machine-gun cover just behind the line. At this time, too, the 17th Rifle Company under Captain Winan was working its way up along the ravine on the right. Minutes later, Turrill's adjutant, Captain Keller Rockey, sent Colonel Neville a message informing him that the 17th Company was "going into deployment from old first line" and that the 8th Machine Gun Company was "already forward." Rockey reported that "things seem to be going well," his only complaint being that no engineers were yet "in evidence. Can something be done to hurry them along."[25]

When Rockey sent this message, Turrill was already forward with the line, where he was joined by Lieutenant Colonel Logan Feland, Neville's second in command. Feland saw for himself that, even though "things seemed to be going well," there was still no tie-in with the French on Turrill's left. Exposing a flank so close to a contested front presented a grave risk. If the Germans managed to sideslip that flank, all they had to do was turn to their left and "roll up" the battalion. Like a rifle or the point of a bayonet, an attacking force is truly effective in one direction only: facing front. Catch it from an exposed flank and you catch it at its second-weakest side (only the rear is more vulnerable). At 6:00 a.m., Feland sent a message to Neville, asking for a company of reserves to "connect Turrill's left with the French. He is ahead of them."[26]

In his *On War,* posthumously published in 1832, the influential early-nineteenth-century military theorist Carl von Clausewitz wrote most famously of the "fog of war," the confusion endemic to any battlefield. That fog was evident in abundance around and in Belleau Wood. Somewhat less well known is the Clausewitzian concept of what he termed "friction" in war, by which he meant the multitude of realities, great and small, that interpose themselves between a plan and its execution. It is one thing to pencil a line from point A to point B, or to send a message calling for "one company of reserves," but quite another actually to move from A to B. The only reserve Neville had available at this point was Frederic Wise's 2nd Battalion, which had just now been relieved at Les Mares Farm. Technically, this unit was now immediately under General Harbord's control, as a brigade (rather than battalion) reserve. To summon a company of this unit, Neville had to telephone General Harbord and plead the case Feland had laid before him. This took some considerable persuading, but, at length, Harbord grudgingly released the 51st Company, 2nd Battalion, under Captain Lloyd Williams, who set out with his company up the ravine that was to the left of Turrill.

The "friction"—time as well as a degree of meaning lost in the message getting from Feland to Neville to Harbord—was related to the fog of war. Each link in the chain of communication failed to convey the urgency of the situation at the front. As Turrill and his company commanders knew from immediate experience, their attack was progressing, yet the situation was nevertheless desperate, subject to reversal at any moment, largely because the offensive had been so poorly prepared for, and the marine battalion had been forced to step off before all of its components were in place. Neville did not convey urgency to Harbord when he requested the release of a company to patch Turrill's left. On the contrary, by 7:00 a.m. he reported to Harbord that "both Turrill and Berry have reached their objectives." Neville further summarized that there had been heavy shell fire, as well as rifle and machine-gun action but, curiously, noted that only "a few men were killed and quite a number wounded but only lightly." Overall, Neville reported, "Our front line has thrown strong points in front of the line and are consolidating their position as rapidly as possible." At practically the same time, the

U.S. liaison officer attached to the French division reported that the division had "practically obtained all its objectives, though fighting still continues." Perhaps most astounding of all was the report of Major Holland Smith, a great marine who would become famous in World War II as Lieutenant General "Howlin' Mad" Smith, the father of marine amphibious assault. Stationed at Turrill's forward command post, he reported shortly after 7:00 a.m. that the marines had "reached our objectives" and were "throwing out strong points and . . . consolidating our positions."[27]

It is not that the reports were untrue but that they were inaccurate, failing to convey the fragility and fluidity of the evolving situation. The result, however, was just as dangerous as if they had been flatly false. For Harbord, they painted a rosy picture when a bloody picture was called for. It was true that Turrill had gained his assigned objectives, but at a terrible cost. Nor did any of the reports reflect Hamilton's desperate situation in front of these objectives. As for the report concerning the French, this was the most misleading. They had yet to reach most of their objectives, hence the gap between them and Turrill's battalion. Finally, Neville had casually reported that Ben Berry's 2nd Battalion was in place, guarding Turrill's right flank, as it was supposed to do. In reality, the 45th Company, 2nd Battalion, had overshot its objective. Instead of tying in with Turrill's right at the ravine below Hill 142, as it should have done, the company had advanced too far forward and too far to its right. The result was not only an enduring gap between the company and Turrill's battalion, but a perilous situation for the 45th itself, which was pinned down by the German 460th Regiment, firing from the woods. Major Berry reported something of this situation to Neville at 8:10 a.m., but was himself confused, writing, "Ravine of creek will be occupied as soon as Major Turrill has gained his objective."[28] He was right that the 45th Company was short of the ravine, but he did not know that Turrill had already reached his objective, that the 45th was pinned down, and that Turrill's right was in imminent peril.

For his part, Harbord was left to assume that all the major objectives having been attained, the first phase of the Degoutte offensive was essentially at a close. He reported to 2nd Division commander Omar Bundy at 8:40 that, as of 7:10 a.m., "our position was being consolidated," signifying that the operation was all but over. Indeed, Harbord felt sufficient leisure to compose, at 9:00 in the morning, a letter to Neville, which he himself characterized as a "lecture." Harbord groused that he "couldn't take a chance on cramping Major Turrill's style by not giving him that extra company"— Williams's 51st, as requested by Feland—"to fill the gap between him and the French," adding that the "facts" appeared to be that the French had actually "attacked through a battalion in line which remained in position and effectually guarded Turrill's left flank no matter what the gap appeared to be." In other words, as Harbord saw it, he had been obliged to send Turrill a company Turrill really didn't need, because the French were actually guarding his flank even though they didn't appear to be. That is, Turrill's crisis was imagined, not real. Had Turrill provided a "proper runner liaison between his left and the French," Harbord lectured, he would have seen that the "gap" was an illusion. To rub it in, Harbord pointed out that the company sent to him was "tired, sleepy, entitled to rest" and might "sometime today" be "really needed." This company "had to be sent to do the duty that might have been done by two or three runners." Despite the fact that Harbord concluded by congratulating Neville and "the 1st Battalion and 3rd Battalion on doing so well, what we all knew they would do," the letter must have stung the 5th Regiment colonel.[29]

At least, it would have stung, if Neville had any opportunity to digest and ponder it. But at the very moment Harbord was composing the letter, Neville was reading a message from Turrill, reporting that the French had gotten "under [their] own artillery fire and retired"—permanently, it seemed. Turrill implored: "Can't they be persuaded to come up to our left." He also asked for ammunition—machine-gun, Springfield, and Chauchat ammunition—and, most revealing, he asked for stretchers. Neville replied that he was sending the requested supplies to Champillon immediately, to which Turrill responded tersely: "I have no men to carry this up." Under fire, he could spare no one to fetch the supplies. It was yet more of the friction of war. Turrill then sent a second message reiterating his urgent need for ammunition, apparently leaving it to Neville to figure out how to get it *directly* to him.[30]

It was all a matter of perspective, and perspective would be a major issue throughout all of the fighting in and around Belleau Wood. The struggle, from start to finish, was always in doubt, always desperate, yet the higher the head-quarters, the more glibly optimistic the assessment of the action, as if the per-ception of the reality of the desperation were, by virtue of some ineluctable mathematical law, inversely proportional to the distance from the scene of bat-tle. Harbord did not appreciate Neville's situation. Neville did not adequately appreciate Turrill's. And Turrill was only made aware of Captain Hamilton's dire predicament when he received a message from him: "Elements of this Company [the 49th] and the 67th Company reached their objective, but be-cause very much disorganized were forced to retire to our present position which is on the nose of Hill 142. . . . Our position is not very good because of [German] salient. . . . We have been counter-attacked several times but so far have held this hill. Our casualties are *very* heavy. We need medical aid badly, cannot locate any hospital apprentices and need many. We will need artillery assistance to hold this line tonight. Ammunition of all kinds is needed. . . . The line is being held by detachments from the 49th, 66th and 67th Company and are very much mixed together. . . . *All my officers are gone.*"[31]

Hamilton's next message was sent at ten minutes past noon. He called for artillery support and for ammunition "as much as can be gotten up"—and reported that several corpsmen had arrived to dress wounds, but noted that evacuation of the wounded would have to wait. "Need water badly," he wrote. Also needed were "Very pistols"—flare guns—and illumi-nating rockets, both essential for battle in the night to come.[32]

Minutes later, Turrill wrote his own message, this one to Neville: "Un-less Berry comes up to my right I will have to fall back, there is nothing on my right between the front and way back to where we started from, as far as I can find out." He followed this up around 1:00 p.m. by repeating that his "first line is on our objective—left weak—right uncovered." He believed that the French were "slowly advancing on our left," but—"As I said before, . . . a strong attack on our right would finish us."[33]

Turrill's men had started out in perfect order, parade order—"lines all dressed and guiding true. Such matters were of deep concern to this outfit."[34] Looking around him now, Turrill saw ragged men, spent men, men taking cover where they could amid the wounded men and the dead men. Ammunition was in critically short supply. Everyone was thirsty, their thirst as galling as any wound. To his left, Turrill knew, was a gap. To his right, another. Up ahead—somewhere—was Captain Lloyd Williams, cut off on all sides.

All this Turrill either saw or knew. What he neither saw nor knew was that he had won the "Battle for Hill 142."

Had he been able to see what the Germans saw and knew, he would have realized it. Between June 4 and that moment, the 197th German Division had lost two thousand men killed or wounded. The 273rd Regiment of this division had alone suffered more than four hundred casualties, all before noon, on June 6 on Hill 142. The German positions there were cut off and could not be reinforced. All the reserves of the 197th had been committed at dawn of this day, and, having failed to defeat the marines, the division drew more men from the German 5th Guards and from the 273rd Regiment. But to no avail. The 197th, its reserves, and the other units it had called on, all had beaten themselves insensible against the wall that was the U.S. Marines. To be sure, the marines, themselves reeling, were vulnerable now, but the Germans had nothing left to attack them there.

"Later," Captain Thomason wrote, "there was a letter, taken from a dead feldwebel in the Bois de Belleau—'The Americans are savages. They kill everything that moves.'"[35]

▪ 9 ▪

A Dark, Sullen Mystery

C aptain John W. Thomason wrote:

> The Boche wanted Hill 142; he came, and the rifles broke him, and he
> came again. All his batteries were in action, and always his machine-guns
> scourged the place, but he could not make head against the rifles. Guns he
> could understand; he knew all about bombs and auto-rifles and machine-
> guns and trench-mortars, but aimed, sustained rifle-fire, that comes from
> nowhere in particular and picks off men—it brought the war home to the
> individual and demoralized him.[1]

At the headquarters of General Harbord and the more distant headquarters of Generals Bundy and Degoutte, the commanders were professionally heedless of the wounded and the dead on both sides. All that
merited their professional notice was the victory achieved at Hill 142 and the
necessity then of beginning the next phase of the offensive—the phase that
had been ordered but left utterly without plan—the taking of Belleau Wood.

About noon, Joseph Degoutte transmitted Order XXI C.A. 87/PC. It
directed the French 167th Division to continue its advance to the Clignon

River and the U.S. 2nd Division to commence the second phase of the offensive: the capture of the ridge west of Belleau Wood, along with Belleau Wood itself and the nearby village of Bouresches. By the time he received this order, General Omar Bundy had already tasked Harbord's marines, the 4th Brigade, with carrying out this phase of the offensive. In turn, James Harbord issued his Field Order Number Two, which identified two phases of the operation: the taking of Belleau Wood and the taking of Bouresches as well as the ridge to the west of Belleau Wood. Major Ben Berry's 3rd Battalion, 5th Marines—with the exception of Captain Conachy's company, temporarily attached to Turrill's battalion—was to attack the woods on its west side, while the 3rd Battalion, 6th Marines, under Major Berton Sibley, would hit the lower lobe of the woods, which hooked to the southwest. Thomas Holcomb was to lead his 2nd Battalion, 6th Marines, on Sibley's right, in conformity with Sibley's progress, supporting his attack. Machine-gun support would be provided by the 77th Machine Gun Company and by unspecified artillery. Assigned overall command of the assault on Belleau Wood was the colonel of the 6th Regiment, Albertus Catlin, who had, by his own account, spent the previous night brooding over the "dark, sullen mystery" of what was now the first of his assigned objectives.[2]

After Belleau Wood was captured, the next part of the attack was to commence. Sibley was to continue his advance east to railroad tracks north of Bouresches while his right flank captured the town. At the same time, Berry was to advance through the northern end of Belleau Wood so that his right protected Sibley's left. Berry was to advance to Hill 133, which was northwest of Bouresches on the Bouresches-Torcy road. While he was thus advancing, Turrill's 1st Battalion, 5th Marines, reinforced by the addition of two companies, would advance from the hard-won (indeed, barely won) Hill 142 to the north, just east of Bussiares, to link up with Berry's left at Hill 133.

It was a complex plan hurriedly cobbled together, involving the coordination of virtually all of the units of the 4th Brigade. If it worked, it would advance Degoutte's line considerably east. This, in turn, would prevent a German breakthrough either to the northwest or, worse, toward Paris.

Degoutte, Bundy, and Harbord were encouraged by the success of the morning's campaign to take Hill 142. But had they cast a colder eye on this victory, they would have realized how narrow and costly a triumph it was. To a more realistic set of minds, the results of the morning of June 6 might well have appeared not as encouragement, but as a cautionary tale on the dangers of launching ambitious offensives without adequate planning and preparation. After all, the taking of Hill 142 had been what the Duke of Wellington called the Battle of Waterloo: "the closest run thing you ever saw in your life."[3] The truth was that, as with the earlier operation, the ends were laudable, but the means were hardly available—at least not on such short notice.

Harbord had set 5:00 p.m. as zero hour for the 4th Brigade to fulfill Degoutte's orders. As of early afternoon, Sibley's battalion, which was to take the lower part of Belleau Wood, was more than a mile from its designated starting point, which was just north of Lucy-le-Bocage. Berry's battalion was in disarray, its companies facing in various directions, along a line from Lucy-le-Bocage northwest toward Hill 142. Although higher headquarters believed the fight for Hill 142 was over and done with, Turrill and his battalion were still in combat there—and two of his four companies had been all but destroyed. Holcomb's battalion, which was deployed in a line from Triangle Farm to Lucy-le-Bocage, was in the throes of reorganizing. Wise's battalion, which, except for the 51st Company, had been held as brigade reserve during the fight for Hill 142. Despite this brief respite, it was badly depleted. Finally, a battalion under Major John A. Hughes was being held as a corps reserve.

In short, the marines that afternoon of June 6 were shot up, depleted in number, disorganized, and lacking in ammunition and equipment. All of these deficiencies could be remedied, given a few days. But the attack on Belleau Wood was scheduled for five that very afternoon.

The greatest deficiency of all was the absence of reliable reconnaissance. "It was supposed to be a surprise attack," General Harbord wrote of it later, "and was, therefore, not preceded by any unusual artillery activity."[4] That is, there would be no artillery preparation to soften up the woods. Von

Hutier's devastating method of attack, Hutier tactics, did away with the prolonged artillery preparation that customarily preceded major attacks on the grounds that such preparation sacrificed the element of surprise. But another ingredient Hutier tactics brought to the attack more than compensated for the absence of preliminary artillery. It was overwhelming numbers attacking with overwhelming ferocity. That was the essence of Hutier tactics, and it was not present in the marine attack on Belleau Wood. Or, rather, there was no way of telling whether it was present, because the marines had no idea whether they possessed overwhelming numbers. They had no idea how many troops the Germans had placed in Belleau Wood.

Harbord would later write: "I am obliged to acquit General Degoutte of any responsibility as to the tactical methods employed [at Belleau Wood]. With the information we had had that the woods were unoccupied by the Germans, we gave it no artillery preparation, thinking thereby to take it by surprise or to find it unoccupied."[5]

Just how murky and confused the situation was in the precious few hours preceding the attack is apparent from the discrepancies between Harbord's recollections and those of Colonel Catlin. Catlin recalled that one of the very few things known for certain about the "dark, sullen mystery of Belleau Wood" was that it was "strongly held." Catlin knew this because he had endeavored to secure his own intelligence regarding the woods. "That something was going on within those threatening woods we knew, for our intelligence men were not idle. *Every day* my regimental intelligence officer rendered a report of the enemy's movements to the Divisional Intelligence Department [that is, to Bundy] and also to me, and I reported in turn to Brigade Headquarters [that is, to Harbord]." On the morning of June 6, the "report . . . was to the effect that the Germans were organizing in the woods and were consolidating their machine gun positions, so that a sortie in force seemed not unlikely." This is a sufficiently astounding contradiction of what Harbord recalled—but there is even more. Catlin wrote, "We had been prepared for [a German sortie from out of Belleau Wood] for nearly two days [June 4–6]" because, on "the night of the 4th Lieutenant Eddy, the intelligence officer of the Sixth [Regiment], with two men stole through the

German lines and penetrated the enemy country almost as far as Torcy," which was on the far side of Belleau Wood. Eddy and his men "lay in a clover field near the road and watched the Germans filing past them. They listened to the talk and observed what was going into the woods." Catlin admitted that such reconnaissance was risky, but that it "brought back valuable information." Besides, "Lieutenant Eddy was a dare-devil, anyway, and loved nothing better than to stalk German sentries in Indian fashion and steal close to their lines. . . . He was the son of a missionary, I believe, born and raised in Asia Minor, and was an American college graduate. How he came by his extraordinarily adventurous spirit, I don't know, but he certainly had it. The Marine service has always attracted men of that type."[6]

Nor was Eddy's the only ominous preattack intelligence. A division intelligence report of June 2 noted that "the Boche are believed to be concentrating in the woods just north Bouresches," and on June 3 a French pilot—one of the few flying in this sector, the air space of which was dominated by the Germans—reported being "under the impression that [Belleau Wood is] occupied by the Boche." This impression was created, apparently, by the fact that the pilot was "fired on by machine gun from the rear of the woods." A second French aviator reported on June 5 the presence of "Several Boche elements in the Bois de Belleau—enemy gun shots fired."[7]

None of this intelligence was definitively informative, of course, but that was precisely the point. The division intelligence report, Eddy's reconnaissance, the reports of the French pilots all cried out for further investigation in the form of more extensive reconnaissance. Yet none was forthcoming, and Harbord, apparently, was content to recall that the only information he and everyone else had was that Belleau Wood was either unoccupied or only lightly held.

(The matter of intelligence may not be the only discrepancy between Harbord's recollection and the facts. Harbord claimed that *no* artillery preparation was devoted to Belleau Wood, whereas his own 4th Brigade War Diary recorded in an entry dated June 6 at 5:00 p.m.—zero hour— "Artillery starting with raking fire on Bois de Belleau and on the northern and eastern slopes" as well as "interdiction fire on the ravine, railroad, and

road between Bouresches and Belleau-Torcy-Licy-Clignon and Bussiares."
It might be argued that this use of artillery fire was not "artillery preparation," because it was almost simultaneous with the marines' incursion into
Belleau Wood. Catlin recalled that the Allied "artillery fired for half an
hour, shelling the woods, but there was no artillery preparation in the
proper sense of the term. They had no definite locations and were obliged
to shell at random in a sort of hit-or-miss fire. It must have been largely
miss."[8] More important than arguing the existence of a discrepancy here is
pointing out that, even if artillery fire did accompany the attack, it was
grossly insufficient.)

As no American officer had complained about Deguotte's precipitous
orders for an offensive—but on the contrary welcomed the opportunity to
fight no matter how reckless the fight would be—so Catlin surely did not
complain about being sent on a mission he likened to "entering a dark
room filled with assassins." Instead, he remarked laconically, "In the afternoon we were ordered to attack at 5 p.m. The Germans must be driven out
of Belleau Wood," and went on to explain that there "were sound strategic
reasons for this remarkable order."[9] He enumerated them:

> Pressure had to be relieved northwest of Château-Thierry before that po-
> sition could be made secure. Belleau Wood . . . formed a dangerous
> salient in our curving line [and was] too strong a natural fortress to be
> allowed to remain in the hands of a powerful enemy on our immediate
> front. . . . For the Germans it formed a base of attack that threatened our
> whole line to the south. So long as they held it a sudden thrust was pos-
> sible at any time, and such a thrust might mean untold disaster, proba-
> bly the quick advance on Paris. For us it was an effective barricade. The
> Allies could not advance with that thorn in their side.[10]

Catlin, indeed, was at pains to justify the attack and even to second Degoutte's haste: "Obviously, Belleau Wood had to be taken, and that right
quickly, whether we were to act successfully on the defensive or on the offensive. It would have been suicidal to wait for the German attack. An

assumption of the offensive was the only solution." This being the case, Catlin put the situation in its most positive light—so far as the reputation of the Corps was concerned: "And so it turned out that the United States Marines, who had been called up to support the French in defence, were ordered to attack, and to attack an enemy position of the strongest kind. That we were expected to succeed speaks volumes for the confidence we had won."[11]

Long after the fact, we now know that on June 2, Major Hans Otto Bischoff, commanding the 461st Regiment of the 237th German Division, captured the village of Belleau. Not that there was much to capture by the time he and his men entered it. The villagers had long since joined the stream of refugees fleeing the front. The village church had been looted, and the château that had dominated the place was a shell. But Belleau did offer a large concavity below a bluff, which provided excellent cover for the regiment's kitchen and headquarters. Once established in the village, Bischoff sent some of his men into Belleau Wood, which the 461st began to occupy on June 4.

Bischoff grasped the value of Belleau Wood as precisely what Catlin had called it, a natural fortress. He sent his second in command, a Major von Hartlieb, to organize three battalions in the woods, two on the line and one in reserve. On his right (north), these were tied in with the German 460th Regiment. From the point of the tie-in, at the northwest corner of Belleau Wood, Bischoff and Hartlieb arranged their battalions down along the upper portion of the western face of the woods. The southern end of the western face they deemed too overgrown for the purposes of adequate defense, so leaving some outposts there, they curved the main line across the woods to its southeastern corner. Large boulders, the size of railroad cars, abounded among the trees. These, along with the many ravines that scarred the ground, Bischoff and Hartlieb exploited for the placement of machine-gun nests as well as trench-mortar emplacements. At the southeast corner of Belleau Wood, Bischoff tied in with the 398th Regiment, German 10th Division, which was well dug in just south of Bouresches and Vaux. Both in Belleau Wood and above and below it, the German position was very strong.

No fewer than fifteen heavy Maxim guns were planted among the boulders. Added to this was a plethora of light machine guns—about two hundred in all. In contrast to the headlong pace of the Allies, Bischoff and Hartlieb moved carefully and deliberately, placing their guns to ensure crossfire so that an attempt to take one machine gun would expose the attackers to flanking fire from at least two others. Nor did the commanders rely solely on the features of this natural fortress. The cover provided by boulders and ravines was supplemented by trenches. There were three lines of these running directly through the woods. The westernmost was behind the southern edge and faced Lucy-le-Bocage and Bouresches. Another line bisected Belleau Wood through its center at its narrowest part, running east to west. Edged with barbed wire, it sheltered trench-mortar teams and connected with rifle pits for snipers. At the northern edge of the woods was another line of trenches, also protected by barbed wire and sheltering more trench-mortar outfits. Manning all of these formidable positions were about twelve hundred men who were, however—and this was key—not in the best of shape. By this stage in the war, Germany was deep in the grip of the British naval blockade as well as the general economic strain of a war that had lasted years longer than anyone had expected. Most Germans lived on a semistarvation diet, the men of the army not excepted. Americans might complain about French rations, but except for periods in the field, they were fed quite well. German soldiers by this time and on this front were subsisting on the coarsest of black bread, the cheapest of cereals (generally barley), and the occasional dried vegetable. Meat was a rarity, subject to the luck of a foraging party. Malnourished, men were chronically ill with a complaint commonly called grippe and characterized by flulike symptoms verging on pneumonia. Endemic, too, was dysentery. Added to these debilitating disorders and diseases was a universal exhaustion and, in some quarters, a gnawing defeatism. Man for man, on the level of physical condition and emotional state, the Germans were no match for the Americans.

At 3:45 in the afternoon, an hour and fifteen minutes before the attack was to begin, Catlin received his orders from Harbord's aide, a Lieutenant Williams, who drove up with them on a motorcycle. Apart from the obvious problem of lack of time, confusion reigned from the start. Catlin, colonel of the 6th Marine Regiment, was also to direct the movements of Major Berry's 5th Regiment battalion; however, Berry "had also received the orders from his own Regimental Headquarters," so it would be by no means clear to him that he was to report directly to Catlin instead of the 5th Regiment colonel, Wendell Neville. Seeing a potentially catastrophic conflict in the making, Catlin sought to nip any problems in the bud with a timely phone call. But Berry, it turned out, was already a mile away from the telephone, and his battalion was well beyond reach. Heavy shelling making it impossible to "run a telephone to him," Catlin "sent runners, but I was sure they couldn't reach him before the attack would have to be made." From the start, then, a complex and ambitious operation whose success depended on careful coordination among the units involved was assailed by a major problem of communications. "I must confess that this situation caused me considerable anxiety. I don't know whose fault it was, but the communications were far from perfect." To be sure, that was an understatement, but understatement though it was, Catlin understood all too well what this deficiency meant: "It looked as though we would have to attack without proper cooperation, and as a matter of fact, that is what we did."[12]

The situation very nearly verged on being a grotesquely bad joke. Yes, it was terrible to attack without proper cooperation, but having to do so quickly emerged, in Catlin's view, as the least of the marines' problems. "I was fully aware of the difficulties of the situation, especially for Berry. He had four hundred yards of open wheat field to cross in the face of a galling fire, and I did not believe he could ever reach the woods." Aside from the fact that, in Catlin's view, Berry was being sent on a suicide mission, it also meant that "Sibley's battalion would have to bear the brunt of the action," and his "stupendous task [was] to lead his 500 [men of the 'first rush'] through the southern end of the wood clear to the eastern border if the attack was not to be a total failure. Even to a Marine it seemed hardly men enough." Indeed, while Catlin thought that the "men knew in a general way what was expected of them and what they were up against," he believed that "only the officers realized the almost impossible task that lay before them. . . .

But I had perfect confidence in the men; that never faltered. That they might break never once entered my head. They might be wiped out, I knew, but they would never break."[13]

Catlin summoned Thomas Holcomb and Berton Sibley to meet with him at Holcomb's headquarters, five hundred yards behind the line. The three pored over the map as Catlin "explained the situation to them without trying to gloss over any of its difficulties." This completed, Catlin drove off to Lucy-le-Bocage, "where [he] could observe the action." As Catlin knew, the village was under heavy artillery fire. "Perhaps I exposed myself unduly, but I was anxious about Berry and it seemed necessary for me to get as near his command as possible and to keep an eye on the whole proceeding."[14]

As the colonel passed through Lucy-le-Bocage, he skirted left of Sibley's men, waiting in their shelter trenches, waiting—in that phrase universal throughout the Great War—to *go over the top*. "They were equipped for action," Catlin noted. "When Marines go into line they travel in heavy marching order [with sixty-pound packs], but when they go in to fight it is in light marching order, with no extra clothing or any blankets. They carry twenty-odd pounds then. They all had their rifles and ammunition, and some of the men were equipped with hand or rifle grenades." To Catlin's eyes, the "men seemed cool, in good spirits, and ready for the word to start. They were talking quietly among themselves. I spoke to several as I passed. Some one has asked me what I said, what final word of inspiration I gave those men about to face sudden death." Catlin denied being a speech maker. "If the truth must be told, I think what I said was, 'Give 'em Hell, boys!'"[15]

Half an hour before the marines began their advance into Belleau Wood, Allied artillery fired, more or less at random, into the former hunting preserve. Whereas the Allied fire was hit or miss, the German artillery fell with increasing intensity just as Sibley's men began to go into line. Berry's position was also shelled, seriously interfering with his nearly frantic efforts to get his men into attack order. In addition to the artillery barrage, Berry's men also had to deal with the outbreak of various individual firefights.

The hour before "going over the top" hardly allowed an interval for quiet reflection. Floyd Gibbons, war correspondent for the *Chicago Daily*

Tribune, went in company with Lieutenant Oscar Hartzell, a former *New York Times* correspondent who was then General Pershing's press officer, to Colonel Neville's headquarters as soon as they heard that General Degoutte had ordered a continuation of the morning's advance. It was four o'clock by the time they announced to Colonel Neville "our intentions of proceeding at once to the front line."[16]

> "Go wherever you like," said the regimental commander, looking up from the outspread maps on the kitchen table in the low-ceilinged, stone farmhouse that he had adopted as headquarters. "Go as far as you like, but I want to tell you it's damn hot up there."[17]

Damn hot. And the battle had yet to begin.

The two reporters arrived "in the woods to the west of the village of Lucy le Bocage," just behind Berry's front. "German shells were continually falling. To the west and north another nameless cluster of farm dwellings was in flames. Huge clouds of smoke rolled up like a smudge against the background of blue sky." It was, Catlin recalled, "a clear, bright day." Shifting his gaze from the smoke-smudged blue of the sky, Gibbons noted that the "ground under the trees in the wood was covered with small bits of white paper. I could not account for their presence until I examined several of them and found that these were letters from American mothers and wives and sweethearts—letters—whole packages of them, which the tired, dog-weary Marines had been forced to remove from their packs and destroy in order to ease the straps that cut into aching grooves in their shoulders."[18]

This far back, "Bits of [machine-gun] lead, wobbling in their flight at the end of their long trajectory, sung through the air above [the] heads [of Gibbons and Hartzell] and clipped leaves and twigs from the branches."[19] The reporters dropped into a hastily dug American machine-gun pit at the edge of Belleau Wood.

> Five minutes before five o'clock, the order for the advance reached our pit. It was brought there by a second lieutenant, a platoon commander.

"What are you doing here?" he asked, looking at the green brassard and red "C" on my left arm.

"Looking for the big story," I said.

"If I were you I'd be about forty miles south of this place," said the Lieutenant, "but if you want to see the fun, stick around. We are going forward in five minutes."

That was the last I saw of him until days later, when both of us, wounded, met in the hospital. Of course, the first thing he said was, "I told you so."[20]

Given the word, Gibbons "hurriedly finished the contents of the can of cold 'Corned Willy' which one of the machine gunners and I were eating. . . . And then we went over. There are really no heroics about it. There is no bugle call, no sword waving, no dramatic enunciation of catchy commands, no theatricalism—it's just plain get up and go over. And it is done just the same as one would walk across a peaceful wheat field out in Iowa."[21]

At any given marine position, it was just that simple, and just that terrible. The hour or so preceding this simple and terrible moment was filled with confusion as the various units struggled to communicate with each other even as they each scrambled to put their own companies into position for an "advance in line of sections." This was the French attack formation all American units learned—and learned by heart as if it were a catechism—when they came to France. It was a highly choreographed attempt to impose order on the chaos of combat. In it, each four-platoon company formed up with two platoons creating a front, and two for support behind it. In turn, each platoon divided itself into four sections of twelve men each, with two sections in the front and two in the rear. This division took the form of vertical columns that, ordered to advance, did so in a horizontal wave, each man five yards from the next. About forty yards to the rear of the front two sections, the rear two sections formed up similarly, and so the pattern continued, all the way to the rearmost wave of the rearmost platoon in the company. Every company in the battalion formed up in this manner.

It is important to maintain discipline in combat, and that does require somehow displacing chaos with order. A battalion arranged in a line of sections would appear as a vast rectangular box, perhaps a thousand yards across and seven hundred or eight hundred yards deep. It was most impressive, especially in motion. Moreover, maintaining the proper intervals gave a man something to take his mind off the falling shells and the raking machine-gun fire. Perhaps because it imposed discipline or perhaps merely because it was a particularly ossified tradition of French infantry doctrine, the line of sections was never subjected to rigorous analysis. The fact of the matter was that, boxed up in this manner, a platoon, a company, a battalion sacrificed most of its firepower while on the march. Only the outermost men could fire, and only the front line could fire effectively at the enemy.

"Instantly," Catlin wrote, "the beast in the wood bared his claws. The Boches were ready and let loose a sickening machine gun and rifle fire into the teeth of which the Marines advanced." Berry's battalion had an open wheat field to cross, "400 yards or more wide—winter wheat, still green but tall and headed out." Sibley's battalion was closer to the woods. Bad communications made it impossible to coordinate between Berry and Sibley. Up front with Berry's men—oblivious of Sibley's—Floyd Gibbons reported what he called "a beautiful sight, these men of ours going out across those flat fields toward the tree clusters beyond from which the Germans poured a murderous machine gun fire." Gibbons later remarked to Catlin that the "platoons started in good order and advanced steadily into the field between clumps of woods. It was flat country with no protection of any sort except the bending wheat. The enemy opened up at once and it seemed . . . as if the air were full of red-hot nails. The losses were terrific."[22]

Berry and his men did get the worst of it, having to march across an open expanse of wheat field, swept by machine-gun fire as surely as by some all-encompassing scythe. At the time, however, Catlin focused his attention exclusively on Sibley's battalion, as mesmerized by his line of sections march as Gibbons had been by Berry's: "I watched [Sibley's] men go in and it was one of the most beautiful sights I have ever witnessed. The battalion pivoted on its right, the left sweeping across the open ground in four waves, as steadily and correctly as though on parade." A year later, in 1919, while still struggling to recover from the shattering chest wound he suffered on the day he was writing about, Colonel Catlin proclaimed: "Never did men advance more gallantly in the face of certain death; never did men deserve greater honour for valour."[23]

To Private Elton E. Mackin, who arrived at the battle on the next day, the vision of combat was far more intimate: "A fellow does not know 'til afterward that little pieces of his heart will rot in graves where friends are fast asleep."[24]

▪ 10 ▪

"Do You Want to Live Forever?"

Five in the afternoon, Belleau Wood, France, June 6, 1918. No bugles, *Tribune* correspondent Floyd Gibbons would write. No flashing swords. Just a general advance through fields of wheat toward a former hunting preserve, tangled, overgrown, and now transformed into one big machine-gun nest. Gibbons, as well as the 6th Regiment's Colonel Albertus Catlin, remarked on the beauty of the marines advancing toward the woods in perfect rank and file, as if on parade, a gloriously doomed march into "a veritable hell of hissing bullets," a "death-dealing torrent," against which the marines bent their heads "as though facing a March gale."[1]

That is how many of the marines began the attack, in the orthodox "advance in line of sections" they had learned so painstakingly under French tutelage. It was a style of advance born of a very human desire to impose order on chaos, to ward off confusion with method. It did not work for long.

Against Benjamin Berry's 3rd Battalion, 5th Marines, who had to advance across the most extensive stretch of open wheat field—some four hundred yards of it—the German fire was longest and hottest. "The headed wheat bowed and waved in that metal cloud-burst like meadow grass in a summer breeze. The advancing lines wavered, and the voice of a

Sergeant was heard above the uproar: 'Come on, you __ _ __! Do you want to live forever?'"[2]

Correspondent Gibbons had heard this cry, too, or so he reported. In his 1918 memoir, "*And They Thought We Wouldn't Fight*," Gibbons wrote of how, when he was a boy, he read "Hugo's chapters on the Battle of Waterloo in 'Les Misérables'" and conceived his "ideal of fighting capacity and the military spirit of sacrifice." In Hugo's classic, an old sergeant of Napoléon's Old Guard, facing annihilation at the hands of the English, refuses the call of his enemy to surrender. "Into the very muzzles of the British cannon the sergeant hurled back the offer of his life with one word. That word was the vilest epithet in the French language. The cannons roared and the old sergeant and his survivors died with the word on their lips. Hugo wisely devoted an entire chapter to that single word." Today, Gibbons continued, "I have a new ideal . . . I found it in the Bois de Belleau."[3]

A small platoon line of Marines lay on their faces and bellies under the trees at the edge of a wheat field. Two hundred yards across that flat field the enemy was located in trees. I peered into the trees but could see nothing, yet I knew that every leaf in the foliage screened scores of German machine guns that swept the field with lead. The bullets nipped the tops of the young wheat and ripped the bark from the trunks of the trees three feet from the ground on which the Marines lay. The minute for the Marine advance was approaching. An old gunnery sergeant commanded the platoon in the absence of the lieutenant, who had been shot and was out of the fight. The old sergeant was a Marine veteran. His cheeks were bronzed with the wind and sun of the seven seas. The service bar across his left breast showed that he had fought in the Philippines, in Santo Domingo, at the walls of Pekin, and in the streets of Vera Cruz. I make no apologies for his language. Even if Hugo were not my precedent, I would make no apologies. To me his words were classic, if not sacred.

As the minute for the advance arrived, he arose from the trees first and jumped out onto the exposed edge of that field that ran with lead, across which he and his men were to charge. Then he turned to give the charge order to the men of his platoon—his mates—the men he loved. He said:

"COME ON, YOU SONS-O'-BITCHES! DO YOU WANT TO LIVE FOREVER?"[4]

The Battle of Bunker Hill gave us "Don't fire until you see the whites of their eyes"; the seagoing duel between John Paul Jones's *Bon Homme Richard* and HMS *Serapis*, "I have not yet begun to fight"; the siege of a San Antonio mission turned fortress, "Remember the Alamo"; and the Battle of Belleau Wood, "Come on, you sons of bitches! Do you want to live forever?" Along with Captain Lloyd Williams's earlier "Retreat, hell! We just got here," they were the most celebrated utterances to emerge from marine throats in World War I, and they became hallowed words in the annals and lore of the Corps. The declaration was universally attributed to Gunnery Sergeant Dan Daly, but nobody has been found who actually heard him say it. Catlin's memoir implied that the sergeant (Catlin does not name him) was attached to Berry's battalion, and Gibbons, who accompanied elements of that unit in its attack on Belleau Wood, implies that he was even within earshot. But Daly, forty-four years old, had shipped out to France as first sergeant (a full rank above gunnery sergeant) of the 73rd Machine Gun Company, and at Belleau Wood was attached not to Berry's battalion but to Sibley's, which attacked Belleau Wood south of Berry's position and formed part of the American center along this entire front. Daly's platoon was on the outskirts of Lucy-le-Bocage when it was either completely pinned down by fire from Belleau Wood or wavered in its advance—sources vary on this—whereupon Daly hefted over his head a bayonet-tipped Springfield and made his deathless declaration. Daly later told a Marine historian that "What I really yelled was: For Christ's sake, men—COME ON! Do you want to live forever?" But, accurately or not, the lore of the Corps has chosen to remember it as "Come on, you sons of bitches!"[5]

Dan Daly was a real marine, who really did fight at Belleau Wood, coming to that battlefield already having received the Medal of Honor twice, once for single-handedly defending the Tartar Wall in the Boxer Rebellion of 1900 and again for defeating four hundred Caco bandits with just thirty-five marines in the Haitian campaign of 1915. John A. Lejeune, who would succeed George Barnett as Marine Corps commandant after World War I, pronounced Daly the "outstanding Marine of all time."[6] Short and slight, standing five foot six and weighing 132 pounds, Daly repeatedly refused offers of a commission throughout his career, protesting that he would rather be "an outstanding sergeant than just another officer." Unassuming, he remained single his entire life and retired from the Corps on February 6, 1929, with the rank of sergeant major. In civilian life, he became a guard in a Wall Street bank and died quietly at sixty-five on April 28, 1937, in his Long Island home.

A real marine in a real battle, Daly really did say something that ended with the rhetorical question, "Do you want to live forever?" That the versions of the legend surrounding Daly and his battle cry vary in the details does not diminish the reality the legend is based on. Both Catlin and Gibbons seized on the phrase, changing its location a bit, and in Gibbons's case even claiming to have heard it personally, for much the same reason that the marines marched against Belleau Wood in the elaborately choreographed line of sections formation: to impose order on chaos, to make sense of it, to extract some greater meaning from it. Even the minor error that all versions of the story share—"demoting" Daly from first sergeant to gunnery sergeant—is significant in the effort to mythologize this aspect of the battle. For while the first sergeant outranks the gunnery sergeant, it is the "gunny" who is the archetypal marine noncom, perceived as the rugged, tough-love layer of command closest to the grunts.

Without such patterns and stories, the Battle of Belleau Wood threatened to emerge into posterity as what Catlin admitted "it has been called"—nothing but "an exaggerated riot," a slaughter, full of sound and fury, signifying—just what?[7]

Even under fire, legends endure far longer than a line of sections. "The ripping fire grew hotter," Catlin wrote. "The machine guns at the edge of the woods were now a bare hundred yards away, and the enemy gunners could scarcely miss their targets. It was more than flesh and blood could stand." Berry's "men were forced to throw themselves flat on the ground or be annihilated, and there they remained in that terrible hail till darkness made it possible for them to withdraw to their original position." Henry Larsen, Berry's adjutant, reported to the brigade after the battle: "three platoons 45th Company went over. Only a few returned," and Catlin wrote: "Berry's men did not win that first encounter in the attack on Belleau Wood," which was another way of saying that not a single one of Berry's marines even reached the edge of the woods, and 60 percent of the battalion became casualties.[8] Among these was Major Benjamin Berry himself. Floyd Gibbons was there when it happened—and he was more than a witness.

Gibbons, with Berry and many of his men, was making his way down a wooded slope, where midway down was a sunken road, littered with French bodies and "several of our men who had been brought down but five minutes before. We crossed that road hurriedly knowing that it was covered from the left by German machine guns." Gibbons, Berry, and the marines came to a V-shaped field, "perfectly flat and . . . covered with a young crop of oats between ten and fifteen inches high." On all sides of the field were dense clusters of trees. Gibbons and the others could hear the machine guns. "We could not see them but we knew that every leaf and piece of greenery there vibrated from their fire and the tops of the young oats waved and swayed with the streams of lead that swept across." After giving orders to follow him at ten to fifteen-yard intervals, Berry "started across the field alone at the head of the party. [Gibbons] followed." The woods around the field "began to rattle fiercely," and Gibbons could see "the dust puffs that the bullets kicked up in the dirt around our feet." Berry was well beyond the center of the field when he turned toward Gibbons and the other men: "Get down everybody."[9]

He did not have to repeat the order. "We all fell on our faces. And then it began to come hot and fast," the volleys of lead sweeping the "tops of the oats just over us." As Gibbons "busily engaged [in] flattening [himself] on the ground," he heard a shout. "It came from Major Berry. I lifted my head cautiously and looked forward. The Major was making an effort to get to his feet. With his right hand he was savagely grasping his left wrist. 'My hand's gone,' he shouted."[10]

In some ways what really had happened to him was worse. Berry's hand had not been shot off, but a bullet had entered his left arm at the elbow, passing down alongside the bone, "tearing away muscles and nerves to the forearm and lodging itself in the palm of his hand. His pain was excruciating," causing him to stand up as he gripped his arm. Gibbons called to Berry: "Get down. Flatten out, Major," knowing that "he was courting death every minute he stood up." Berry in turn called over to Gibbons: "We've got to get out of here. We've got to get forward. They'll start shelling this open field in a few minutes." Gibbons replied that he was crawling over to him. "Wait until I get there and I'll help you. Then we'll get up and make a dash for it."[11]

Gibbons crawled, pushing "forward by digging in with my toes and elbows extended in front of me. It was my object to make as little movement in the oats as possible."[12]

> And then it happened. The lighted end of a cigarette touched me in the fleshy part of my upper left arm. That was all. It just felt like a sudden burn and nothing worse. The burned part did not seem to be any larger in area than that part which could be burned by the lighted end of a cigarette.[13]

A bullet had gone through the biceps of the upper arm and come out the other side. Gibbons looked down at his sleeve and could not even see the hole where the bullet had entered.

> Then the second one hit. It nicked the top of my left shoulder. And again came the burning sensation, only this time the area affected seemed larger.[14]

Feeling surprisingly little pain, Gibbons continued to crawl toward Berry.

> And then the third one struck me. In order to keep as close to the ground as possible, I had swung my chin to the right so that I was pushing

forward with my left cheek flat against the ground and in order to ac-commodate this position of the head, I had moved my steel helmet over so that it covered part of my face on the right.

Then there came a crash. It sounded to me like some one had dropped a glass bottle into a porcelain bathtub. A barrel of whitewash tipped over and it seemed that everything in the world turned white. That was the sensation. I did not recognize it because I have often been led to believe and often heard it said that when one receives a blow on the head everything turns black.[15]

Gibbons asked himself, "'Am I dead?' . . . I wanted to know. . . . How was I to find out if I was dead? . . . I decided to try and move my fingers on my left hand. I did so and they moved. I next moved my left foot. Then I knew I was alive."[16]

Floyd Gibbons's left eye had just been shot out of his head, along with part of his skull. With his remaining eye, he watched Major Berry "rise to his feet and in a perfect hail of lead rush forward and out of my line of vision."[17] Despite his wound, Berry continued to command, led his men in destroying a German machine-gun nest, and later received the Distinguished Service Cross from General Pershing. Gibbons, with his fellow journalist Hartzell (who was unwounded), remained in the oat field for three hours, until 9:00 p.m., not daring to move until they judged it was sufficiently dark to risk crawling back to the American position. After a series of agonizing stops at various forward dressing stations, Gibbons was loaded into an ambulance and evacuated to a hospital. Astoundingly, he was on his feet and once again covering the war within ten days of having been wounded.

If the line of sections advance in all its archaic formality failed to work for long, in some places it did not work at all. The poverty of communications and the level of confusion were so profound on the afternoon of June 6 that some units never even formed up to join the "parade." They were not aware of the attack until after it had actually begun.

Lieutenant George Gordon, commanding a platoon in one of Berry's companies, was standing—*standing*—at the periphery of the wheat field "watching the shells as they dropped along the edge of the woods across the wheatfield." He was talking with a friend, who remarked of the shelling, "I wonder what this is about. . . . They must have something spotted over there." Several minutes passed before Captain Larsen ran up to Gordon and his friend. "Get your platoons ready immediately," he shouted. "You should have started across with the barrage." Gordon later remarked:

> This was the first information we had received regarding an attack and did not know one had been planned. No objective was given as to where it was to stop and no maps had been distributed; the only thing we were sure of was the direction and we knew that.[18]

Attacking from Lucy-le-Bocage, well south of Berry, Sibley's 3rd Battalion, 6th Marines was, in Catlin's words, "having better luck." Catlin thrilled to the sight of these men "sweeping across the open ground in four waves, as steadily and correctly as though on parade." As if to justify on some pragmatic terms the ostentatious grandeur of this procession under fire, Catlin explained: "They walked at the regulation pace, because a man is of little use in a hand-to-hand bayonet struggle after a hundred yards dash." The obvious response to this observation would have been to ask the colonel just how much use a dead man was. But who could have dared such impertinence as Catlin looked on? "My hands were clenched and all my muscles taut as I watched that cool, intrepid, masterful defiance of the German spite." He saw "no sign of wavering or breaking."[19]

> Oh, it took courage and steady nerves to do that in the face of the enemy's machine gun fire. Men fell there in the open, but the advance kept steadily on to the woods. It was then that discipline and training counted. Their minds were concentrated not on the enemy's fire but on the thing they had to do and the necessity of doing it right. They were listening for orders and obeying them. In this frame of mind the soldier

can perhaps walk with even more coolness and determination than he can run. In any case it was an admirable exhibition of military precision and it gladdened their Colonel's heart.[20]

Interviewed in October 2003, upstate New Yorker Eugene Lee—who at age 104 was then the nation's "oldest living marine"—recalled the grim journey across the wheat field Catlin watched from afar. "They split us out into formation. They had the first wave go so far. They kept on firing in the woods there. The next wave would come and jump over them and they'd go so far, and would fire till they got in the edge of the woods."[21] The object of this leap-frog advance was to allow the first wave to cover the farther advance of the second wave, and the second to cover that of the third, and the third to cover the fourth as it finally reached the woods. Once the fourth had been delivered to the objective, the marines of the preceding waves—those who survived—would follow it in. Lee was in the third of the four human waves.

Unlike Berry's men, many of Sibley's, who had much less open field to traverse, made it to Belleau Wood. Yet their entry into the objective was somehow anticlimactic. Catlin wrote that the "Marines have a war cry that they can use to advantage when there is need of it. It is a bloodcurdling yell calculated to carry terror to the heart of the waiting Hun. I am told that there were wild yells in the woods that night, when the Marines charged the machine gun nests, but there was no yelling when they went in." Catlin also noted a report that the marines "advanced on those woods crying 'Remember the *Lusitania!*' If they did so, I failed to hear it." Quite rightly, he observed that this did not "sound like the sort of thing the Marine says under the conditions." In fact, so far as he could observe, Catlin did not believe "a sound was uttered throughout the length of those four lines. The men were saving their breath for what was to follow."[22]

Having written of this wordless entry into Belleau Wood, an entry bought at the price of many dead and wounded, the colonel of the 6th Marine Regiment feared that he had "given but a poor picture of that splendid advance." True, there "was nothing dashing about it like a cavalry charge," yet it was nevertheless "one of the finest things I have ever seen men do."

Catlin fully appreciated that these marines "were men who had never before been called upon to attack a strongly held enemy position." What lay
before them was a "dense woods effectively sheltering armed and highly
trained opponents of unknown strength." Indeed, within the depths of this
dark space "machine guns snarled and rattled and spat forth a leaden death.
It was like some mythical monster belching smoke and fire from its lair." Yet
these marines, the vast majority entirely new to combat, marched "straight
against it . . . with heads up and the light of battle in their eyes."[23]

Months after the battle, Private W. H. Smith, recovering from wounds
in the Brooklyn Naval Hospital, related to Catlin what it had been like
marching into Belleau Wood. He said that there "wasn't a bit of hesitation
from any man. You had no heart for fear at all. Fight—fight and get the
Germans was your only thought. Personal danger didn't concern you in the
least and you didn't care." Smith explained that he and about sixty others
had gotten ahead of the rest of the company. "We just couldn't stop despite
the orders of our leaders." Reaching the edge of the woods, they "encountered some of the Hun infantry" and then "it became a matter of shooting
at mere human targets." At first, it was almost easy. The marines fixed their
rifle sights at three hundred yards and, "aiming through the peep kept picking off Germans. And a man went down at nearly every shot." But then the
enemy "detected us and we became the objects of their heavy fire."[24]
Colonel Catlin, who had no field telephone, "felt obliged to see what was
going on." He took his stand on a "little rise of ground protected by a low
line of bushes about 300 yards from the woods." The position was near a
road, the point at which the left flank of Thomas Holcomb's battalion made
contact with the right flank of Berry's battered battalion. "The shelter
trenches did not cross the road," so Catlin was fully exposed as he watched
the advance through his binoculars. "Bullets," he recalled, "rained all
around me, the machine gun crews near me forming a target for the Germans." The "racket of rifle and machine gun fire and bursting shrapnel and
high explosives" was "like the continuous roll of some demoniacal drum,
with the bass note of the heavy guns that were shelling Lucy." Through his
binoculars, Catlin watched "a number of our brave lads fall" as the German

machine gunners made sure to aim low, sweeping the ground, thereby "catching most of the men in the legs." Those who were thus disabled "lay right in the line of fire and many of them were killed there on the ground" whereas those "who were able to stand and keep going had the best chance." Some of these men "went through the whole fight with leg wounds received during the first ten minutes."[25]

Vivid as his perceptions of battle were, Catlin was not destined to be an eyewitness for long. "Just about the time Sibley's men struck the woods a sniper's bullet hit me in the chest. It felt exactly as though some one had struck me heavily with a sledge. It swung me clear around and toppled me over on the ground. When I tried to get up I found that my right side was paralysed." Catlin's French interpreter, Captain Tribot-Laspierre—a "splendid fellow," Catlin called him, "who stuck to me through thick and thin"—had been "begging [Catlin] to get back to a safer place." Now he sprang out of his cover and rushed to Catlin's side. "He is a little man and I am not, but he dragged me head first back to the shelter trench some twenty or twenty-five feet away."[26]

Like Gibbons on Berry's side of the attack, Catlin on Sibley's was more fascinated than horrified by the sensations of being wounded. "I have heard of men getting wounded who said that it felt like a red-hot iron being jammed through them before the world turned black," but nothing of the kind happened to Catlin. "I suffered but little pain and I never for a moment lost consciousness." Nor did he think of death, "though I knew I had been hit in a vital spot. I was merely annoyed at my inability to move and carry on."[27]

The colonel took a peculiarly professional and analytical interest in the circumstances of his wounding, concluding that it had been a "chance shot and not the result of good marksmanship, for the bullet must have come some 600 yards." It passed "clean through" Catlin's right lung, "in at the front and out at the back, drilling a hole straight through me." Catlin related that ballistics experts calculated that a "bullet fired at short range—less than five hundred or six hundred yards—twists [so that] when it strikes an obstacle it wabbles." Catlin therefore reasoned that had he been shot at close range, the bullet would have "torn a piece out of my back as big as my fist." However, had the bullet been fired from a range greater than about six hundred yards, it would have been "already wabbling, and would have made a big hole in the front of my chest and perhaps would not have gone clear through." Because the holes going in and out were both small, Catlin concluded that he had been shot from a range of about six hundred yards. "[For that] I am thankful."[28]

Catlin calmly sent word of his wounding to the command post, ordering his second in command, Lieutenant Colonel Harry Lee, to assume command of the 6th Regiment. Forty-five minutes elapsed before the regimental surgeon, Dr. Farwell, came under intense fire to Catlin's side. Farwell had brought stretcher bearers with him, but heavy shelling prevented immediate evacuation, and when gas shells began to detonate nearby, the stretcher men put a mask on the colonel. "I never knew before how uncomfortable one of those things could be. It is hard enough for a man to breathe with a lung full of blood without having one of those smothering masks clapped over his face." What gave Catlin comfort was the sound of the fire gradually receding, which told him that "Sibley's men were advancing." However, when the firing grew louder on the left, he "knew that Berry's outfit was being beaten back."[29]

At length, the pace of the shelling eased, and four men raised Catlin's stretcher to their shoulders. "Carrying a 215-pound man on a stretcher over rough country under fire is no joke," Catlin observed, "but they got me to Lucy," then to an ambulance, and on to hospitals at Meaux and Paris.[30] The colonel remained hospitalized until July 22, when he was sent home on leave.

In Catlin's absence, the men on Sibley's left flank, most of them, clawed their way into Belleau Wood, via its southwestern hook. On contact, the combat was a combination of close rifle fire and fierce bayonet work. Both the U.S. Army and the Marine Corps administered bayonet training, and soldiers and marines made ample use of the bayonet in the Great War— more, certainly, than they had in any previous conflict. Yet U.S. Army soldiers tended to dread the weapon, whereas marines, at least in the attack, reveled in its use. In a war fought to such a great extent by the weapons of high technology—high-explosive artillery, gas, the machine gun, the airplane, and even the tank—it was as if marines craved contact at its most warriorlike. The isolated German outposts in the southwestern end of Belleau Wood fell prey to the marines' bayonets, but the terrain, with its tangle of undergrowth, soon broke up the cohesiveness of the attacking units. Isolated and slowed, Captain Dwight Smith's company of Sibley's marines, after they had penetrated a few hundred yards into the woods, made easy marks for the German machine guns. The machine-gun fire became so intense that the attackers were deflected northward from their due-eastward push.

Another of Sibley's companies, led by Lieutenant A. H. Noble, followed Dwight Smith's men into the woods, desperately trying to maintain contact with the lead company but failing to do so amid the rugged terrain and the outpouring of machine-gun fire. As if shivered and split by the stream of fire, the left flank of Noble's company sheered off to the north—just as Smith's men had done—but the right flank, advancing along the ravine at the southern tip of Belleau Wood, continued due east. This flank consisted of two platoons, one under Lieutenant Louis Timmerman and another under a lieutenant named Hurley. The attack on the woods, which had begun in parade-order "line of sections," increasingly broke up within Belleau Wood itself. Yet, in doing so, it did not falter or flag. Instead, as companies divided into platoons and platoons into sections and sections into fire teams or even individual marines, the fragmented fight only intensified.

In Timmerman's case, his platoon soon lost contact with Hurley's, and then the sections of the platoon itself lost contact with one another. Marines set up machine-gun positions within the woods wherever they could. This was necessary, of course, but it also added to the confusion of this most chaotic combat. Timmerman and the men who were still with him passed one marine machine-gun company, so he naturally assumed that the machine-gun fire he heard to his rear was coming from them. In fact, what he heard was the sound of German machine gunners pinning down all of Smith's company along with Sibley's other two companies and the two sections of Timmerman's own platoon that had veered to the north. Unaware of this, Timmerman just kept going. In its advance, the platoon stumbled across a German outpost. The marines and the enemy were equally surprised, but it was the Germans who gave up, and Timmerman sent back the prisoners under a single man while he and the others kept moving.

That's when Timmerman got his second surprise. He was suddenly shocked to discover that he had broken through to the east side of Belleau Wood, finding himself at a point slightly to the north of Bouresches.

Just before the attack, the company commander, Lieutenant Noble, had passed on to his platoon commanders the orders he had received. They were for the platoons on the right flank to move through Belleau Wood and capture Bouresches. Like all neophyte lieutenants, Timmerman was anxious to follow orders, and he assumed everyone else was too. Finding himself and the two platoon sections with him—about twenty marines in all—on the east side of Belleau Wood, and entirely unaware that the rest of the marines in the southern end of the woods were being held down and held back by German machine guns, Timmerman experienced a moment of panic. It was not panic born of an awareness of the actual situation: that he and twenty other marines were alone in enemy territory, separated from the rest of their unit by a dense woods exploding in hostile fire. Instead, it was panic born of the fear that everyone else had made it through Belleau Wood before him and that *he* was behind in the assault on Bouresches.

Sending one wounded private—a marine named Henry—to the rear, Timmerman deployed his two sections into a line of skirmishers, sent a Corporal Larsen and Private Swenson ahead as scouts, then led his men along the ravine they had followed through the woods until they reached a wheat field. On the other side of this field, about two hundred yards away, was Bouresches. As with the wheat fields on the western face of Belleau Wood, this one (as pictured in Timmerman's diary) "was thrashing to and fro with machine gun bullets."[31]

Timmerman watched as Larsen and Swenson reached "a sort of mound of earth parallel to our line of advance." They signaled a halt there, and Timmerman advanced his men to the mound. Suddenly, "[I] noticed that we were coming under fire from all directions," despite being "sheltered from the enemy in front."[32]

Who was firing from the rear?

It was a profoundly disorienting moment. After no more than a minute, however, the disorientation blossomed into disbelief as Private Henry—the wounded marine Timmerman had sent to the rear—"came running back yelling something." Timmerman could not make out what Henry was trying to say, so signaled for him to come over. What he was saying was, "The woods in back of us were full of Germans." At first, the lieutenant simply did not believe him. After all, "[they] had just come through there." But the sight, sound, and sensation of "the bullets kicking up dust and landing all around our side of the barricade" soon made a believer out of him.[33]

Clearly, Timmerman realized, he and his two sections—now reduced from twenty to "about fifteen" men—could not long stay behind a mound that offered no shelter. Timmerman yelled to his marines, ordering them back into Belleau Wood. "Luckily I hit the edge of the woods just where the Germans were."[34]

There were seventeen German privates and two noncoms manning a pair of machine guns in a patch of low ground that led off from the ravine. The machine gunners were second-line troops, and they did not expect a swarm of marines to descend on them from the *east*. In the lead, Timmerman kicked the faces of the first two Germans he encountered, knocking both unconscious. The others, confronted with the marines' bayonets, threw down their weapons and laid themselves prostrate before the attackers. Some tore open their uniform blouses, baring their chests, as if to say in a language that required absolutely no translation, *We are unarmed!*

At this point, a sergeant from Hurley's platoon broke through Belleau Wood with a couple of marines. Timmerman put his prisoners into their custody and instructed them to take them to the rear. Still under the unshakable conviction that most of the other marines had broken through the woods and were already attacking toward Bouresches, Timmerman could not afford to be encumbered by POWs. He further assumed that capturing the machine gunners had put an end to German resistance in the south end of Belleau Wood. He therefore resumed his interrupted advance and returned to the mound. This time, machine-gun fire opened up from the town, then also from his left flank, coming from a rise just fifty yards off. To this was added fire from Timmerman's left rear as well. "I faced around and saw Swenson lying dead with a bullet hole through the forehead." Timmerman shouted, "Open fire to the right," and pointed "toward the hillock where a terrific fire was coming from." No sooner had he done this than he himself was hit on the left side of the face. "[Timmerman] fell forward thinking, 'I've got mine,'" believing that a bullet had ripped through under his eye. He lost consciousness momentarily but then "felt better." He said, "[Although] I was covered with blood I realized I had not been dangerously hit." Nevertheless, Timmerman's "men were dropping around there" and so "[Timmerman] told them to follow [him]" and, once again, they "ran back for the shelter of the woods."[35]

Lieutenant Louis Timmerman had begun the advance on Belleau Wood commanding a platoon of fifty marines as part of a company of some two hundred. This mass of men broke apart inside the woods, leaving Timmerman with fifteen men on the other side. By the time he retreated to the eastern perimeter of Belleau Wood, shot through the face, he commanded just six marines. They hunkered down in the German machine-gun position they had captured minutes ago. Only then did it occur to him that Belleau Wood had neither been taken nor even traversed—at least not by very many of the marines who had entered it. Beyond these realizations, the lieutenant knew only that the battle, which had been ahead of him in Belleau Wood when Belleau Wood had been ahead of him, was now ahead of him in the little town of Bouresches. But the battle was also on either side of him and, not least of all, it was raging yet in the ruined tangle of trees, rocks, and ravines that now lay behind him.

▪ 11 ▪

Taking Bouresches

Lieutenant Louis Timmerman and a half dozen tired marines were a crew too small to feed, fire, and defend the two German machine guns they had captured. But by the time they had retreated to this position, a Sergeant Fadden and some other marines managed to wiggle through Belleau Wood to Timmerman's position. They did so just in time to man the weapons as Timmerman spotted a column of troops approaching no more than forty yards away. Through the smoke, it was difficult to make out their uniforms, but Timmerman was sufficiently persuaded that they were Germans to order his men to let loose with the machine guns. The column quickly broke up.

Because he occupied a covered position at the edge of the woods, was in possession of machine guns, and was staying put, Timmerman suddenly became the nucleus around which ragged marines gathered in ones and twos and threes. Some ran in from Belleau Wood. Others crawled, wounded. They came from the rear, from the right, and from the left. They were from various platoons and companies, and there were even some men from Berry's battalion who, instead of retreating from the wheat field when that battalion's attack on Belleau Wood failed, had waited for the fire to die down and one by one, crawled into the woods, eventually emerging in Sibley's sector, well to the south of where Berry's men were supposed to be.

By the time that about forty marines had gathered around the captured German machine-gun position, Sibley's intelligence officer showed up. He told Timmerman to hold on where he was and await reinforcements. It certainly had not been planned like this—of course, very little had been planned—but Timmerman now found himself in possession of the first piece of the first objective that had been assigned to the marines. Because he had gotten through the woods and was holding ground on the east side of the woods, Timmerman was deemed worthy of reinforcement.

Timmerman's achievement notwithstanding, most of Sibley's battalion was still fighting it out within Belleau Wood, or "Hellwood," as Sibley's marines had taken to calling it. Albertus Catlin, put out of action by a bullet through the lung, later gathered reports on what happened after he was taken from the field. In his account of the struggle at Belleau Wood, he called Major Berton Sibley "one of the most picturesque characters in the Marine Corps," describing him as short, swarthy, and wiry, "one of those men whose looks are no indication of their age; he might be anywhere from thirty-five to fifty. I fancy that is why he is affectionately known as 'the old man.'" Catlin praised Sibley as "particularly thorough" and impossible to rattle. "His men love him and would follow him anywhere." Into Belleau Wood, Catlin claimed, "They followed him as warriors of old followed their chieftain."[1]

The reality was not nearly so straightforward. The 79th Company, under Captain Randolph Zane, was one of the first of Sibley's units to penetrate the woods. As it did, it came under what platoon commander Lieutenant Graves B. Erskine called "murderous fire, mainly automatic weapons, some artillery and mortar." The artillery barrage included gas shells. "My platoon consisted of fifty-eight men in addition to myself when we jumped off. About forty minutes later, five of us were left." It was at this point that Erskine grabbed a wounded marine as the man made his way to the rear. He asked him to tell Captain Zane, who was some distance in the rear, that the platoon was "pinned down and could advance no further."

After an hour or so, "this poor kid"—he had been badly wounded in the nose—"crawled back to report the captain's words: 'Goddamnit, continue the advance.' This was at early nightfall. We continued the advance."[2]

To the right of Erskine's rapidly dwindling platoon, the men of Captain Donald Duncan's 96th Company were advancing through the ravine at the extreme southern end of Belleau Wood, which led to Triangle Wood, little more than a clump of trees below the tip of Belleau Wood and in line of sight with Bouresches to the northeast. Firing from Bouresches, German machine guns raked this wooded patch. Duncan deployed three of his platoons to the eastern perimeter of Triangle Wood, then sent his fourth platoon, under Lieutenant Clifton Cates, to shift to the left and make contact with Major Sibley. Cates moved left to Zane's right flank in Belleau Wood proper, then, reasoning that Sibley must already have moved forward of this position, he led his platoon due east to the eastern margin of the woods. Pausing there, he saw before him, nestled at the foot of a gentle seven-hundred-yard slope, the village of Bouresches.

There was Bouresches, but there was no sign of Sibley. It was still possible that Sibley was somewhere ahead, and Cates also knew that Bouresches was one of the day's objectives. Both of these facts argued for a continuation of his advance. Just as he was deciding whether to do this, he saw the rest of Duncan's company on his right beginning to advance east of the woods. That decided him. Cates stepped out of the cover of Belleau Wood and turned to his platoon: "All right, men, the guide is left, remember, hit their line together, boys," and with that, Cates's platoon began its advance on Bouresches.[3]

On Cates's right, a platoon under Lieutenant Lockhart pulled ahead of the entire company. Seeing this, Captain Duncan and his first sergeant, a marine named Sissler, walked heedlessly through the machine-gun and rifle fire pouring out from Bouresches and approached Lockhart's advanced position. Donald Duncan was a supremely confident, cool, and collected marine. In the British fashion, he carried a swagger stick rather than a cane, and regardless of circumstances, he invariably had a straight-stem pipe clenched between his teeth and a smile on his face. He reached Lockhart's position, halted him, and ordered him to await the rest of the company so that the attack would be with maximum strength.

Sergeant Al Sheridan saw what happened next. A friend who had grown up with Duncan in Kansas, Sheridan wrote a letter to the captain's family. In it, he pictured Duncan "talking to Mr. Lockhart our platoon leader" while "the bullets were singing all around us." He wrote that Lockhart asked the captain "as a joke if he thought we would see much action." Duncan broadened his smile at this: "[O]h! yes we will give and take but be sure you take more than you give." Sheridan elaborated: "I guess he meant lives." Then he went on: "anyway [Duncan] started away up the hill and it was not a minute till down he went."[4] A heavy machine-gun bullet had drilled into Donald Duncan's stomach. First Sergeant Sissler yelled out for a corpsman. Sheridan, together with dental surgeon Weedon Osborne and a navy corpsman, ran through the fire. They carried Duncan "to a small clump of trees, all the time he was gasping, hit through the stomach," Sheridan continued in his letter. "We no more than laid him on the ground when a big 8 in. shell came in and killed all but myself, I was knocked down but my helmet saved me, so I left them and rejoined my platoon."[5]

Duncan's second in command, Lieutenant Robertson, took over the company. Wasting no time, he waved his pistol above his head and shouted, "Come on, let's go."[6]

Hugging the ground, Lieutenant Cates watched. "We really didn't know where we were going but this town was right in front of us."[7]

Rising to his feet, Cates began moving toward Bouresches, the single-file line of his platoon following behind him. Inclined as it was toward Bouresches, the slope offered this procession of marines to the German gunners in that town as if serving them up on a platter. At every few steps a man dropped. Cates himself went down when a bullet skimmed his British-model, washbasin helmet. He fell on his face, nose buried in the earth, whereupon Robertson took the lead.

Despite appearances to the contrary, Cates was not dead. He rose to his knees and felt his head where a large, bloody, and very tender knot had erupted. Finding his dented helmet, he gingerly fitted it back on, then looked around him before coming fully to his feet. The machine-gun fire reminded him of hail hitting the ground, and his very first thought—a sane thought, at that—"was to run like hell to the rear." Looking to the rear and then side to side, he saw no one, "except the wounded and dead." But then he looked forward. In that direction he saw four men advancing through the ravine. He "beat over to them."[8]

Beat over to them? It was more like stumble-staggering vaguely in their direction. Cates gave the appearance of a man who had been drowning his sorrows in more than a few glasses of beer. The four faces that materialized before his still blurry vision were familiar to Cates, all members of his platoon: a pair of corporals, Finn and Dorrell, Sergeant Belfry, and Private Tom Argaut. Seeing that Cates looked far from all right, Argaut gently lifted the lieutenant's helmet, gasped or grimaced at the clotted lump poking through a thatch of hair, unscrewed the top from his canteen, and poured some of its contents over the wound. It was not water.

"Goddamn it, Tom. Don't pour that wine over my head, give me a drink of it."[9]

And with that, the four men knew their lieutenant was going to be OK.

Seizing a French rifle that had been abandoned on the field much earlier, Cates led his four marines down the ravine and toward Bouresches. These men were now the sum total of his entire command.

On the periphery of the village, Cates saw some Germans lurking in the buildings at the southern tip of Bouresches. Turning to his men, he motioned toward them, and the marines opened fire, scattering the Germans. When he sees his enemy run, a marine does not hesitate to fill the resulting vacuum. Cates and the four others quickly exchanged the wheat field for the streets of the village. Looking back, they were surprised to see Lieutenant Robertson leading about two dozen more marines.

"Come on," Cates called to Robertson. "Let's take the rest of the town. There's no one in there now."[10]

Robertson turned the men over to Cates, telling him that he would run back to fetch reinforcements. Now with about thirty marines to deploy, Cates divided them into three assault groups. He assigned Gunnery

Sergeant Moorey to lead one group from the west to seize the northwest corner of Bouresches. Sergeant Belfry was tasked with leading the second group to take the center. Assuming that the south end of the little village was already reasonably secure, Cates took the others north to occupy the railroad station.

Earlier in the day, some three hundred or four hundred Germans had held Bouresches, using its buildings as cover for the machine guns with which they swept the southern portions of the wheat fields west and south of Belleau Wood. To Cates, the town now appeared mostly empty, the Germans having withdrawn as the marines fought their way through the woods and began emerging at its east end. But Cates was wrong. As they approached the heart of the village, a machine gun suddenly opened up on them. Several of Cates's marines fell, and a bullet passed harmlessly through the lieutenant's own already battered helmet. In short order, another tore a hole through his tunic, pinging audibly against his silver lieutenant's bar and cutting a gash into his shoulder.

Ordering his men back, he divided them into a pair of fire teams. He sent one team around the left side of the machine-gun position and the other around the right. After a crackling burst of rifle fire, it was all over. The machine gun was silenced, and the surviving gunner surrendered.

Cates had won—but at a price. The encounter with the machine-gun nest had reduced his total occupation force from thirty marines to twenty-one. Nevertheless, he did hold the town, becoming the first marine to attain one of the objectives Degoutte had assigned, and he had accomplished this not with the three companies allocated to the mission—about six hundred men—but with no more than the ragged remnant of a single, shredded platoon. When Cates declared to himself that the town was his, night had fallen. It was about a quarter to ten.

Lieutenant Clifton Cates deployed his meager resources through the dark streets and environs of the village in four so-called Cossack posts—independent positions, unconnected with one another. One he placed in an apple orchard adjacent to the village, another behind a wall facing the railroad station, and two in the south end of Bouresches. His men were soon joined by the reinforcements Robertson had managed to recruit from a number of shattered platoons still emerging from the woods. Later in the night, these newcomers were bolstered by survivors of the 79th Company under Captain Randolph Zane, to whom Cates relinquished command.

The reinforcements were sorely needed, for although Colonel Catlin later crowed that Cates's "twenty men started in to clean up that town in approved Marine fashion," there was a full German regiment just north of the town—part of the German 237th Division—and it had started to push back. The fire fight grew hot, and the marines in Bouresches sent back word that they were running critically short of ammunition. Hearing of the need, Lieutenant William B. Moore, a Princeton athlete, and Sergeant Major John Quick volunteered for the hazardous duty of driving a truck packed with ammunition, under fire and over shell-cratered roads, to Bouresches. From fifty other marines who volunteered to go with them, Moore selected a small crew. They loaded the truck, piled in, Quick's foot came down on the clutch pedal, his hand shifted the gear, and letting out the clutch slowly, Quick eased the explosives-packed camion into motion.

It was a hellish ride, brilliantly illuminated by the enemy's starburst shells and phosphorous flares, which quite effectively lit up the lumbering, lurching target. "It rolled and careened fearfully over the gullies and craters," Catlin related, "shells shrieked and whistled over their heads and burst on every hand, and as they neared the town they drove straight into the fire of the spouting machine guns." Miraculously, the truck arrived unscathed and, Catlin succinctly observed, "saved the day."[11]

It made for an exciting story—and the heroism of Moore and Quick was later recognized with the appropriate military decorations. Yet their mission was entirely unnecessary. The critical shortage of ammunition at Bouresches was a figment of someone's fevered imagination. The fact was that the defenders of the newly liberated town had so much ammunition on hand that for four full days they left what Moore and Quick had brought exactly where they had hurriedly dumped it: at the edge of town.

Shortly after 11:00 p.m. Captain Zane reported that the Germans had been driven out of Bouresches. A counterattack at 2:30 a.m. on June 7 was "smothered by our machine gun fire."[12]

The town continued to be an object of contention throughout June 7 and even into the eighth. But during these two days, U.S. Army engineers helped the marines dig into secure defensive positions, and fresh reinforcements were put in place. Each German counterattack was repulsed, and by the end of the eighth, the garrison of Bouresches had tied in with the line of Sibley's men who were still fighting it out in Belleau Wood, and also with Holcomb's battalion, which extended the line from Bouresches down to Triangle Farm due south of the village. This American line now enveloped Belleau Wood on its southern end, effectively containing the German forces that were still making existence hellish there.

Colonel Albertus Catlin, who had to content himself with vicarious pride since he had been taken out of the action, remarked that in capturing Bouresches, his marines "were obliged to get along without direct telephone connection with headquarters" and instead depended entirely on intrepid runners, who dashed "through machine gun and shell fire" to keep "open the lines of communication."[13]

The platoon or battalion runner was invariably a volunteer. He got no glory, but, as Private Elton Mackin made clear in his remarkable memoir, *Suddenly We Didn't Want to Die*, the runner did get plenty of opportunities to be killed. Mackin described how, during the Battle of Belleau Wood, his sergeant summoned him.

"Rest your bones, son, maybe I got a job for you. . . . You and me have the same nickname, it seems. Made me think of you." Sergeant "Slim" explained to Private "Slim" that "Battalion wants a new runner. 'Itchy' Fox was killed last night comin' out. They got a vacancy to fill."[14]

"Bad news," Mackin's third-person narrator observed. "Not of Fox. That was just an ordinary matter, another fellow gone. 'Battalion wants another runner.' It came like an easily spoken sentence of death to the lad who heard it." Private Slim suddenly recalled "talk of jobs too dangerous; jobs certain to mean death. Runners didn't last. Everyone knew that." Stirring within him were "fear and protest," and he mentally groped to "find a good excuse. A fellow didn't have to take a runner job. All a fellow had to do was say no. . . . Suicide squad. That's how the fellows spoke of it. A runner didn't have a chance."[15]

> The noncom's eyes were wells of patience, understanding men. He read your innermost thoughts and knew your fear. He let you fight it out with yourself.
>
> "Want the job, son?"
>
> Could any man who had pride refuse and let that stern old soldier see the coward inside? . . . "Sure, Sergeant. I'll take it."[16]

For all their heroism, runners were poor substitutes for efficient communication by field telephone on a modern, fluid battlefield. Shot through the lung, Catlin had ample time to collect firsthand information while convalescing *after* the battle. "It is not the general who wins such a battle," he wrote of Belleau Wood, "but the captain, the sergeant, the private. . . . The men who went through that Turkish bath of fire and steel are the best judges of what it was like."[17] So he collected *their* stories.

Catlin collected the tale of Private W. H. Smith of Winston-Salem, North Carolina, who was interviewed "after he had been invalided home." He told how the "German machine guns were everywhere" in Belleau Wood, in "the trees and in small ground holes." To survive, the marines dug one-man pits to fire from. These, Smith remarked, "gave us just a little protection." The bullets "came so close at times I could almost feel their touch. My pack was shot up pretty much but they didn't get me." And that fact led Smith to think he was "bullet proof." He "didn't care a damn for all the Germans and their machine guns," he said, but observed that "every blamed tree must have had a machine gunner," the "potting" of whom "became great sport" for the marines. "Even the officers would seize rifles from wounded Marines and go to it." But one of those machine guns finally got Smith. "Five shots hit right in succession. The elbow was torn into shreds,

but the hits didn't hurt. It seemed just like getting five little stings of elec-
tricity." When the captain ordered two men to help him back, Smith responded that he could make it alone, and he "picked up part of the arm that
was hanging loose and walked" two miles to the dressing station. "I got
nearly to it when everything began to go black and wobbly. I guess it was
loss of blood. But I played in luck, for some stretcher bearers were right
near when I went down."[18]

Of images such as these was the intimate picture of battle made. They
were images of which higher headquarters, hobbled by hasty and inadequate planning (the result of an impulsive attack decision) and crippled by
poor communications, was woefully ignorant. General James Harbord,
commanding 4th Brigade from his headquarters at La Loge Farm, received
only the most fragmentary word from the front, so that he was forced to
view the battle as if through a kaleidoscope. And as if the fragmentary nature of the information were not bad enough, those fragments were, more
often than not, inaccurate in themselves, almost always glibly optimistic,
painting a picture of the marines' "beautiful deployment in beautiful line,"
mentioning but "one casualty at the dressing station," giving assurance that
"things are going fine."[19]

Confusion, miscommunication, and even the total absence of communication were present from the very beginning of the attack. At the southern-
most end of the American line where the marines tied in with the army,
Colonel Paul Malone, commanding the army's 23rd Infantry in this sector,
ordered the two marine battalions to his left to attack along with the others
at 5:00 p.m. When Malone reported these orders to 3rd Brigade commander
E. M. Lewis, the brigadier exploded. *Attack?* Malone's regiment and, with it,
the two tied-in marine battalions were supposed to do no more than stand
fast, attacking only if marine action on the left made it necessary for them to
do so. Stunned, Malone tried desperately to communicate with the marine
battalions, to order them back, but without field telephones, he could not
reach them in time. The result was a costly advance that achieved nothing.

At 3:15 a.m., June 7, Malone finally got a message through to the majors commanding the two marine battalions: "It is desired that you merely

reoccupy the position which you occupied before the advance this afternoon. . . . No advance is desired." At 3:45, 2nd Division commander Omar
Bundy sent one of his staff officers to 3rd Brigade to find out why two battalions had advanced without authorization. General Lewis replied that "he
did not know, as it was not intended," and he assured Bundy's staff officer
that "he understood perfectly that there was to be no advance," as if that assurance was somehow supposed to make up for 340 men killed and
wounded in a ten-hour action that accomplished nothing in the end and
that was never supposed to have taken place to begin with.[20]

▪ 12 ▪

Armies of the Night

After nightfall, that June 6, amid heroism and sacrifice, the confusion only intensified. General Harbord, operating from a headquarters close enough to the front to be shelled but too far from it to receive a continuous flow of timely and comprehensive reports, struggled to get his arms around the "exaggerated riot" that was the Battle of Belleau Wood. Harbord was an enthusiastic army commander who had quickly learned to love the marine brigade assigned to him, but the fog of war was frustrating him, doubtless frightening him, and finally angering him. Earlier, this had led him to send a shrill epistolary lecture to Major Julius Turrill on the importance of liaison. Now, just before 9:00 p.m., it prompted a message to Lieutenant Colonel Harry Lee, who had assumed command of the 6th Marine Regiment from the wounded Catlin. "I am not satisfied with the way you have conducted your engagement this afternoon," Harbord began. "Your own regimental headquarters and this office have not had a word of report from you as to your orders or your positions." Harbord complained to Lee that Major Sibley, whose battalion belonged to the 6th Regiment, had been "asking your regimental adjutant for orders." He further complained that Major Berry, whose battalion belonged to the 5th Regiment but "over whom you should have asserted authority," was "reporting to his own Regimental Commander." Figuratively seizing Lee by the shoulders, Harbord scolded: "I want you to take charge and to push this attack with rigor." He then proceeded to give a string of orders, most of which were made irrelevant either by circumstances or developments on the front.[1]

It is probably most fortunate that Lee was in no position to receive Harbord's sputtering message. The very circumstances that prevented his sending reports to headquarters or even communicating effectively with the battalion commanders prevented his getting the general's ill-tempered missive. The hard fact was that at nightfall, absolutely no one had the true picture of the situation in Belleau Wood. Company- and platoon-level commanders were, on their own, either struggling to survive, holding in place, or grimly pushing through the woods. Those on the extreme right (south), like Clifton Cates, were able to squeeze through. Those farther left were forced by walls of machine-gun fire to divert to the north from their eastward push, a turn that left them stranded in the woods and in the thick of the firefight. Those even farther to the left—the men of Berry's battalion—were either killed, disabled by wounds, or turned back in the initial advance. Some, who had been pinned down for hours in the wheat, managed to crawl into the woods and, if they were lucky, linked up with others who were fighting it out.

Harbord received word late in the night that one entire unit of marines was stuck in a hard fight at the northern edge of the woods, but actually that part of the objective contained no marines at all. Only the south end was occupied. The truth was that the attack had no cohesion whatsoever. That fact would have frustrated and alarmed Harbord even more—had he known it. Intended to be an attack of coordinated companies, the Battle of Belleau Wood was now a fight of platoons and squads, and, most of all, of individual marines. Despite its fragmented nature, however, it was an attack both fierce and determined.

Harbord did not have an accurate picture of the battlefield, but for him there was no uncertainty as to the big picture. He firmly believed that "more than Belleau Wood was at stake, more than standing between the invader and Paris. It was a struggle for psychological mastery." He conceded that the "stage was small"—no more than a patch of French forestland—"but the audience was the world of 1918."[2]

Harbord could also rest assured that everyone saw the same big picture. Cut off and confused as they now were in the dark realm of Belleau Wood, Turrill and Lee, as well as every marine noncom and private, understood that the world was watching them—or, rather, reading the headlines they made. Certainly, the marines fought as if this were the case. At the same time, they had no doubt about their most immediate mission, which was to kill the Germans who were killing them, and to kill them wherever they found them. Despite these two islands of crystal clarity—the knowledge that they fought upon a world stage but had to deal with death just yards or feet or inches away—the marines were, that night of June 6–7, precisely in the situation the English poet Matthew Arnold had evoked in his 1867 "Dover Beach"—bewildered:

> . . . as on a darkling plain
> Swept with confused alarms of struggle and flight,
> Where ignorant armies clash by night.

Majors Berton Sibley and Thomas Holcomb struggled to consolidate their positions in the southern end of Belleau Wood. Farther north, on the left, Lieutenant Colonel Logan Feland had yet to lead his attack, although it was almost half past ten. He had earlier requested a preparatory artillery barrage, then asked for another. Harbord replied to Feland that a barrage had been "put down at your request about 8:50. Your later request . . . for barrage cannot be honored because of ignorance of your whereabouts."[3] Frederic Wise was holding with his entire battalion (except for Lloyd Williams's 51st Company, sent in earlier) in a reserve position, south of Champillon, to the rear and north of Belleau Wood. During that hellish night, however, that position yielded no safety. German shells rained down on it. Lieutenant E. D. Cooke recalled that one shell landed "right in the headquarters group and three more exploded in the trees overhead." The concussion blew the company runner, a marine Cooke identified only as Steve, against him, and knocked them both to the ground. "I grabbed him and rolled into a hole, but Steve was dead. Two other fellows were killed and a half dozen more torn and bleeding." In an effort to save the battalion before it was blown to bits waiting to be called in to the attack, Captain Lester Wass "raged about, making men scatter, take cover, dig in." Others "pulled the wounded behind trees. . . . It was a messy ten minutes." From that point on, "we kept digging and ducking shells. . . . A grim business, crouching in a shallow hole, wondering if it were to prove a selfdug grave." When shortly after midnight the order finally came to move out, to the relief of Berry's beleaguered 3rd Battalion, the marines advanced into the battle proper "with no regrets."[4]

Wise's marines may have felt relieved to be out from under the falling shells, but Wise himself was utterly bewildered. His orders from Harbord told him to take three companies "into the line on right of Feland between him and the 3d Battalion." The order went on to explain that "Feland's right is supposed to be about one kilometer south of Hill 126. Berry's left near Hill 133." Then it instructed Wise, when he arrived "approximately in position," to "report by runner to Feland," who would give him further orders. Flabbergasted, Wise later wrote, "[It] was the damndest order I ever got in my life—or anyone else ever got. It went on the calm assumption that all the objectives of the First and Third Battalion had been secured." Wise was close enough to the action to know that this assumption was quite unwarranted. Nevertheless, "Starting at two a.m. I was to go along the Lucy-Torcy road, find Colonel Feland, second in command of the Fifth Marines, whose P.C. [post of command] was supposed to be somewhere near Champillon, and get orders from him what to do." Whereas Wise's marines were happy to leave a place that amounted to a magnet for artillery fire, Wise himself understood that he "was between the devil and the deep sea. If I didn't move, I knew I'd catch hell"—both from the German artillery and General Harbord. "If I did move, I knew I was going right down into Germany."[5]

But, given an order to advance, a marine advances. "It was dark as pitch. Finding Feland would be a miracle."[6]

The Lucy-Torcy road passed to the left of Belleau Wood and paralleled very closely its entire western margin. To get to the road in the absolute darkness, Wise, in company with Lieutenant Bill Mathews and his section of scouts, personally led all three companies in single file northeast toward the road. Each man, bat blind, held onto the man in front of him. Once they reached the road, they had the luxury of shelter to the east. For approximately a half mile north out of Lucy-le-Bocage a slope or ridge separated the road from Belleau Wood. After this, however, the ridge gave way to "sloping grain fields, like a bottle-neck opening into a bottle." Harbord's orders assumed that Wise's advance up the Lucy-Torcy road would be at least somewhat protected by Berry's battalion, which was supposedly holding the north end of the woods.[7]

Of course, Berry's shattered battalion was doing no such thing.

As his column marched sightlessly along the road, Wise called a halt at the "bottleneck." All was quiet.

And that was precisely the problem.

If an entire battalion was positioned just to the right (east), how could there be no noise? Taking his adjutant and two squads, Wise ventured ahead on the road. Within two hundred yards they were met by a burst of rifle fire—not from the right, but from the left. Wise knew from the sound that the rifles were Springfields, not Mausers, and he called out to cease fire.

The shooting stopped. A moment of silence followed. Then someone shouted: "Look out. The Germans are on your right in the Bois de Belleau."[8]

So much for meeting up with Lieutenant Colonel Feland and Berry's battalion.

With his adjutant and squad members, Wise turned to head back to his halted column. At that point, however, the Germans opened up with machine guns and artillery, killing half of Wise's men as they scrambled back to the others. As he approached the officers at the head of his battalion, Wise was professionally laconic, crisply barking out to them: "About face to the rear—on the double."[9]

It is one thing to give such an order to a squad and quite another to relay it to some six hundred marines—in single file, no less. The order had to be passed down the line, and as it was, the well-trained marines responded not by instantly executing the order but by returning the regulation reply: "By whose command?" This was a safeguard to prevent unauthorized retreats and other movements. As future marine commandant Lieutenant Lemuel Shepherd explained, the order traveled down the line and the reply "went all the way back up the line" to be answered with, "By Colonel Wise—we're in the wrong spot."[10]

But that left another very big problem. Lieutenants Gil Jackson and E. D. Cooke, the officers at the rear of column, had been watching German artillery explode behind them just as they received Wise's order. Cooke recalled: "Jackson and I looked at each other inquiringly. We knew there wasn't any such thing as going to the rear because of the shells." In response to the order, they "made the tail of the column stand fast." This brought to them Captain Wass at a dead run. "To the rear!" he bellowed, facing down Jackson and Cooke. "By order of Lieutenant Colonel Wise. To the rear!" In an instant, the dilemma was resolved. "We couldn't run from the Boche, but if Fritz Wise and Captain Wass said to run it was time to get going," shells or no shells.[11]

Not that the single-file column could get going very quickly. "We could move a few steps and then halt, then a few steps and halt," Cooke later wrote. "This kept up until day was breaking."[12]

Wise's battalion did not run from the Germans. As soon as it had withdrawn down the Lucy-Torcy road to a defensible position alongside the western face of Belleau Wood, Wise again halted the column, turned it back around, and began its deployment. He sent Captain John Blanchfield's 55th Company forward to assume the first position fronting the woods. The company's task was to begin suppressing some of the fire from the woods. As Blanchfield and Shepherd organized a reconnaissance to locate the source of fire from a projection out of the western face of Belleau Wood, Blanchfield turned toward the sound of the fire. At that moment, another machine gun crackled from the body of the woods. A bullet caught Blanchfield, spinning him around before it knocked him to the ground. He sprawled across the Lucy-Torcy road.

Seeing Blanchfield fall, Private Paul Bonner at first followed his buddies, who scattered at the burst of fire. But "then I thought of Blanchfield and started back. . . . [I] rushed across the road, machine gun bullets whipping the air everywhere, and I made the captain's side. He was still alive." Like Albertus Catlin, John Blanchfield was a big man, "twice my size," Bonner judged, "but I picked him up and carried him back."[13]

Despite Bonner's efforts, Blanchfield died, and command of the company fell to Lemuel Shepherd. He continued positioning the platoons along the edge of the woods. Suddenly, his orderly, a Private Martin, went down. When Shepherd bent to help him, he caught a bullet in his hip. "One of my men came along, pulled us back to the edge of the road, then got us to a dressing station."[14]

While 55th Company deployed along Belleau Wood to the right of the road, the other companies took up positions in a small woods on the road's left. Back at brigade headquarters, General Harbord believed this end of the woods had been occupied, if not secured. The marines to the west of the woods knew this was hardly the case. Now, however, they heard men deploying along the western margin of Belleau Wood and along the Lucy-Torcy road. E. D. Cooke vividly recalled the result this produced. "Daylight came suddenly as we lay alongside of the road." Cooke heard some talking up ahead, "then shouts and the chug-chug of a heavy machine gun. Several other guns joined in and the air was full of bullets." Cooke hollered to the men, "Keep down!" It was a superfluous command. Their noses were already "buried in the dirt." The firing came from "our own guns," from marines who assumed that anyone at the end of Belleau Wood this far north had to be German.[15]

Panic sent the "blood pounding into my head and emptied my stomach of courage," Cooke admitted. "It was bad enough to be shot at by the Boche but there was no sense in being killed by friendly troops." Worse, Cooke saw that his own men "looked wild and fingered their triggers, ready to return the fire of our other battalion." Cooke knew that "something had to be done and done quick."[16]

"And Captain Wass did it."[17]

Not that he meant to. Wass yelled to Lieutenant Jackson: "Where are you?" The response was "Right here. Across the road." To which Wass returned: "Stand up, so I can see you."[18]

Above the "crackling roar of machine-gun bullets," Jackson shouted back: "Captain, if you want to see me, *you* stand up." Suddenly, it was over. "American humor can lick anything," Cooke observed. "Smothered chuckles ran down the line," and the friendly fire ceased.[19]

It was six in the morning, June 7. Wise was in position on the western margin of Belleau Wood, roughly along its center. He had managed to tie in with what remained of Berry's battalion, which was deployed to his left, running farther up the woods. With others who soon joined them, they attacked Belleau Wood at this location a little later in the morning. When they did, they discovered that the Germans had withdrawn.

It was by no means a victory, final or intermediate. Belleau Wood was still thickly occupied by the enemy, who had merely pulled back, deeper into its recesses. General Degoutte had ordered that Belleau Wood be taken. That objective, intended to be achieved in a day and night's fighting, was far from having been attained. But no one knew just how far.

As the morning of June 7 progressed, Harbord began to learn what had been accomplished and what had not. He reported to General Bundy at 8:30 a.m. that his brigade from right (south) to left (north) held a line extending from Triangle Farm to Bouresches "through the wood, then practically a line east and west through the Bois de Belleau from the northern edge of the town Bouresches to about Hill 181" and then "in a line running southeast-northwest to near north edge of woods about two kilometers north of Lucy." Behind the lines either fronting or through portions of Belleau Wood, Harbord reported another line continuous from "southeast of Bussiares to Triangle Farm."[20]

The victory was not final. The mission was not yet completed. At best, it was a start. And considering the impulsiveness of the offensive, commenced on the spur of the moment and virtually without preparation let alone careful reconnaissance, it was a remarkable start. But it was far from a consummation. Moreover, it had a cost—well, Harbord did not yet know: "No numbers as to casualties are available. Losses known to be heavy."[21]

To the marines fighting in Belleau Wood, June 7 promised to be another day of hard, confusing combat. To General Harbord, June 7 brought a strong dose of harsh reality, as he reported his tentative and rather meager gains to his superior officer, Omar Bundy. But to the correspondents of America's newspapers, this chaotic battle, just barely begun, loomed as a triumphant breakthrough of nearly miraculous proportions.

As early as June 6, the *Chicago Daily Tribune* trumpeted:

U.S. MARINES SMASH HUNS

GAIN GLORY IN BRISK FIGHT ON THE MARNE

CAPTURE MACHINE GUNS, KILL BOCHES, TAKE PRISONERS

On June 7, the *Tribune* continued in this vein:

MARINES WIN HOT BATTLE

SWEEP ENEMY FROM HEIGHTS NEAR THIERRY

Even the customarily more reserved *New York Times* was ecstatic:

OUR MARINES ATTACK, GAIN MILE AT VEUILLY, RESUME DRIVE AT NIGHT,

FOE LOSING HEAVILY[22]

In newspapers across the nation, the headlines run during these two days were similar. The stories they led were not false, so much as they were misleading. Or, rather, they were not so much news as they were premature celebrations.

The exuberance of the headlines and the stories was the product of two things. The first was a long frustration among journalists and the public alike with the hitherto modest role of the AEF in Europe, as General Pershing struggled to avoid committing American forces into battle piecemeal and before they had been thoroughly trained. The second contributor to the burst of journalistic rhapsody was, ironically enough, Pershing's strict policy of censorship. Correspondents were forbidden to identify army divisions or other units by name, nickname, or number. They were forbidden to identify troops as from a particular state or region. They were forbidden to distinguish among the army's service branches, such as artillery, cavalry, infantry. They were forbidden to make reference to the size of a unit, so they could not use such words as "regiment" or "battalion." All of these restrictions made reporting both difficult and unappealing. After all, in any good story it is essential to know the names of the characters, but Pershing's censorship policy enveloped in dull anonymity the entire American enterprise in the Great War.

With one exception. When the U.S. 2nd Division went to Europe, correspondents pointed out to Pershing's press officer that the U.S. Marines were a service separate from the army. They were not a branch—like the cavalry or the infantry—so it stood to reason that correspondents should be permitted to identify them by name—that is, "marines" as opposed to "army." Pershing agreed.

And now America's journalists had a name—and a character, a most remarkable character—to insert into their stories. Given this, the "anonymous" army receded into obscurity beneath the headlines, more and more of which were devoted to "our Marines."

Many in the United States Army were not happy, and with good reason. Major General Robert Lee Bullard, commanding officer of the 1st Division, complained that the brigade of marines constituted just one third of the 2nd Division, yet was accorded all the glory for the victory at Belleau Wood. "To prevent valuable information from reaching the enemy," Bullard explained in his 1925 *Personalities and Reminiscences of the War*, "our censorship regulations prohibited press reports from mentioning organizations. To say 'Marines' did not violate this regulation: It mentioned no organization. So the press reports of the 2nd Division shouted, 'Marines,' 'Marines,' 'Marines,' until the word resounded over the whole earth and made the inhabitants thereof, except a few Americans in the army in France, believe there was nothing in the 2nd Division, and, indeed, nothing in front of the Germans, but Marines."[23]

One evening, while news "reports were resounding at the highest and American readers were acclaiming the Marines as the saviours of Paris and the war, General Pershing came on a visit to me," Bullard recounted.[24]

> "General," I said to him at dinner, "I see that the 2nd Marines (emphasizing the 2nd as though that division was all Marines) have won the war at Belleau Wood."
>
> "Yes," he answered dryly, "and I stopped it yesterday as I passed there."
>
> But had he? He stopped only what was yet to come, not what had already gone forth. That he could not stop, and it was, I say, enough to convince all good enthusiastic Americans that at Belleau Wood there was nothing but Marines and, of course, dead Germans, their victims and theirs alone.[25]

On June 9, the *New York Times* reported that according to "recruiting headquarters in New York . . . application for service [in the Marine Corps] has increased more than 100 percent in the last two days."[26] Young men picked up newspapers, read about the marine "triumph" at Belleau Wood, and rushed to the recruiting office.

The U.S. Congress was not far behind them. On July 1, 1918—as it turned out, the day after Belleau Wood was finally secured—lawmakers authorized the expansion of the Corps to 3,017 officers and 75,500 men. To be sure, this was still a small and elite force, but it represented a massive increase from the 15,000 men with the Corps who had entered combat, and it brought an absolute end to all talk among legislative as well as executive circles of ever abolishing the marines.

Even as the newspapers printed their headlines, the 4th Marine Brigade set about collecting and evacuating its wounded and counting its dead. On June 6 alone, thirty-one officers of the brigade became casualties (twenty-five wounded, six killed) as did 1,056 enlisted marines, of whom 222 were killed in action or later died of their wounds.

▪ 13 ▪

"Cheap Successes"

The United States Marines were making more than headlines at Belleau Wood, although the headlines they made counted for a great deal, and not just the aggrandizement of the Corps. Additional *New York Times* stories of June 7 were headed "Our Troops Resistless" and "Whole Detachments of Germans Wiped Out. No Holding Back Our Men." Paris, which the marine intervention had surely saved, was still very jumpy, as a June 8 letter from U.S. embassy official Lee Meriwether attested. He wrote of the city's having "lived through seven frightfully anxious days—the seventy-five-mile guns dropping shells on the city daily." By night, Meriwether wrote, Germany's heavy Gotha bombers staged frequent raids. Indeed, Meriwether had a more realistic view of the situation than the newspapers had—perhaps even more realistic than some of the generals. "Terrific fighting is still going on barely forty miles from here where I am writing these notes; thus far the enemy is being 'held,' but whether he will continue to be held, or whether he will succeed in advancing again, and near enough to put Paris within reach of his marine [heavy] guns, remains to be seen." The French government was certainly not resting easy. Meriwether reported that it had "appointed a 'Committee for the Defense of Paris'" on

June 7, although the appointment had been accompanied by an announcement that it was "only a precaution and . . . the public must not become alarmed or imagine that the government believes the Germans will really enter the capital, or that they will even come close enough to bomb it with ordinary big cannon."[1]

While Paris was hardly out of danger, French generalissimo Ferdinand Foch not only praised the marines for having "won the admiration of the French troops with whom they fought,"[2] he recognized that, while American headlines certainly exaggerated their achievement, that achievement was already far out of proportion to the tiny amount of territory the marines had managed to reclaim during June 6–7. Foch's intelligence was reporting that the 5th Prussian Guards and the 28th Infantry, historically two of the best divisions in the German Seventh Army—the army that posed the greatest threat to the French position in the Noyon-Montdidier sector—had been withdrawn and transferred south to deal with the U.S. Marines. Since the end of May, the German strategy had been to threaten Paris, forcing the French to cover the line south of Belleau Wood, closest to the capital, by transferring troops from Noyon-Montdidier, the sector north of Belleau Wood, leaving it more vulnerable to a German breakthrough above Paris. Ludendorff had hoped to drive his latest offensive through Belleau Wood and the environs and through the Noyon-Montdidier sector while the French concentrated most of their troops to the south in the defense of Paris. The performance of the marines in and around Belleau Wood, however, turned the tables on Ludendorff, forcing *him* to transfer troops from the north to the south.

As Foch would probably have seen it, the transfer of the 5th Prussian Guards and the 28th Infantry was not only a great relief to his French troops but a kind of German tribute of honor to the marines. Clearly, Ludendorff regarded the Teufelhunden as the equivalent of what the Prussian Guards were: storm troopers, elite soldiers who specialized in spearheading attacks and counterattacks. As for the German 28th Infantry, it was one of the Great War's most storied units. Nicknamed the "Conquerors of Lorette," the 28th had been victorious at Verdun, Cambrai, and the Somme.

For the Germans, defeating the marines was not first and foremost a question of gaining territory. Like U.S. 1st Division commander Robert Lee Bullard—albeit for very different reasons—Germany's generals were distressed by all the headlines the marines were grabbing. As General Max von Boehn, commanding the 28th Division, wrote in his special order of June 8, the Americans not only intended to gain at Belleau Wood "immobilization of the German forces and local improvement of [the Allied] line," but also "cheap successes," which will "be headlined in the newspapers. It will be said that *one* American division has been sufficient to stop the German attacks without difficulty." The consequences of such headlines, should "the Americans on our front gain the upper hand even temporarily," would be "most unfavorable" for "the morale of the Central Powers and [for] the continuation of the war."[3] Von Boehn's special order suggests that, perhaps even more than the French, the English, or the Americans themselves, the German military placed a supremely high value on the significance of its first encounters with the AEF:

> In the fighting that faces us . . . it is not a matter of possession or non-possession of a village or a wood, of indifferent value in itself, but a question of whether English-American publicity will succeed in presenting the American army as one equal to the German army or as actually superior troops. The renewed employment of the 5th Guard and the 28th Infantry divisions in the front line of Corps Conta is to be considered from this point of view.[4]

What von Boehn failed to mention—and what the public did not see—was the blood behind the headlines. During the day of June 7, Harbord continued his struggle to get accurate reports and to consolidate what little his marines had managed to gain during the night. Even along parts of the line, including within Belleau Wood itself where major German concentrations had been cleared out, consolidation was hampered by sniper fire, fire from isolated machine-gun nests, and fire from light artillery. The agile German 77-millimeter field piece launched whizbangs, shells whose flat trajectories never announced their presence, so they were especially lethal against unsuspecting personnel.

Any activity in and around the woods was likely to draw German fire, including the movement necessary to gather and evacuate wounded men who had lain on the field, in some cases, overnight and for many hours. Bringing in the wounded under fire was strictly a job for volunteers, but since it is a byword among marines that no man is to be left behind, there was never a shortage of volunteers. In Wise's battalion, for example, a Sergeant Patterson who had been crawling into the fields all through the night of June 6–7 to bring in the wounded was exhausted by daybreak. But in the daylight when he saw an arm "through the waving stems" of wheat, he and another volunteer started crawling through the wheat. The other man was stopped by gunfire, but Patterson "insisted he was able to make it." Under intense fire, he crawled "the entire way to the wounded man and carried him back and placed him on a stretcher to be taken to the hospital." As the bearers started away with the rescued marine, Patterson, spent, "chanced to sit on the edge of a fox hole, to talk to his group and was hit in the throat as he was taking a chew of tobacco, receiving a ghastly wound from a shell fragment, and died instantly."[5]

The wounded could not be ignored, but under conditions like these, there was no question of attempting to gather the dead. They were left in the fields and in Belleau Wood wherever they had fallen. Some would be there for days, even weeks, Americans and Germans alike. Albertus Catlin quoted Private F. E. Steck of Camden, New Jersey, who, while making with his buddies one of several unauthorized nocturnal forays to rescue wounded marines, "came across a German officer seated comfortably with his knees crossed."[6]

> Before him was spread a little field table on which was cake, jam, cookies, and a fine array of food. A knife and fork was in either hand.
>
> Beside the officer was seated a large, bulky Sergeant who had been knitting socks. The darning needles were still between his fingers. Both their heads had been blown off by a large shell.[7]

The volume of wounded overwhelmed the marines' small complement of stretcher bearers, corpsmen, and surgeons. "Dressing stations"—little more than improvised dispensaries of the most rudimentary first aid—were set up wherever cover could be found, behind rocks, in dugouts, next to walls, in the cellars of half-ruined buildings. The records of a battalion surgeon noted the nature of the wounds, which were typical of those produced by the weapons of the Great War. They were "chiefly" of the "tearing, lacerating, crushing, and amputating types, accompanied by all degrees of fractures, hemorrhage, and destruction of soft tissue." Most common, the surgeon recorded, were injuries of the extremities, "followed by those of the abdomen and chest." Thanks to heroic treatment by corpsmen at the scene, shock was far less common than anticipated.[8]

Harbord planned no major attack for June 7, but did, in conventional military fashion, set his men to straightening the line they held. The object of such consolidation was to ensure a continuous line without gaps. An open flank was always vulnerable to attack. North of Lucy-le-Bocage, Harbord wanted to secure a "rectangular wood about 200 yards in depth and about 400 yards long," through which he proposed to straighten the line. The 55th Company, under Lieutenant E. D. Cooke, was sent to relieve an exhausted company under Captain Conachy and to occupy the little woods. En route, Cooke reported, "we passed dead men—plenty of them. A German here and there, and whole squads of Americans," among whom was "an officer and three men" lying behind some saplings. "The officer had been hit high up on the thigh, had pulled down his pants to dress the wound but had died before being able to stop the blood."[9] As the celebrated British World War I poet Wilfred Owen had already written, those who saw such sights of ignominious death would never again "tell with such high zest / To children ardent for some desperate glory, / The old Lie: Dulce et decorum est / Pro patria mori."

Once he reached the assigned patch of woods and relieved Conachy, Cooke "felt sort of lonely and inadequate. If any friendly troops were across the ravine on my left I didn't know where they were [and there] was no one on my right and the Lord knew how many Germans in front of me. . . .

Night was coming on. . . . We were out of touch with all friendly troops and the United States of America was three thousand miles away. I all but burst out crying."[10] Not knowing what to do in this isolated situation as night came on—but knowing he should do something—Cooke fell back on a military tactic that was hundreds of years old. He arranged his company into a "British square," the classic defensive posture in which four platoons form the outward-facing sides of a hollow square, so that every side of the formation is a front, without flank. Shopworn though it was, the British square proved an effective tactic in defending against an attack that came later in the night.

By late afternoon on June 7, General Harbord decided that he would do more than merely consolidate his lines. He determined to order his marines to make a fresh advance into the woods early on June 8. Once this decision had been made, much of the late afternoon and night of June 7 had to be devoted to shifting and positioning forces for the advance. There was much of the usual confusion in all of this movement, especially after night fell, and there was also a massive German barrage to cope with, which hit late at night and was spread over an area that encompassed the southern part of Belleau Wood as well as Bouresches, south of the woods, and farther south-west into the army lines of Malone and Upton. Shortly after midnight, the barrage was followed by a German advance, which was arrested by the marines. Repulsed by the Devil Dogs, the Germans hit the army lines farther south but were also effectively resisted and withdrew.

The cessation of the German attack gave the marines time to do what they had been unable to do for many days: enjoy a decent meal of corned beef on bread, which they washed down with lukewarm but palatable coffee. Knowing that they would be ordered to attack before daybreak, the men wolfed their meals. Commanders, it seemed, never tired of ordering armies to attack in the twilit hours before dawn. For time out of mind, it had been common knowledge among military men that this was the time an enemy was most vulnerable, the inertia of human fatigue at maximum, the tendency to panic greatest. At 4:00 a.m., Lieutenant Louis Timmerman was polishing off "a piece of the warm, stringy beef and drinking coffee from a canteen cup." When the attack order came, he hooked his cane over one arm, rose, and "led the men forward," but had to "admit [he] was more interested in finishing the meat and coffee than in the attack."[11]

Soon enough, however, it was the attack that claimed Timmerman's attention. To the shock of all, German machine-gun fire opened up from unseen nests. Above the sustained continuous note of the Maxims and lighter machine guns, German rifles sounded off, many of them propelling grenades.

The marines were stopped cold. Anxious eyes sought to penetrate what was now the smoky, predawn gloom, searching in vain for the source of all the fire. As it soon became apparent, there were so many sources that within two hours the marine companies had captured two German machine guns each. "The most effective method [of capturing an enemy machine gun] was to run to the rear of each gun in turn and overpower the crew," Colonel Catlin wrote. But, in Belleau Wood, "each flanking position was covered by another gun." No sooner would the marines take one machine-gun nest than another would open up on them. Bischoff, the German commander, had positioned his machine guns with great skill. Each was in the crossfire of two others. This was not new to the marines; they had encountered the tactic during the attack on June 6, in which Catlin characterized the effort to neutralize the German machine-gun positions as a "furious dash from nest to nest, with no time to stop for breath."[12] But the machine-gun fire during the attack on the eighth was even worse, especially because the marines had assumed that they had knocked out practically all of the German resistance in the woods.

Under fire from multiple directions, Timmerman and his platoon clawed the very earth for shelter. "Not having any mess gear I was digging in with my fingers," the lieutenant recalled. When a runner from the company captain approached him with orders to "take some men and flank the guns"—that is, carry out the very tactics Catlin described—Timmerman despaired. "I had already seen that we were up against intersecting fire, in other words there weren't any flanks to take. I found myself unable to even attempt to carry out the order."[13]

By 10:00 a.m., Major Berton Sibley was on the field telephone to regimental headquarters. "They are too strong for us," he gasped. "Soon as we take one machine gun, another opens." He reported losses so heavy that he had to re-form "on the ground held by the 82d Company last night. All of the officers of the 82d Company wounded or missing." Incredibly, after reiterating that "these machine guns are too strong for our infantry," Sibley closed with, "We can attack again if it is desired."[14]

Harbord ordered no second attack and instead played for time, ordering Sibley, "Get cover for your men in the ravine (gully) at south edge of woods"—the ground that had been taken on sixth. "Let your men rest. I will have artillery play on the wood. Any further orders will be given you later for other movement by you."[15]

That message was sent at 12:30 p.m. A runner delivered Sibley's reply to Harbord at 2:30: "Regret to report officers and men too much exhausted for further attack on strong resistance until after several hours rest."[16]

James C. Harbord was neither a fool nor reckless with the lives of his marines. Whenever he had chided his field commanders, he had done so out of an ignorance born of faulty communications. When he knew the facts, he could face the facts, and he decided that new tactics and a better plan were in order before he launched a new attack. He conferred on June 8 with his fellow army officer, Brigadier General William Chamberlaine, who commanded the artillery brigade of 2nd Division. Harbord's intention this time was to combine artillery and infantry in a much stronger attack on June 10.

The attacks on June 6 and on June 8 had made relatively little use of artillery. In the case of the June 6 attack, the official reason for omitting prolonged artillery preparation was to preserve the element of surprise in the manner of Hutier tactics. In reality, the preemptory—indeed, impulsive—nature of Degoutte's attack order left no time for an artillery preparation. The omission of artillery on June 8 was more genuinely an attempt to preserve surprise. Moreover, Harbord—and others—had assumed that the action on June 6–7 had largely cleared the Germans from much of Belleau

Wood. That assumption was proved wrong by the German repulse of the June 8 attack. For the June 10 attack, therefore, Harbord decided to make use of a full and intensive artillery preparation, to commence early on the evening of June 9 and to carry on through the night and into the early morning. No fewer than thirty batteries of the famed French 75s and a dozen of the heavy 155s would pound Belleau Wood. Once the marine advance stepped off at 4:30 a.m., June 10, the artillery would play a "rolling barrage" just ahead of their advance.

To the marines, hoping to grab a few fugitive hours of sleep before zero hour, the barrage that night sounded like "sharp thunder."[17] In all, the Franco-American artillerists laid down a barrage of twenty-eight thousand 75-millimeter shells and six thousand 155-millimeter rounds. In response, the Germans launched a counterbarrage but lacked the local firepower to match the intensity of the Allied preparation. Nevertheless, the garrison holding Bouresches took incoming German shells on the night of June 9 at the rate of one a minute. To add insult to injury, long-range friendly fire was hurled into the mix late in the night. Such mistakes were to be expected. As usual, communication with headquarters and from unit to unit was almost exclusively by runners—who were now obliged to pick their way through a shell-cratered landscape even as the shells of both sides rained down on them.

The plan, issued in the form of Harbord's orders at 6:30 p.m. on June 9, was for Major John A. Hughes to lead his battalion of the 6th Marines— a fresh battalion hitherto held in reserve—in a sweep of the southern portion of Belleau Wood. He was to reach a line running east-west at the point where the southwestern hook of Belleau Wood joined the main north-south body of the woods. Having extended his line of advance to this position, Hughes was to consolidate and tie in on his right (his east flank) with the defenders of Bouresches and on his left (his west flank) with Frederic Wise's 2nd Battalion. This would cut off the bottom third of Belleau Wood from the top two-thirds, putting the marines into position (Harbord hoped) to roll up the German flank within that upper portion of the woods. Sibley, who already occupied part of the territory Hughes was to sweep, was ordered to withdraw to the ravine known to French locals as Gobert and to the marines as Gob Gully. Here Sibley's men would take cover during the long and heavy preparatory barrage.

When Hughes moved his men out through the by-then familiar bleakness of 4:30 a.m., he was thrilled to encounter surprisingly light resistance. At 4:51, Hughes sent a runner to Harbord, notifying him that the artillery barrage was "working beautifully." Despite three or four casualties, he reported, all was "O.K." A half hour later, Lieutenant Colonel Lee's intelligence officer sent a message to Harbord, telling him that "Action in woods deemed finished.... Only a few short bursts of machine gun fire noted during advance." By 7:12, Lee reported to Harbord a message from Hughes: "Everything going nicely. No losses coming across. . . . Artillery has blown the Bois de Belleau to mince meat." Although Major Edward Cole was wounded severely enough to require evacuation, by 8:00 a.m. Harbord concluded that the attack had been successful. Now he told Hughes, "Push your reconnaissance north of you in the Bois de Belleau . . . and let me know at the earliest possible moment whether you think it possible to take part of the wood north of your present position."[18]

Harbord, at this point, must have felt a mixture of relief as well as pride—relief that the attack, so thoroughly prepared for with artillery, had apparently succeeded, and pride that his marines had prevailed against two famous German units, the 5th Guards and the 28th Division. As in the previous actions, however, Harbord had a very imperfect picture of the battlefield.

First, while it was true that two crack German units had been brought in to defend Belleau Wood against the marines, they were located mostly outside of the woods, along its western face on the northern end of the woods and then up to Torcy, due north. The woods proper were held by a single reinforced battalion commanded by Major von Hartlieb. It was supposed to tie in on the left (south) with the newly arrived 28th Division, which was taking up a position from Vaux, southwest of Belleau Wood, up to the woods itself. But by the time the 28th had reached Belleau Wood, it was far from being the division that had performed with such magnificence in earlier battles. Its ranks were thinned, its equipment worn and depleted, and its morale depressed. As for the German battalion that was in closest contact with Hughes's advance on June 10, manning an east-west line across the southern portion of the woods, it had been reduced from six to two companies in the line, with a third company in reserve at the eastern margin of the woods, and a fourth, farther east, along the railroad track outside of Belleau Wood. All of these German companies were bolstered by machine-gun units, but on his immediate front, Hughes faced a weaker force than had been present on June 6, 7, and 8. As for the elite outfits that had been sent to ensure the defense of Belleau Wood, they were, at least to a degree, ghosts of their former glorious selves—under-strength and underequipped—and, in any case, Hughes's marines had yet to tangle with them.

There were two more critical pieces of information unavailable to Harbord—or to Hughes. To begin with, burdened as he was by the usual bad French maps, Hughes did not realize that he had stopped very short of the line assigned to him, the line running east-west across the narrow waist of Belleau Wood about one-third of the way up the extent of the woods. All that he had done was to reoccupy the territory that Sibley, as ordered, had withdrawn from. The intended east-west line was at least eight hundred yards farther northeast. Had Hughes actually reached this point, he would have been in close contact with the German battalion deployed along this line. Although, as just mentioned, that battalion was deployed at significantly reduced strength, its machine-gun emplacements were still formidable, and it was tied in with the German units adjacent to the northern portion of the woods. To compound this error—which made both Hughes and Harbord believe that the attack, in its first two hours, had accomplished far more than it actually had—was yet another. The artillery barrage, intensive as it had been, did destroy a large part of Belleau Wood, yet had remarkably little effect on the German machine-gun nests. It was one thing to bombard a treeless no-man's-land or a line of trenches, but quite another to loft artillery shells into a forest. The ordnance employed had simple contact fuses, designed to detonate on impact. Such fuses are very effective when the shells hit ground level, but the densely packed trees of Belleau Wood detonated most of the incoming shells prematurely, so they exploded well above their intended targets. To be sure, the Germans were showered with shrapnel, boughs, and branches, but hunkered down in their well-prepared dugouts, most of them escaped death or even injury. In short, the long, vicious barrage gave Hughes and Harbord confidence that German resistance had been largely flattened, but it was the kind of confidence most destructive in combat. It was false confidence.

Reconnaissance during the rest of the day on June 10 began to dismantle Harbord's sense of achievement, as it was revealed that Hughes's attack had certainly gained less than had been thought. The reconnaissance did not reveal just how much less, but it did make Harbord aware that his report to General Bundy—his announcement that Belleau Wood had essentially been cleared—was premature. After chewing on this disappointing revelation, Harbord dispatched a sidecar-equipped motorcycle to fetch Frederic Wise and deliver him to brigade headquarters. Tired and dirty, the battalion commander stood before the commander of the brigade who handed him an order—Field Order Number Four—directing his 2nd Battalion, 5th Marines, to attack the northern portion of Belleau Wood.

As he handed Wise an order for yet another attack, Harbord knew that the northern portion of the woods had plenty of Germans in it. He did not know how far short of its assigned objective Hughes's attack had stopped, so he had no way of knowing that the German positions still also extended much farther south into the woods. In sum, yet again, the marines were being sent into the unknown. Also as before, it was an unknown about which many overly optimistic assumptions had been made.

Harbord's orders instructed Wise to attack the southwestern edge of the northern part of Belleau Wood across a five-hundred-yard front. He would be supported by artillery and machine-gun barrages. Hughes's battalion, in the southern lobe of the woods, would participate in this new attack as well, in an attack from south to north that was to conform to Wise's progress. Once Wise reached Hill 133 on the northeastern margin of

Belleau Wood, he was to consolidate his position and tie in his line with Hughes. Zero hour was set for 4:30 in the morning, June 11.

To say that Harbord was driving his marines hard would be a spectacular understatement. Wise's battalion, assigned to take the lead in the new attack, was 25 percent understrength. Even more significant, all of the marines were exhausted and had eaten precious little. During the evening of June 10, Wise laid out his map on the ground, kneeled beside it, and showed his company commanders what they were expected to do. Advancing from positions just west of the center portion of Belleau Wood, the 43rd Company under Captain Charles Dunbeck would attack on the left (north) in two waves, and the 51st Company under Captain Lloyd Williams would attack on the right (south). Both companies were to turn sharply left once they entered the woods, pushing their attack due north and spreading out as they progressed, with platoons moving east and west to sweep clear the northern reaches of the woods. Most of the 51st Company was tasked with capturing Hill 133 at the northeastern edge of the woods, then hooking about to attack the Germans from the rear, thereby bagging a substantial number of prisoners. In the meantime, the 43rd Company would continue to press its attack due north. As Harbord had planned it, this would not be a simple frontal attack, but would flank the German positions, then even come around for an attack on the rear.

Through the night, Franco-American artillery bombarded the northern portion of the woods. Lieutenant E. D. Cooke recalled the night vividly, how the shells passed overhead in a "rustling swish" at first and then, louder and louder, until "a hurricane of steel lashed and tore at the borders of Belleau Wood." Cooke was having a smoke with Captain Lester Wass as the barrage died down. When the captain suddenly rose to his feet and looked to the east, Cooke asked "What's the matter?" With a glance at the radium dial of his wristwatch, Wass replied in a "tight, hard voice": "Four thirty. So long."[19]

There was a thick mist that morning as the men of the assault waves rose and followed their captain. When the German Maxims opened fire, the marines' forward lines stumbled, but only for a moment. They pressed on through the wheat, which provided blessed concealment. But then they came to a fence, beyond which the wheat field stopped and the level ground was entirely open. "No more concealment," Cooke wrote, "except for the heavy clinging mist; that was a gift of Providence."[20]

But Providence provided only so much that morning. The first wave advanced across the misty field, not angling northeast and directly into the upper portion of the waist of Belleau Wood—as Harbord's orders had specified—but due west, across more of the fields, in the direction of the lower portion of the waist. This was a critical blunder for three reasons. First, it kept Wise's men exposed in the field longer. Second, as an attack due west rather than hooking to the north, it was a frontal assault rather than the combination frontal and flanking attack Harbord had envisioned. Third, the failure to turn put Wise's men precisely at the point that harbored the strongest concentration of German forces within Belleau Wood—Hartlieb's battalion and, nearby, the line at which that battalion tied in with the 2nd Battalion of the German 40th Fusiliers.

There could have been no worse place to attack Belleau Wood. As Lieutenant Sam Cummings of the 51st Company later wrote, "Men were being mowed down like wheat." When a whizbang landed on Cummings's right, an automatic rifle team "which was there a moment ago disappeared, while men on the right and left were armless, legless, or tearing at their faces." About fifty yards from the woods, Cummings—as the phrase went—"got his." "Something hit me and I spun around and hit flat."[21]

The 43rd Company fared a little better in that it approached slightly closer to the margin of Belleau Wood before the German guns began to mow down its lines. Major John Hughes, waiting with his battalion in the south end of Belleau Wood, heard the action but could see nothing. He sent Sergeant Gerald C. Thomas (who would eventually retire from the Marine Corps as a general) to report on Wise's front. Thomas made his way up, identified himself to Wise, then listened to the exchange as a runner from the 43rd Company approached the 2nd Battalion commander.[22]

"Colonel," the runner reported, "our men are being shot to hell in the wood"—actually, they were barely at the margins of the woods—"we need some help."

In response, Wise ordered the 18th Company "to get up there to the woods," but then he shot back at the runner: "Who told you your company's in trouble?"

"The wounded."

"Hell, don't you know that wounded are very poor witnesses?" With that, Wise countermanded his order about the 18th Company, then turned to Thomas: "I tell you what you can do for me. One of your companies was supposed to attack on our right and I haven't seen them. I want you to find that company commander and tell him I want him to move out."

Sergeant Thomas had "no real idea of what was happening, except that Wise was getting the hell shot out of him," but he managed to work his way down to a company commanded by Lieutenant Megan Overton and gave him Wise's message.

"Well, I've done what I was supposed to do," Overton responded, by which he meant that he had successfully attacked the last machine-gun nest on Wise's flank. "If Wise had brought his outfit into the woods instead of deploying them out there in the wheatfield, he wouldn't have lost all those men."

Still, Wise's companies kept coming. Cooke's 55th Company "entered a deep indentation of the woods and the shadows moved to surround us. Without the slightest warning those shadows suddenly were split apart by chattering, stabbing flames." As the machine guns crackled into flaming life, the order came: "Down! Down! Take cover!" But, as Cooke recalled, some "were already down—down to stay."[23]

Cooke tumbled into a shell crater, then when "the holocaust of steel subsided," he peeked over the crater's edge. Seeing a man down, he "crawled forward and shook his leg. The man was dead." Beside him "lay another, doubled up, both arms locked rigidly about his shattered middle." A third man crawled toward Cooke, dragging his right leg. "It was Lieutenant Cummings of the 51st Company and his ankle was smashed." Cooke dragged him back into the shell crater, bound up his ankle, and asked him the whereabouts of his outfit.[24]

"The machine guns got 'em. As far as I know I'm the only one left out of ten officers and two hundred and fifty men."[25]

Surely it must have seemed to Cummings that he was the last of the 51st, but, incredibly, that company had actually penetrated far enough into the woods to attack the 2nd Battalion of the German 40th Fusiliers on its flank. Outnumbered, however, Williams's 51st was being worn away, even as Overton's company struggled to suppress the German machine-gun fire on the flank of the 51st. At the same time, to the left of the 51st, the battered remnant of Captain Dunbeck's 43rd Company was battling through against the left flank of Hartlieb's battalion.

Having been told that the 51st was finished, Cooke could only assume that the 43rd was in danger of suffering the same fate. "For the first time since the battle started I actually shucked off fear like an old coat. Duty, responsibility, and something like rage took command of my thoughts. Those damn Boche couldn't go shooting up our whole outfit and get away with it like that."[26]

Electrified, Cooke stood up, he later wrote, "in plain sight and blew a blast on my whistle. From holes, furrows, and clods of dirt, faces looked up. Eyes, thankful to see someone in authority, watched expectantly." Cooke pointed to his right front, then walked forward with two others. He half expected that the three of them were entirely alone in their advance, but he looked back to discover about "twenty men . . . right behind us. And more came running, eager to do anything that was wanted."[27]

Cooke and his men advanced due east, and observed that it was not only the marines who were badly cut up. A German machine gunner surrendered to him, as did a larger force of exhausted, demoralized Germans. Soon, Cooke found himself in contact with the survivors of the 51st Company, the 43rd, and the 18th under Lester Wass. The thick undergrowth that the artillery exploding in the trees above had left largely intact, meant that the companies were mostly unaware of one another's movements. Indeed, even within a company, platoons were often out of contact. This was a serious problem, and for any force other than the U.S. Marines it would have been final and fatal. But acting much as Cooke had, on their own and in whatever isolated groups could be assembled, the marines kept moving forward. It was a fragmented, even shattered attack. Yet it *was* an attack.

By six in the morning, Captain Charles Dunbeck knew he had killed a lot of the enemy and that the enemy had killed or wounded many of his men. He also knew that he had reached the edge of Belleau Wood. He did not know—but he assumed—that this was the northeastern margin—the objective assigned to him—and so he reported to Wise at 6:11: "All objectives reached and am mopping up with machine guns."[28]

Dunbeck was as mistaken about what he had achieved as Hughes had been the day before. Dunbeck had advanced not northeast, up the long shaft of Belleau Wood, but due east, across its relatively narrow waist. His line of advance was actually along the line Hughes was supposed to have occupied. Although he did not know it, Charles Dunbeck was lost. As for Frederic Wise, when Dunbeck told him that "all objectives" had been reached, he had every reason to believe that this latest attack on Belleau Wood—the attack James Harbord had assigned to him—was a success. After all, Dunbeck's report had been preceded by reports from the 5th Marines liaison officer that "Everything seems to be going along nicely" and "Everything going well," with the "Germans retiring over hill." At 7:00 a.m., Hughes added the southern perspective on this rosy picture, reporting to Harbord that "everything is O.K. and in good shape."[29]

"Eternal waiting, waiting, waiting . . . seems to characterize a Brigade Commander's duties," James C. Harbord wrote in his war diary on June 23, 1918.[30]

You know your people have started forward, and the outcome is on the knees of the gods. You can do nothing more, but you wish you could, and it is sometimes hours before you know what is happening. The telephone wires are cut; runners are killed; your men are out of sight and hearing. . . . By and by, when you are frantic for news, a message arrives by runner, but is almost illegible and quite generally very vague, being written on some officer's knee with a soft pencil, and carried through brush and shell fire, and probably written under fire.

You wish more than anything else in the world to know the exact position of your troops, and exactly where the enemy is with reference to them. . . . Officers under fire are oblivious to the passage of time and forget the importance of reports. You can't help them unless you know where they are, how they are and when. . . . Meanwhile one waits, and walks the floor, or smokes (some play solitaire), or worry over whether you have left anything undone or not.[31]

By 7:00 a.m., drinking in a blessed stream of very positive reports, Harbord decided that the waiting was over. He sent a message to General Bundy at 2nd Division headquarters: "The northern end of the Bois de Belleau belongs to the 5th Marines."[32] It was not true. Not yet.

• 14 •

A Mad Lust

"**C**ertainly it is no exaggeration to say that the *liaison* is of the very highest importance," James C. Harbord noted in his war diary. "*Liaison* generally speaking consists in keeping *everybody* informed of *everything* he ought to know."[1]

That was far easier said than done. As Harbord himself pointed out, "Telephone wires are cut; runners are killed; your men are out of sight and hearing."[2] But even this pessimistic assessment assumes that the fighters at the front have something true and accurate to tell the commanders at headquarters—if only they could. More often, the perception of the fighters themselves is limited, partial, and distorted by a combination of fear, pain, relief, and exultation. In combat, all information is strictly local, and that was especially the case in a battle fought within and about a tangled woods, whose trees and twisted undergrowth, boulders, ravines, and hills separated one unit from another, making both liaison and coordinated action all but impossible.

The marines, having approached and then entered Belleau Wood from the wrong direction and at the wrong place, were being torn to shreds. There was no denying that. Yet, disorganized and disoriented in the woods, they were nevertheless giving better than they got. Attacked on its flank, the German 2nd Battalion, 40th Fusilier Regiment, 28th Infantry was being rolled up by Wise's marines even as Hughes hammered it from the south. Bischoff rushed reinforcements to it. At some point after the battle, a letter was recovered from the body of a German soldier, a Private Hebel. "We are having very heavy days," he wrote, "with death before us hourly. Here we have no hope of coming out. My company has been reduced from a hundred and twenty to thirty men. Oh, what misery! We are now at the worst stage of the offensive, the time of counterattacks. We have Americans opposite us who are terribly reckless fellows." German commanders complained that the Americans did not fight like soldiers but, rather, attacked in "gangs of ten to twenty men, primed with alcohol." We do know that at least some of the marines filled their canteens with French wine instead of water. "Some of their wounded kept on in the attack." We also know that wounded marines who could still move—maybe even still fight—had a much better chance of survival than those who lay in the wheat fields or forest waiting for help. The German commanders seemed especially outraged by what they saw as the marines' disregard for military convention. "They had no idea of tactical principles. They fired while walking with their rifles under their arms." In World War II, General George S. Patton Jr. called this "marching fire," and far from regarding it as an unauthorized, unconventional approach to combat, he made it an official battle doctrine. "The proper way to advance . . . is to utilize marching fire and keep moving," he wrote. "This fire can be delivered from the shoulder, but it is just as effective if delivered with the butt of the rifle halfway between the belt and the armpit." Patton even specified a rate of fire: one round "every two or three paces." He articulated what the marines instinctively understood at Belleau Wood, that "the whistle of the bullets, the scream of the ricochet, and the dust, twigs, and branches which are knocked from the ground and the trees have such an effect on the enemy that his small-arms fire becomes negligible." The marines' "marching fire" was just part of an attempt to intimidate. The German commanders complained that the marines used "knives, revolvers, rifle butts and bayonets. All were big fellows, powerful, rowdies."

Practically everything went wrong with the attack on June 11, but because of the fighting qualities of the individual marine, it nevertheless took a terrible toll on the German defenders of Belleau Wood.[3]

Yet, despite the optimistic reports company commanders were sending Wise, who in turn was sending Harbord, the Germans still held Belleau Wood and held it tightly. Of all the companies committed to the attack on June 11, only Headquarters Company of Wise's battalion under Captain de Carre had actually attacked an objective specified in Harbord's orders. He reported to Wise's intelligence officer, Lieutenant Bill Mathews, that he had captured a German company near Hill 169. Carre also commented that to his left (north) there was not a single marine in Belleau Wood. Mathews was stunned. He rushed back to battalion headquarters and reported Carre's information to Wise. As he had earlier refused to credit reports from the wounded as inherently pessimistic, so Wise now refused to believe Carre's assessment of the situation. This was not a simple case of denial. After all, Wise had earlier received a message from Captain Dunbeck claiming that "all objectives" had been reached, and this was reinforced by a subsequent message from Captain Lloyd Williams that his company was "holding everything," despite fire from machine guns, which was "causing damage on our right rear."[4] Even that caveat, however, reinforced the impression that the northern reaches of Belleau Wood—the principal objective of this attack—were being occupied. Machine-gun fire on his right rear suggested that Williams's company was indeed oriented toward the north.

Well into the morning, Wise kept receiving positive, optimistic messages from his company commanders. Yet none of the communications gave an accurate picture of where the companies were—their leaders were disoriented—and because a marine does not complain, they did not indicate just how badly shredded they were either. Wise did understand that "we have lost quite a few officers,"[5] but no one seemed especially alarmed by this. After all, marine officers were supposed to be shot at—and sometimes hit.

It was not until late in the morning, toward eleven, that Wise yielded to Mathews and once again dispatched him to reconnoiter to the north.

Matthews and his intelligence section were delayed by the "scores of wounded" they encountered along the way, all "lying unattended calling for help." They paused to give first aid as best they could, and as they were doing this a marine gunner named Mike Wordazeck "came marching out of the woods with a large group of prisoners." Mathews remarked that they could find no one in the north part of the woods, and he "asked Mike what was over there." The gunner answered with one word: "Nothing." Mathews sought the company commanders, Dunbeck, Wass, and Cooke. They were all standing together.[6]

"Are you sure you have reached your objectives?" Mathews fired point-blank.[7]

Without hesitation, all answered yes, Dunbeck bolstering his response by pointing to Torcy and Belleau, which he knew to be at the north end of the woods. What none of the men standing there knew at the time—Mathews included—was that the village Dunbeck identified as Torcy was really Belleau, and what he thought was Belleau was Bouresches. Belleau was well south of Torcy, and Bouresches south not only of the village of Belleau, but also Belleau Wood. The marines were much farther south than they thought. Mathews had no more than an inkling that the marines were badly turned around. He pointed out that a "great mass of the woods to the left was totally unoccupied," to which the men responded that "it was all behind them and therefore safe."[8]

If Torcy and Belleau were ahead of them, as Dubeck thought, and the unoccupied woods was to the left—that is, to the north—how could that portion of the woods be *behind* the marines who had attacked from the south?

Convinced now that the objectives had not been attained, Mathews knew that he had to rush this intelligence back to Wise. Leaving part of his intelligence section in the woods as observers, he beat it back to battalion headquarters and told Wise that "the whole left flank" of the marine attack "was absolutely unprotected."[9]

Now even the most charitable would have to concede that Frederic Wise was in denial. He snapped at his intelligence officer: "You goddamn young bonehead, you don't know what you're talking about. I have messages from my company commanders saying they are at the north end of the woods."[10]

A marine never surrenders, not to the enemy and not even to his own commanding officer. On his own initiative, Mathews returned to the northern part of Belleau Wood to make a more definitive reconnaissance. What he did not know was that despite the commander's flare-up of temper, his report had already made an impression on Wise, who sent a runner to Harbord: "I think my left flank is rather weak." That was, of course, a spectacular understatement, although far closer to reality than the assumption that the northern portion of the woods had been taken. "The Germans are massing in our front. I can hardly spare any men. They could easily filter through tonight for counter-attack." But Wise did not elaborate on this last sentence and instead closed with, "Nothing new to report except increased artillery activity." If this was an alarm, it was tepid rather than hot, and Harbord dismissed it—largely because it paled in comparison to the message he had received earlier from Colonel Wendell Neville, commanding the 5th Marine Regiment: "Do not need any more companies now. Everything O.K. Believe our casualties slight. From ravine . . . to Wise's flank O.K."[11]

In the meantime, Mathews kept probing. He sent back to Wise an on-the-spot map he hurriedly sketched to demonstrate that the north was entirely unoccupied. "My messenger came back with the message that Wise could not understand my map. I had drawn it as the woods actually were at that point and of course he could not reconcile it with the French map he had." Exasperated, Mathews reported to Wise in person "and pleaded the importance of filling this gap and pointed out that something must be done quickly." As luck would have it, while Mathews pleaded with his commanding officer, a marine came in with a prisoner. He was a hospital orderly who "told us that had we acted sooner all of the enemy in the woods would have surrendered, but that by now they had been reinforced. Wise now realized that I was not dreaming." Once again Mathews "urged the importance of getting the gap filled quickly." Wise looked his intelligence officer in the eye: "Where in the hell am I going to get them?"[12]

Mathews suggested that Wise send in "the 6th Regiment men who were lying along side the woods north of battalion headquarters." Wise replied that he could not, but then, walking just behind a platoon of the 6th Regiment, Wise "proceeded to reconnoiter" for himself. Mathews added: "about six hours too late."[13]

Even as Mathews was probing and Wise was denying—then finally accepting—that Belleau Wood was far from having been won, the editors of the *New York Times* were composing the headline for the morning edition of June 12:

BRILLIANT VICTORY IN WOOD

AMERICANS CAPTURE GUNS AND TRENCH MORTARS IN FIGHT AT BELLEAU[14]

The captured German hospital orderly was probably accurate in his speculation that had the northern part of the woods been properly and timely attacked, the Germans would have withdrawn. But if soldiers like Private Hebel were thoroughly demoralized, commanders like Hartlieb were still determined. Instead of pulling out under attack, he reinforced his battered battalion and counterattacked along the west side of the woods. The marines lacked the resources—and, indeed, the coordinated leadership—to occupy the positions from which they had pushed the Germans, so in the course of the counterattack, Hartlieb quickly reoccupied those positions. When the marines neglected to press their attack north, Hartlieb was reinforced by a fresh battalion of the 28th Division, which positioned itself throughout the northern tract. Even as the *Times* was composing its headline trumpeting the marines' conquest of Belleau Wood, Hartlieb's men were firmly establishing a new defensive line, bristling with machine guns and artillery.

As the afternoon of June 11 wore on, evidence of a counterattack mounted. Neville received word that shortly after noon German troops were "reported massing on our front in the direction of Belleau and Torcy and think counter-attack is on foot." Facing this were the 43rd, 51st, and 18th Companies, each of which "have about thirty men . . . lost," and the

55th Company, which, according to Neville's adjutant, had lost "about eighty-three. I can hardly believe the latter." Shortly after this message was sent, word came that Overton had beaten off a counterattack, and a prisoner reported the presence of an entire German division in the village of Belleau. When Wise apprised Harbord of the possible presence of the division, the general replied that artillery was "very watchful on your left flank." Therefore, Harbord advised, "You need have no fear of [the enemy division]." He went on to congratulate Wise on what he called "Your affair today," which he lauded as "certainly well handled and . . . the biggest thing in prisoners that the American Expeditionary Force had yet pulled off. We are all delighted."[15]

Harbord also advised Wise that "approximately 1,000 replacements" were arriving. Replacements were code-named "overshirts," and the marine companies that received them needed them badly yet looked upon them with a mixture of pity and contempt. They were babies. Certainly, their introduction to Belleau Wood was unceremonious enough. "At ten o'clock [on the night of June 11] we were given two boxes of hardtack and a double handful of prunes apiece . . . and started out," one of the replacements recalled. "There was no smoking and no talking." The overshirts passed through a deserted village and, traversing a woodcutter's path, started through the woods. "A few minutes later Heinie artillery started coming in. There was a flash and a roar from somewhere up ahead and I heard a man cry out. . . . There was a little group of marines in the brush alongside the path. A wounded man was groaning, 'Oh, Jesus! Jesus Christ! Oh, Jesus!' and I caught a glimpse of blood-stained bandages. My knees felt suddenly weak and I wanted to sit down. 'Move along there,' the sergeant growled, 'unless you want your Ma to stick a red star in her window.' . . . I guessed we were in Belleau Wood."[16]

In the meantime, Wise's personal reconnoitering had fully opened his eyes. "Do we hold the extreme point of the woods at this end?" he demanded of Captain Lester Wass.[17]

"No, sir, we don't. . . . There are a lot of Germans over in that northeast corner. We didn't have enough men to extend over there."[18]

Wise observed laconically: "There was a problem. The Germans were evidently in that point of wood in some force. Yet I didn't have the men to attack them. I knew now that over half of my battalion was gone. . . . God alone knew what minute the counter-attack was coming."[19]

Wise borrowed a company from Hughes's battalion and brought it up north to reinforce his thinly held position. Receiving Harbord's message to have no fear of the enemy battalion on his flank, Wise later wrote that he found "damned little satisfaction in that for me."[20] Wise later claimed that he began bombarding Harbord with reports of his severe casualties, but none of these messages survive in the 4th Brigade records. Whether or not Harbord read, heeded, or even received the messages is not known. What is clear from the documents that do exist is that as of the end of the day of June 11, Harbord was still reporting a successful attack that had put the marines in possession of Belleau Wood.

To the relief and surprise of Frederic Wise, the German counterattack did not materialize on June 11, and early on the morning of June 12, he returned to the front line to find that replacements had arrived and that engineers had done some serious digging in. The line was also "well sprinkled with machine guns now—our own and captured German weapons." Wise felt "much better satisfied" and recorded, "I wasn't afraid . . . of any break through." He then reported to a meeting with Harbord, Neville, and Feland. His confidence bolstered, he "expressed the opinion that with a certain amount of artillery preparation he could capture the remainder of the Bois de Belleau." Harbord jumped at the offer of another attack and quickly ordered an artillery barrage on the northwestern section of the woods "until 5 p.m. when an attack is to be made."[21]

It was as if Wise had suddenly become infected with the same impulsiveness that had moved General Joseph Degoutte to put the whole offensive into motion to begin with. Evidence of German reinforcement mounted. Wise's battalion had been seriously mauled, and although replacements had been brought in, they were raw recruits, untested in battle.

What moved Wise to order an attack under these conditions? Doubtless, he—with Harbord—was motivated by a desire to make good on all those premature reports of victory, reports that had gone beyond Bundy and had been published to the entire world. Yet, for the first time, the marines in the field did not share their commanders' enthusiasm. "We didn't want to make an attack," E. D. Cooke wrote later. "Hundreds of our men lay stiff in death already. A large part of our effectives were replacements." Worst of all, "the attack of the day before had left us low in morale and courage."[22]

At the very start, there was a major blunder. The artillery preparation began on time that afternoon, but it was directed ahead of the line Wise had *reported* he reached. That meant that the Franco-American shells fell not only a full thousand yards ahead of where the marines actually were but also well behind the current German positions as well. Wise contacted Neville, who sent a message to Harbord warning that the barrage had been ineffective. Harbord responded by prolonging the barrage, which, however, was still registered much too far north to be effective.

No thought was given to canceling or postponing the attack, which stepped off at 5:30 p.m. The Germans were well prepared. Cooke recalled that they "gave us all they had," including light machine guns firing from trees, heavy machine guns on the ground, hand grenades, rifles, pistols, "everything was turned loose at once." Cooke watched a Sergeant Brown in front of him, "bent nearly double, pulling his men forward with beckoning arms. A burst of bullets smashed into a man's jaw beside me, carrying away the lower part of his face. A grenade fell on the other side, tearing a youngster's legs to shreds."[23] Captain Dunbeck soon fell, wounded, his command assumed by Lieutenant Dink Milner, who had earned a reputation for his mild manners—until it came to fight. Then he turned into a marine.

From Cooke's description of the action, a reader nearly a century later can only assume that the marines, shot up and fatigued to begin with, were doomed against what were now highly reinforced enemy positions. But at Belleau Wood, the marines did not behave like ordinary soldiers. Facing a stream of hot lead and a torrent of jagged steel, their comrades dropping at their sides, they seemed to take rather than lose heart. The slaughter was like meat to a starving beast. Even as the enemy fire whittled them down, the remaining marines charged forward and in less than half an hour overran the advance positions of the enemy, dropping into position to take out the heavy machine guns. This required killing the men who protected the guns, infantry riflemen on the ground and light machine gunners camouflaged in trees. Such combat was hand to hand—a style of fighting at which the marines excelled—but to get close enough to grapple with the enemy, there was yet more fire to face. "One of my lieutenants went down, writhing and clawing at his face," Cooke recalled, "begging to be gotten out of there. A sergeant ducked behind the tree next to mine just as a bullet hit and exploded the canteen on his belt. We both thought we were drenched with blood." The Germans seemed unable to believe the willingness and capacity of the marines to wade into them. To Cooke's left, "a group of gray-clad figures got up like a covey of frightened quail. Big, husky Huns, running over the ploughed ground with stilted awkwardness in their heavy boots." Cooke confessed to staring at them, stupefied, his mouth gaping. But in an instant, "clawing out my automatic, I let go an entire clip at their retreating backs." Cooke's whole company "discharged a scattered volley" at them, but "never hit a damn one!" Elsewhere, to the right, a sergeant of the 18th Company ran up the side of a rocky cliff, going "after a machine gun, like a cat chasing birds on a tin roof" while Captain Wass chased "a frightened Heinie over a pile of cordwood." Cooke appreciated the transformation that was before him: "Fear, hunger, fatigue—everything seemed forgotten in a mad lust to ram two feet of steel into some Heinie's innards." The lust carried Cooke along "much against my better judgment. . . . The hot blast of guns beat against our faces, grenades curved over our heads, underbrush and men dying clogged our feet. . . . The Boche . . . slipped into the underbrush and [ran] . . . [with] scattered remnants of our battalion . . . hot in pursuit."[24]

In terms of organization, the marine attack had fallen apart, but the marines themselves, more as men enraged than as disciplined soldiers, kept surging forward. When they encountered heavier German fire, they spread out even wider, becoming much less a cohesive force yet never letting up on the forward momentum. The attack on Belleau Wood had become a mob action, and the Germans, overwhelmed by a sheer, raw ferocity that apparently knew no discipline and that was beyond anyone's commanding, either ran or surrendered, hurling down weapons, throwing hands into the air, yelling, pleading, crying "Kamerad! Kamerad!"

As a military operation, the marine attack into the reinforced northern tract of Belleau Wood had been a failure. Losses were heavy, discipline nonexistent. Yet Hartlieb's left, reinforced though it was, had been forced out of the woods. At 8:30 p.m., June 12, Wise's ragged marines began to emerge from the northeastern edge of Belleau Wood. It looked as if Wise had made good on his earlier message to Harbord. Maybe the headlines were at last backed by reality.

Lieutenant Milner of the 43rd Company offered a wounded German officer that currency of universal value, an American cigarette. The officer, who had just surrendered with his men, spoke halting English. He asked Milner to give him a guide to take him and his forty-two men to the rear to surrender. Doubtless in some embarrassment, Milner explained that he did not know where his battalion headquarters was. Much better oriented, the German officer gave Milner his bearings, then, seemingly in a spirit of gratuitous comradeship, warned Milner that a counterattack was in the works. Dink Milner communicated this information to Wise, who passed it on to Harbord, identifying the wounded officer as a "dying German officer," thereby giving the information the credibility of what lawyers call a "dying declaration."

According to the officer, a fresh German division was to attack that very night. Wise accordingly called for artillery. He assured Harbord, "We are in full spirits" but closed with the news that he had "now 350 old men left and seven officers. They are shelling very heavy."[25]

It was the continuous shelling even more than the "dying declaration" of a German officer that persuaded the marines of the imminence of a major counterattack. The Germans were calling it Uberseefahrt—Operation Overseas Voyage—and it was to take place all along the entire American front, including Belleau Wood, Bouresches, and the army's (3rd Brigade) positions south of the Metz-Paris highway. While waiting for it, men crouched in the holes they had dug, some big enough to stretch out in, some even improved with straw to serve as beds. They talked with one another, they cleaned their equipment, they read the letters from home they had tucked into their pockets.

At 1:00 a.m. on June 13, the tempo of the shelling increased, and for the next two hours, Berton Sibley's battalion—now shifted to the left, just west of Belleau Wood, in preparation for dealing with the counterattack—and the battalions of Wise and Hughes in the woods, as well as that of Major Maurice Shearer garrisoning Bouresches, all fell under heavy bombardment. Artillery batteries from three German divisions joined in. It was the heaviest enemy barrage of the Belleau Wood battle. Many of the shells were big 150s and giant 210-millimeter trench mortar rounds. In Hughes's battalion alone, casualties from the barrage topped 20 percent. Those who survived in all the battalions were essentially deaf, certainly shaken, deprived of sleep, and angry. Very angry.

A sudden diminuendo of the German barrage signaled a change from harassing and neutralizing fire to rolling fire, the kind that moves ahead of an attack. That came at 3:00 a.m., but to the surprise of the marines, the counterattack fell most heavily not on Belleau Wood but on Bouresches— by the 109th Grenadiers and 40th Fusiliers, both units of the celebrated (but battle-weary) 28th Infantry Division.

Attacking from the south, the grenadiers overran several marine positions, including farmhouses and the ruins of the village church. The marines consolidated their defense behind barricades in the streets of the little village and, thus lodged, refused to be dislodged. They proved as fierce in the defense as they had been in the attack. The grenadiers and the marines alike held their ground, the grenadiers knowing that the 40th Fusiliers were to attack from the east and north, thereby enveloping the marine position. All they had to do was wait.

That attack, however, did not materialize. Marine machine gunners and light artillery pounded the 40th, forcing it into retreat. By 9:30 on the morning of June 13, the German attack on Bouresches was called off. Yielding their hard-won ground, the grenadiers limped out of the village.

Things had quieted in Belleau Wood as well, although Hughes's battalion—in the woods but closest to the action in Bouresches—had been mauled badly. In the northwest corner of Belleau Wood, the German 237th Division consolidated what it held. As for the marines, "Lines appear to be holding," Wise reported, adding that "losses must be very heavy." But, while the Germans also held, the anticipated counterattack in this sector had never been launched. That fact gave some comfort but not very much. None of the marines—not Wise, not his company commanders, and not General Harbord—were repeating the assumptions of the days just passed. Belleau Wood did not yet belong to them, and they knew it.

▪ 15 ▪

Bois de la Brigade de Marine

B y June 13, reality percolated up, even to the highest levels of command. Major General Omar Bundy, commanding the U.S. 2nd Division, sought to give his marines and soldiers a chance to reorganize by shortening the sector the 2nd Division was responsible for. He arranged for the French 167th Division to take over part of the line on the left (north), and he bolstered the marines holding Bouresches by moving the U.S. Army's 23rd Regiment into the village. General Harbord decided to relieve Wise's battered battalion with Holcomb's more rested men. The relief was to take place on the night of June 13, and in preparation at about 5:00 p.m., Major Thomas Holcomb went forward to meet with Wise and inspect his battalion's position. With his visitor in tow, Wise ventured out of his command post, he later wrote, "on the same route I took in my regular morning inspection." At that very moment, the "Germans cut loose with a bombardment." By that time, Wise had a connoisseur's ear and could easily identify among the incoming ordnance of 155s, 77s, and Austrian 88s—the whizbangs. "Great masses of earth and roots, of limbs and fragments of trunks, mixed with shell-fragments themselves, began to fly through the air. The din was deafening—a solid, continuous roar." Holcomb looked at the commander he had been assigned to relieve: "Is this celebration due to my arrival?"[1]

It was an example of the dry gallows humor born of Belleau Wood. At that, Wise neatly topped it with his response: "No . . . This is only routine."[2]

The shelling continued through the evening and into the night. Holcomb's men were alerted to move out to relieve Wise's battalion beginning at midnight. Lieutenant Clifton Cates was in command of one of Holcomb's companies. His outfit was in foxholes in a thick, forested patch on a hillside near Belleau Wood. German artillery was shelling on the marines' front and right. Just before zero hour, Cates crawled out of his foxhole, ready to lead his men toward their new position. "I had not gone over twenty feet from my fox hole," he wrote, "when I heard a salvo of shells heading our way." Like Wise—like any marine who had survived long enough to be called a veteran of the Battle of Belleau Wood—Cates had developed a fine ear for incoming rounds. "From the whistle I thought they were gas shells." When they "hit with a thud and no detonation my fears were confirmed. Soon I smelled the gas, and I gave the alarm to the men, and they all put on their masks." There was by this time "a steady stream of incoming shells—gas, air bursts, shrapnel, and high explosives. I reached for my gas mask, but it wasn't there. Naturally, I was petrified."[3]

As the corrosive mustard gas began to singe his nose, throat, and eyes, Cates fought back the panic. The mask—it *had* to be in his foxhole. But where was his foxhole? Amid the din and smoke of the incoming shells, Cates was thoroughly disoriented. The thought suddenly crossed his mind that Private Hall, one of his men, had earlier picked up a German mask as a souvenir of war. That seemed now his only hope. Cates crawled through the woods, which was exploding above and around him. He called out, "*Hall! Hall!*" over and over again.

At length, there was a muffled response and a half-pronounced sentence: "Here I am, over here. What do you . . ."[4]

Cates jumped into Hall's foxhole, seized the captured mask, and clapped it to his face.

The gas component of the German barrage consisted of seven thousand mustard gas shells combined with about two thousand high-explosive shells containing 10 percent diphenylamine, a major active ingredient in Adamsite, a gas originally developed in 1913 and designed to induce uncontrollable vomiting and sneezing. It was a diabolical combination. Propelled by the high explosives, the sneezing-vomiting agent dispersed into the air just before the heavier mustard agent did. Those who had not yet put on their masks began retching, vomiting, and sneezing too violently to get their masks over their heads. Breathing convulsively, they drank in the mustard, drawing it deeply into their lungs. Mustard gas was not a gas at all, but an aerosolized liquid, what physicians call a vesicant, a chemical that burns and blisters human tissue on contact, especially the mucosa—the membranes of the nose, throat, and lungs. In a lung filled with mustard, the chemical reacted with the moisture in that organ, churning it into a burned cud. Men literally coughed up their lungs and drowned in their own semi-liquefied tissue. Some of the marines who had managed to put on their masks tore at them frantically as the retching began. The experienced hands around them wrestled with them, forcing them to keep the masks on. Better to inhale one's own vomit than a deep draft of mustard.

The gas had caught the battalion unawares. There was a mixture of panic and heroism, as when Gunnery Sergeant Fred Stockham removed his own mask from his face and put it over the mouth and nose of a wounded marine, then, heedless of his own safety, went on to help more of the wounded before collapsing. He died in a field hospital a few days later and, posthumously, received the Medal of Honor.

Heroism was possible under such an attack, but not glory. The devastating effectiveness of the bombardment revealed just how green most of the marines—many of them newly arrived replacements—were. They had been given little training in defense against gas, and most of them in the panic, the darkness, and the confusion, forgot what little they had been taught. Many failed to put on their masks. Others put them on too late. Still others fumbled and put them on incorrectly. After the attack, most of the marines failed to follow through with the protocol for mustard gas. Because it was a liquid, a heavy liquid at that, the mustard agent clung to everything it came into contact with, soaking into clothing and hair. Troops were instructed to strip and rinse their bodies as thoroughly as possible with soap and water. Uniforms could not be washed in the field, but the next best thing was to beat the fumes and droplets out of them, letting the agent evaporate in the air. Those who failed to do these things—and most failed to—received slow, severe, blistering burns over many parts of their bodies. These were as disabling as any other wound.

Military historians typically minimize the overall effectiveness of poison gas in World War I, invariably concluding that it was not a "decisive" weapon. This was generally true, but what is "nondecisive" in general can nevertheless be devastating in a particular case. The night of June 13–14 was one of those cases. The bombardment did not kill a large number of marines, but it disabled many, taking them out of the battle. The purpose of gas was never to kill masses of men—at least not directly—but rather to create panic and to tie up resources by creating casualties that had to be attended to. Even those who managed to get their gas masks on and who avoided injury, disability, or death were rendered less effective by the very fact of having to wear the mask. Cumbersome and suffocating, the gas masks of the day greatly reduced the fighting man's ability to move and to see—especially at night.

Holcomb advanced to Wise with eight hundred men. The gas attack reduced his effectives to fewer than three hundred. Wise reported to Harbord: "I did not consider that they were sufficient to relieve me, and remained in position." Two more gas barrages fell, on June 14 and 15. In total, the attacks inflicted about eight hundred marine casualties in and around Belleau Wood, including Major John Hughes, who had been temporarily but totally blinded. Although Wise informed Harbord that he was remaining in place, he also advised him that his "men [were] physically unable to make another attack." As a result of a fresh reconnaissance, Wise also reported that he considered his "present line unsafe unless whole woods are in our possession." He did not have enough troops to take the whole woods, he reported, let alone hold the woods once taken. Accordingly, Wise requested "permission to withdraw slightly to make the line safer" and also requested that "Holcomb be given more men as many of them here have had gas."[5]

At the moment, Harbord had no men to give Holcomb, and he could not give Wise permission to withdraw either. "Regret necessity of having to put your fine battalion in again with so little rest, and when so many have been gassed," Harbord replied to Wise, "but do it with perfect confidence that you and they can be depended upon under adverse circumstances."[6]

Brigadier General James C. Harbord had learned to love his marines. That much was evident in his response to an impromptu ceremony that took place in the midst of the latest crisis in Belleau Wood. Wendell Neville greeted Harbord when the general came calling at his battalion headquarters. During the visit, he handed Harbord a pair of eagle-anchor-globe collar insignia.

"Here," Neville said. "We think it is about time you put these on."[7]

Neville pinned them on and said he thought that Harbord—who was already sufficiently unconventional about matters of uniform to wear a French Adrian, or "coal-scuttle," helmet in preference to the army regulation British-style wash basin—later said that he "wore those Marine Corps devices until after [he] became a Major General." Harbord explained further: "No officer can fail to understand what that little recognition meant to me, an Army officer commanding troops of a sister service in battle. It seemed to me to set the seal of approval by my comrades of the Marines Corps, and knowing the circumstances, it meant everything to me."[8]

Harbord never lost faith in his marines, but he had lost faith in Frederic Wise. Shortly after assuring him of his "perfect confidence," Harbord sent Logan Feland, Neville's second in command, to relieve Wise as overall commander of the defense of Belleau Wood. Meeting with Wise, Feland pulled no punches: "General Harbord is sore as hell because you didn't clean out the wood." Wearily, Wise responded, "We've done the best we could." He explained that in the original attack—when his battalion entered Belleau Wood too far to the right (south)—his men had "naturally drifted toward" the machine-gun fire they were drawing from the right in order to "take the machine guns in that sector." Having drifted in this way, the simple fact was, "[They] . . . didn't have enough men to cover the whole front." Perhaps to fend off a charge that he had not tried hard enough, Wise told Feland, "More than half the battalion are casualties now. I've got one captain left." With that, he turned the show over to his replacement: "Now you know where we stand. You've got a map. You can read it as well as I can."[9]

Feland did not rely on a map, but made a personal tour of inspection and accepted the advice of company commanders that an attack could be made in order to push through to the left of Wise's position and seal off the northern part of Belleau Wood, thereby preventing further German infiltration attacks. When Neville disagreed with this approach, Feland responded not by arguing but by asking to be relieved of the command he had just been given. That was sufficient to change Neville's mind. He agreed, and a company of the 5th Marine Regiment, well supported by heavy machine-gun fire, attacked on the morning of June 15, penetrating the northern part of the woods along its western face. By 8:00 a.m., the north was sealed off—at least for the moment. Feland next scrambled to consolidate what he had gained, but his forces were depleted, and even many of those who had not been evacuated were nevertheless weakened by the effects of the gas attacks.

Fortunately for Logan Feland and his marines, 2nd Division commander Omar Bundy had been engaging tirelessly in a military campaign of his own. He had laid siege to General Joseph Degoutte, urging him to release French relief for the entire marine brigade. In the middle of this siege, however, Degoutte was kicked upstairs to assume command of the whole French Sixth Army and was succeeded as corps commander by General Stanislaus Naulin, who stood his ground. He would give the Americans nothing more than the French 167th Division and suggested that Bundy draw relief from his own U.S. Army's 3rd Brigade. Bundy deemed this out of the question because the 3rd Brigade already had its hands full defending its own sector. At this point, Bundy's chief of staff, Preston Brown, acted on a brainstorm, arguing that the French were not making much use of the

U.S. Army's 7th Infantry Regiment. Why not "lend" it to reinforce the marines at Belleau Wood? Naulin objected to removing the 7th Infantry Regiment from French control. But now it was Bundy's turn to stand *his* ground. He more or less politely told the French general that, if the 7th were not yielded to him, he, as senior American officer in the area, would assume command of all U.S. troops in the entire sector. Naulin immediately agreed to transfer the 7th Infantry Regiment to the U.S. 2nd Division.

No time was wasted in getting the men of the fresh army regiment into position to bolster Feland's new line. During the night of June 15, Wise's battalion was relieved. Judging from Lieutenant E. D. Cooke's recollections, the relief came in the proverbial nick of time. "My nerves were completely shot," he wrote. "I cowered in a foxhole at the sound of every shell and cringed at any unexpected noise. If a man had suddenly yelled in my ear I'd have probably shot him dead." As they were relieved, the men of the battalion "kept no formation. Each man simply followed the one in front. No one was going to let himself be left behind. We wanted to hurry but our legs acted as though gripped by an undertow." Shortly after dawn on June 16, Wise and his only remaining captain, Lester Wass, assembled the remnant of the battalion near a farmhouse. Wise wrote: "It was enough to break your heart. I had left . . . on May 31 with 965 men and 26 officers. Now, before me, stood 350 men and 6 officers." A short time later, when Wise's wife, who was in Paris, asked him "How are the Marines?" Wise could think of only one reply: "There aren't any more Marines."[10]

Devastated though he was, the battalion commander was also filled with pride. He knew that for "17 days [these men] hadn't had a cup of hot coffee or a bite of hot food. They hadn't taken off their shoes. They hadn't had a chance to wash their faces." Nevertheless, "they had driven trained German veterans out of fortified positions by frontal attack; had walked into the fiercest kind of woods fighting in France; had taken nearly twice their own number in German prisoners and captured more than 50 machine guns. . . . They had made a record never surpassed in the war."[11]

■ ■ ■

Relieved of command at Belleau Wood, Frederic Wise was understandably anxious that all he and his marines had done, suffered, and sacrificed should add up to victory. Everything Wise wrote about his battalion's record at Belleau Wood was true—as far as it went. As far as it went, he and his marines had achieved victory—*a* victory. Belleau Wood had belonged to the German army. Now, it no longer belonged to them. But neither was it yet the property of the U.S. Marines. Like any other disputed ground lying between opposing lines, Belleau Wood could now most accurately be designated as no-man's-land.

"Honest," Clifton Cates wrote in a letter home on June 18, "when I look out at the few men left I really cry—I am the only officer out of two companies and I am in charge of the remains of both companies—one good platoon. I didn't realize how I loved the old bunch until it had been broken up."[12]

Wise—and all the others up to now—had made a down payment on the former hunting preserve. The cost had been exorbitant, but it was still no more than a down payment.

That is not how Logan Feland saw it. He believed that much more had been accomplished, and he judged that enemy resistance in Belleau Wood as of June 16 consisted of just "forty or sixty Germans with several machine guns" positioned on "a small knoll in the western part of the north end of the wood."[13] As usual, this was a significant underestimate of remaining German strength in Belleau Wood. Worst of all, contrary to what Feland believed, the enemy was not cut off and isolated within the woods. The defenders were still tied in with larger German forces to the northeast. But their long engagement in this sector had bled all German forces and had worn them down. The German ranks were thinned by death and by wounds, as well as by malnutrition and exhaustion, both of which made the soldiers vulnerable to so-called Spanish influenza, the disease that before the year was out would assume the proportions of a global pandemic. By the third week in June, when the Americans were planning a final push to clean out Belleau Wood once and for all, the ground was being defended by sick and tired men who had been there since the end of May and also by comparatively fresh troops, brought in, unknown to the marines, via the north.

As for the unit that relieved Wise's battalion, it too was fresh. In fact, the U.S. 7th Infantry was "unblooded"—had yet to see combat. Writing about the relief of the marine battalion, Clifton Cates observed that the untested army unit had been put in "a tough spot . . . for [its] first baptism of fire. I felt sorry for them last night when they came in," especially because no sooner had they arrived than "all hell broke loose. The Boche in our rear started firing, then our men returned it, the Germans to our front started firing, we answered, then both their artillery and ours opened up." It was, Cates conceded, "a madhouse. Imagine the poor Army boys that have not been under fire before."[14]

A battalion of the 7th Infantry made an abortive attack on June 20, but the green soldiers became disoriented, and the attack failed miserably. The confusion of the untested troops and their officers was increased by English-speaking Germans who donned American uniforms and infiltrated the infantry's lines.

Harbord attributed the failure of the attack entirely to the inexperience of the 7th's officers. He refused to consider that Belleau Wood was held by anything larger than a very small band of German die-hard defenders. He therefore ordered the 3rd Battalion, 5th Marines, now under the command of Major Maurice Shearer—Major Berry having been evacuated—to relieve the 7th Regiment battalion on the night of June 21. Harbord instructed Shearer to use snipers to "reduce the German positions without much expenditure of men" and to proceed with "wiring-up" the east and north of Belleau Wood—that is, constructing a trench line defended by barbed wire to further contain the remaining Germans so that they could be more readily extirpated. Harbord told Shearer that it was "not practicable to withdraw" his troops in order that "further artillery preparation" could be made. In other words, no artillery support would be provided.[15]

Shortly after General Harbord issued his orders to Shearer, interrogators learned from a German deserter that German troops still held all of the northern end of Belleau Wood. On June 22, Logan Feland corroborated this with his personal reconnaissance. Shocked by this information, Harbord reported to General Bundy that "undoubtedly the Germans have access to that part of the woods, and have been free to come and go." He continued, defensively: "The undersigned has been misled as to affairs in that end of the woods, either consciously or unconsciously, ever since its first occupation by the battalion under command of Lieutenant Colonel Wise and later by the battalion of the 7th Infantry." Doubtless, Harbord really did feel put upon, but accusing his subordinates of misleading him was, at the very least, unbecoming. Even worse, although it was now apparent that the infantry tactics he proposed that Shearer employ would be insufficient to envelop a large German position in the northern part of the woods, Harbord insisted that Shearer nevertheless make the attack as planned—without reinforcement and without artillery preparation.

The attack began at 7:00 p.m. on June 23 over ground so rocky that the marines could not even dig in. From the start, it was a catastrophe. The marines were once again cut up by machine-gun nests placed such that each was covered by the crossfire of at least two others. In under three hours, one hundred thirty marines had fallen, and progress was minimal. Lieutenant Laurence Stallings led a supporting platoon of the 47th Company. As a supporting outfit, his platoon's job was to "plug gaps"—that is, to supply men to take the place of those in the front line who were killed or wounded. This meant crawling, under machine-gun fire, past or over the dead and wounded almost as soon as they were hit. "The cries of men as blood drained from them and they lost self-control were almost not to be endured," Stallings wrote. Worse, the officers—such as himself—were forced to restrain "men who wished to administer first aid." Doing so would delay their plugging the gap; therefore, the officers "hazed the kindhearted into gaps littered with corpses." Thus hazed, the men crawled "forward hugging the ground, the blood of other men on their sleeves, their hands, their faces." Stallings wrote: "This last failure in Belleau Wood would be remembered by some as the worst afternoon of their lives no matter what fortune later befell them."[16]

(Stallings left one of his legs at Belleau Wood, but he did indeed carry that afternoon with him throughout his life, and he would spend a significant part of his life putting it and his other war memories on paper, on stage, and on film, beginning with an autobiographical novel titled *Plume* and then its silent screen version, director King Vidor's 1925 *The Big Parade*. With the playwright Maxwell Anderson, Stallings would write the Broadway dramatic hit *What Price Glory?* which was made into a silent film directed by Raoul Walsh in 1926 and remade by John Ford in 1952.)

Shearer broke off the attack and reported to Harbord that "the enemy seems to have unlimited alternate gun positions and many guns. Each gun position covered by others. I know of no other way of attacking these positions ... and am of opinion that infantry alone cannot dislodge enemy guns."[17]

To Harbord's great credit, he took Shearer's "opinion" to heart, and on June 24 met with Bundy and the marine commanders in addition to General William Chamberlaine, the 2d Division's artillery commander. If infantry alone could not do the job, then artillery would be called in after all. Moreover, it would be a massive barrage using American as well as French guns and lasting from three in the morning on June 25 until five in the afternoon. At that point, the artillery preparation would become a rolling barrage in the lead of a new advance by Shearer's marines. Harbord and the others were betting that fourteen hours of artillery fire directed not over the whole woods but concentrated on a target only two hundred yards across would kill, wound, or simply stun enough of the enemy to allow the marines, at long last, to claim Belleau Wood.

Although they had been shredded in their previous attack, Shearer's marines embarked on the attack of June 25 in high spirits. Thwarted and hurt earlier, they fought "like a bunch of wild cats" now.[18] The artillery barrage had indeed taken a terrible toll on the German defenders of Belleau Wood, and what is more, it had thoroughly intimidated the divisional commanders above them. Higher German headquarters now refused to commit major reserves to reinforce faltering positions in the woods. Everywhere, the enemy began surrendering. Yet the terrain of Belleau Wood kept each German unit out of the sight of others. On an open battlefield, one unit would have seen another surrender and most likely joined that action. In the tangle of the woods, comrades were cut off from one another. The surrender of one position did not induce the surrender of another. Fighting, therefore, continued from position to position, all through the night of June 25–26. By first light, the marines at last neared the northernmost margin of Belleau Wood. They passed through what had been the most strongly held German positions, positions manned now only by the blasted remnants of mangled torsos. At around 7:00 a.m., Shearer sent Harbord a simple message: "Belleau Woods now U.S. Marine Corps entirely."[19]

There was mopping up to be done, and men would still be killed on both sides near Belleau Wood, but this patch of ruined ground was no longer no-man's-land. It had been won.

On June 30, General Harbord proudly published an order issued by French Sixth Army commander General Joseph Degoutte:

> In view of the brilliant conduct of the 4th Brigade of the 2d U.S. Division, which in a spirited fight took Bouresches and the important strong point of Bois de Belleau, stubbornly defended by a large enemy force, the General commanding the VIth Army orders that henceforth, in all official papers, the Bois de Belleau shall be named "Bois de la Brigade de Marine."[20]

General Pershing was not happy about all the attention lavished on the marines. When France's premier, Georges Clemenceau, visited 2nd Division headquarters, no marine commanders were invited—including the army's own marine commander, James Harbord. Army high command even tried—without success—to cancel Degoutte's order conferring the new name on Belleau Wood. When that attempt failed, high command saw to it after the armistice that the Battle of Belleau Wood was entered into the combat history of the AEF as nothing more than a local engagement, not a battle in itself, but only a phase of the defense of the Aisne-Marne sector.

General Robert Lee Bullard, as we have already noted, denigrated the achievement of the marines in his 1925 *Personalities and Reminiscences of the War*, but his book has long been forgotten, along with the official army designation of the battle. Army General Harbord, in his war diary, published immediately after the war, refused to slight the marines he had been assigned to command. "The effect [of the marine action at Belleau Wood] on the French has been many times out of all proportion to the size of our brigade or the front on which it has operated. . . . They say a Marine can't venture down the boulevards of Paris without risk of being kissed by some casual passerby or some *boulevardière*. Frenchmen say that the stand of the Marine Brigade in its far-reaching effects marks one of the great crises of history, and there is no doubt they feel it." As for his own feelings, Harbord resorted to a most unmilitary three exclamation points: "What shall I say of the gallantry with which these marines have fought!!!" He continued: "I cannot write of their splendid gallantry without tears coming to my eyes. There has never been anything better in the world."[21]

In truth, it is difficult to calculate the significance of the Battle of Belleau Wood. General Tasker Bliss told Pershing that he believed the battle had "stopped the German drive and very possibly saved Paris"—something the French had no doubt about. In 1936, General Bullard himself offered this assessment: "The marines didn't 'win the war' here, but they saved the Allies from defeat. Had they arrived a few hours later I think that would have been the beginning of the end." Yet, years later, no less a figure than General Matthew Ridgway thought Belleau Wood should be added to the tragic gallery of "prize examples of men's lives being thrown away against objectives not worth the cost." Belleau Wood, he said, was "a monument, for all time, to the inflexibility of military thinking in that period."[22]

Was Belleau Wood worth winning? Those present thought it was, that as a "natural fortress," it was just too dangerous to leave it in German hands. But did winning it demand the sacrifice of so many marines?

Probably not.

As we have seen, artillery bombardment alone was not always effective in a densely wooded area, but an intensive bombardment with mustard gas might well have gone a long way to clearing the woods of the enemy *before* the marines were sent in.

But that, of course, would have required planning—and General Joseph Degoutte's impulsive decision to shift from a defensive to an offensive posture precluded virtually all planning. Once the marines were committed to taking the objective—this patch of old hunting preserve, a kidney-shaped forest maintained for the amusement of the idle rich—they could not bring themselves to surrender the attempt. The initial defense of the Belleau Wood sector almost certainly saved Paris; however, the offensive attack on Belleau Wood that followed probably did no such thing. It was at that point a psychological objective, symbolic in import, an item of currency, as it were, rather than of intrinsic value. Or, rather, its value was directly proportional to the number of lives each side was willing to spend on it.

In those terms, it was a most valuable prize. Between June 1 and July 10, the 2nd U.S. Division gave up 217 casualties among its officers and 9,560 among its enlisted ranks. The 4th Marine Brigade alone lost 126 officers and 5,057 men killed or wounded. German losses in and around Belleau Wood are more difficult to calculate, but they were doubtless even higher.

For the U.S. Marine Corps, this investment in blood has never been subject to question or controversy. It was a mission. That in itself is all that really matters. Beyond this, however, it was a test of American military capacity and American character, and the marines felt fortunate that they were given the responsibility for taking and passing this test.

"How are the Marines?" the wife of Lieutenant Colonel Wise had asked after the battle.

"There aren't any more Marines," Wise replied.

And so it must have seemed to one who had lived through the thick of the fight and saw the fall of so many he commanded there. Yet in the hell of Belleau Wood the Corps did not die. The reputation of the marines as America's fiercest warriors, the nation's elite fighting force, was forged in this battle. After Belleau Wood, the marines claimed the right to be regarded as the American vanguard, the first to fight, and if necessary the last to leave. The Marine Corps emerged from Belleau Wood in possession of a legend unlike any the army or navy could claim. That legend would animate the Corps through the next world war and through the wars in Korea, Vietnam, and Iraq.

The Battle of Belleau Wood was a very small part of a Great War fought with the weapons of modern industrial technologies and driven by the political motives of modern industrial economies. Such weapons and such motives produced death on an industrial scale—massive and anonymous—and yet the combat at Belleau Wood endowed the marines with a warrior legend that seems to come from some age distant from our own, perhaps even from some other people, certainly not from a modern industrial nation founded on the principles of rational democracy. Those who fought at Belleau Wood, like those who would fight later at Tarawa and Iwo Jima, at Pork Chop Hill, at Khe Sanh, and at Fallujah, seemed closer to the Spartans at Thermopylae than to their fellow Americans of 1918, 1943, 1945, 1953, 1968, or 2004. Certainly, since that combat in a French forest named for the spring that still flows beside it—clear, cold, pure—the marines, though bound in service to America, have been universally seen for what they are: a band apart.

▪ Notes ▪

INTRODUCTION: A PATCH OF WOODS

[1] Albertus W. Catlin, *"With the Help of God and a Few Marines"* (1919; repr., Nashville, TN: The Battery Press, 2004), p. 4.

[2] Catlin, *"With the Help of God,"* p. 4.

[3] The following account of the beginning of World War I, including the military plans of the major combatants and all quotations from original sources, is drawn from Alan Axelrod, *America's Wars* (New York: Wiley, 2002), pp. 369–71; Alan Axelrod, *The Complete Idiot's Guide to World War I* (Indianapolis: Alpha Books, 2000), pp. 29–40, pp. 47–50, and pp. 53–56; and Barbara Tuchman, *The Guns of August* (1962; repr., New York: Ballantine, 1994), pp. 17–55.

[4] The following account of the United States' shift from neutrality to involvement in World War I, including all quotations from original sources, is drawn from Alan Axelrod, *Political History of America's Wars* (Washington, DC: CQ Press, 2007), pp. 356–61.

CHAPTER 1: BELLHOPS AND STEVEDORES

[1] Allan R. Millett, *Semper Fidelis: The History of the United States Marine Corps* (New York: Free Press, 1991), p. 139.

[2] Millett, *Semper Fidelis*, p. 140.

[3] Charles Reginald Shrader, ed., *Reference Guide to United States Military History 1865–1919* (New York: Facts on File, 1993), p. 98.

[4] Millett, *Semper Fidelis*, p. 293.

[5] Richard Suskind, *The Battle of Belleau Wood: The Marines Stand Fast* (New York: Macmillan, 1969), p. 28.

[6] United States Marine Corps, "Major Albertus W. Catlin, Medal of Honor 1914, Vera Cruz," at http://www.usmc.mil/moh.nsf/0/000003c919889c0385255fa200626e80? OpenDocument (accessed January 25, 2007).

[7] Blake's comments are cited in Millett, *Semper Fidelis*, p. 708, n. 9; Catlin, *"With the Help of God,"* p. 19.

[8] Kemper F. Cowing, comp., and Courtney Riley Cooper, ed., *"Dear Folks at Home—": The Glorious Story of the United States Marines in France as Told by Their Letters from the Battlefield* (New York: Houghton Mifflin, 1919), quoted in Robert B. Asprey, *At Belleau Wood* (1965; repr., Denton: University of North Texas Press, 1996), p. 15.

[9] Millett, *Semper Fidelis*, p. 709, n. 26.

CHAPTER 2: "A QUIET SECTOR"

[1] First World War, "Sir Douglas Haig's 'Backs to the Wall' Order, 11 April 1918," http://www.firstworldwar.com/source/backstothewall.htm (accessed January 25, 2007).

[2] Catlin, *"With the Help of God,"* p. 101.

[3] W. A. Carter, *The Tale of a Devil Dog* (Washington, DC: Canteen Press, 1920), quoted in Asprey, *At Belleau Wood*, p. 20.

[4] Interview with General Lemuel C. Shepherd, Asprey, *At Belleau Wood*, p. 21.

[5] G. S. Vireck, *As They Saw Us* (New York: Doubleday, Doran, 1929), quoted in Asprey, *At Belleau Wood*, p. 24.

[6] Report of Paul H. Clark to John J. Pershing, May 1918, Papers of Paul Hedrick Clark, 1918–1922, Library of Congress, quoted in Asprey, *At Belleau Wood*, pp. 48–49.

[7] S. T. Hubbard, *Memoirs of a Staff Officer 1917–1919* (Tuckahoe, NY: Cardinal Associates, 1959), quoted in Asprey, *At Belleau Wood*, p. 49.

[8] Report of Paul H. Clark to John J. Pershing, May 1918, Papers of Paul Hedrick Clark, Library of Congress, quoted in Asprey, *At Belleau Wood*, p. 55.

[9] John J. Pershing, *My Experiences in the World War*, vol. 2 (New York: Frederick A. Stokes, 1931), p. 224.

[10] Suskind, *The Battle of Belleau Wood*, p. 3.

Chapter 3: Orders

1 Catlin, *"With the Help of God,"* p. 73.

2 Catlin, *"With the Help of God,"* p. 73.

3 Catlin, *"With the Help of God,"* pp. 67–68.

4 "Decoration Day" was officially proclaimed on May 5, 1868, by General John Logan, national commander of the Grand Army of the Republic, to honor the Civil War dead, in part by decorating soldiers' graves with flowers. "Memorial Day" was first used in place of "Decoration Day" in 1882, but it was not commonly employed until after World War II. In 1967, federal law made Memorial Day the holiday's official name.

5 James C. Harbord, *Leaves from a War Diary* (New York: Dodd, Mead, 1925), pp. 281, 284–85.

6 Fielding S. Robinson to Asprey, quoted in Asprey, *At Belleau Wood*, p. 63.

7 Interview with Shepherd, Asprey, *At Belleau Wood*, p. 63; Harbord, *Leaves from a War Diary*, p. 285.

8 Catlin, *"With the Help of God,"* p. 14.

9 Catlin, *"With the Help of God,"* pp. 15, 80.

10 Major E. D. Cooke, "We Can Take It," *Infantry Journal*, May–December 1937, quoted in Asprey, *At Belleau Wood*, p. 65.

11 Catlin, *"With the Help of God,"* p. 81; Harbord, *Leaves from a War Diary*, p. 288.

12 Catlin, *"With the Help of God,"* p. 81.

13 Harbord, *Leaves from a War Diary*, pp. 288–89.

14 James G. Harbord, *The American Army in France, 1917–1919* (Boston: Little, Brown, 1936), p. 276.

15 Harbord, *Leaves from a War Diary*, pp. 289–90.

16 Harbord, *Leaves from a War Diary*, pp. 289–90; Cooke, "We Can Take It," quoted in Asprey, *At Belleau Wood*, pp. 76–77.

17 Catlin, *"With the Help of God,"* p. 82.

18 Catlin, *"With the Help of God,"* pp. 82–83.

19 Catlin, *"With the Help of God,"* p. 84.

20 Harbord, *The American Army in France*, p. 281.

21 Oliver L. Spaulding and John W. Wright, *The Second Division American Expeditionary Force in France, 1917–1918* (New York: Hillman Press, 1937), quoted in Asprey, *At Belleau Wood*, p. 89.

CHAPTER 4: IN THIS LINE

1 U.S. Army, *Translations, War Diaries of German Units Opposed to the Second Division (Regular), 1918*, vol. 1, *Château Thierry* (Washington, DC: Army War College, 1930–1932), quoted in Asprey, *At Belleau Wood*, p. 82.

2 Harbord, *The American Army in France*, p. 281.

3 Harbord, *Leaves from a War Diary*, p. 291.

4 Harbord, *Leaves from a War Diary*, p. 291.

5 Harbord, *Leaves from a War Diary*, pp. 291–92.

6 Harbord, *The American Army in France*, p. 283; Alan Axelrod, *Patton on Leadership* (Paramus, NJ: Prentice Hall Press, 1999), p. 59; Harbord, *The American Army in France*, p. 283.

7 Harbord, *Leaves from a War Diary*, p. 292.

8 Jean de Pierrefeu, *French Headquarters 1915–1918* (London: Geoffrey Bles, 1929), quoted in Asprey, *At Belleau Wood*, p. 96.

9 Pierrefeu, *French Headquarters*, quoted in Asprey, *At Belleau Wood*, p. 97.

10 Catlin, *"With the Help of God,"* p. 100.

CHAPTER 5: FIRST BLOOD

1 Elton E. Mackin, *Suddenly We Didn't Want to Die: Memoirs of a World War I Marine* (Novato, CA: Presidio Press, 1993), p. 66.

2 Mackin, *Suddenly We Didn't Want to Die*, pp. 67–68.

3 Suskind, *The Battle of Belleau Wood*, p. 19.

4 Suskind, *The Battle of Belleau Wood*, p. 18.

5 Suskind, *The Battle of Belleau Wood*, p. 19.

6 U.S. Marine Corps, *History of the Sixth Machine Gun Battalion* (Neuwied, Germany, 1919), quoted in Asprey, *At Belleau Wood*, p. 104.

7 U.S. Marine Corps, *History of the Sixth Machine Gun Battalion*, quoted in Asprey, *At Belleau Wood*, p. 104.

8 Cooke, "We Can Take It," quoted in Asprey, *At Belleau Wood*, p. 105.

9 Cooke, "We Can Take It," quoted in Asprey, *At Belleau Wood*, p. 106.

10 Cooke, "We Can Take It," quoted in Asprey, *At Belleau Wood*, p. 106.

11 Cooke, "We Can Take It," quoted in Asprey, *At Belleau Wood*, p. 106.

12 Cooke, "We Can Take It," quoted in Asprey, *At Belleau Wood*, p. 106.

[13]Interview with Shepherd, Asprey, *At Belleau Wood*, pp. 106–7.

[14]Interview with Shepherd, Asprey, *At Belleau Wood*, p.107.

[15]Floyd Gibbons, *"And They Thought We Wouldn't Fight"* (New York: George H. Doran, 1918), pp. 316–20.

[16]Suskind, *The Battle of Belleau Wood*, p. 21.

[17]Frederic M. Wise and Meigs O. Frost, *A Marine Tells It to You* (New York: J. H. Sears, 1929), p. 239.

[18]Clyburn O. Mattfeldt, comp., *Records of the Second Division (Regular)*, vol. 5 (Washington, DC: Army War College, 1925-27,), quoted in Asprey, *At Belleau Wood*, p. 109.

[19]Mattfeldt, *Records of the Second Division*, 6, quoted in Asprey, *At Belleau Wood*, p. 111.

CHAPTER 6: RETREAT, HELL!

[1] Mattfeldt, *Records of the Second Division*, 5, quoted in Asprey, *At Belleau Wood*, p. 112.

[2] Spaulding and Wright, *The Second Division American Expeditionary Force in France*, quoted in Asprey, *At Belleau Wood*, p. 115.

[3] Mattfeldt, *Records of the Second Division*, 5, quoted in Asprey, *At Belleau Wood*, p. 117.

[4] Mattfeldt, *Records of the Second Division*, 5, quoted in Asprey, *At Belleau Wood*, p. 118.

[5] Mattfledt, *Records of the Second Division*, 5, cited in Asprey, *At Belleau Wood*, p. 114.

[6] Mattfeldt, *Records of the Second Division*, 5, cited in Asprey, *At Belleau Wood*, p. 119.

[7] The source of this exclamation is discussed in Asprey, *At Belleau Wood*, p. 120.

[8] See Asprey, *At Belleau Wood*, p. 120.

[9] Mackin, *Suddenly We Didn't Want to Die*, p. 28.

[10]Mackin, *Suddenly We Didn't Want to Die*, p. 28.

[11]Mackin, *Suddenly We Didn't Want to Die*, pp. 28–29.

[12]Mackin, *Suddenly We Didn't Want to Die*, p. 29.

[13]Interview with Shepherd, Asprey, *At Belleau Wood*, p. 121.

[14]Catlin, *"With the Help of God and a Few Marines,"* p. 95.

[15]Catlin, *"With the Help of God and a Few Marines,"* p. 92.

[16]Catlin, *"With the Help of God and a Few Marines,"* p. 95.

[17]Catlin, *"With the Help of God and a Few Marines,"* pp. 95–96.

[18]Catlin, *"With the Help of God and a Few Marines,"* p. 94.

[19]Catlin, *"With the Help of God and a Few Marines,"* p. 94.

[20] Catlin, *"With the Help of God and a Few Marines,"* pp. 94–95.

[21] Craig Hamilton and Louise Corbin, *Echoes from Over There* (New York: Soldier's Publishing, 1919), quoted in Asprey, *At Belleau Wood*, p. 200.

[22] Catlin, *"With the Help of God and a Few Marines,"* p. 96.

[23] Interview with Shepherd, Asprey, *At Belleau Wood*, p. 123.

[24] Interview with Shepherd, Asprey, *At Belleau Wood*, p. 123.

[25] Interview with Shepherd, Asprey, *At Belleau Wood*, p. 123.

[26] Catlin, *"With the Help of God and a Few Marines,"* p. 93; Cowing and Cooper, *"Dear Folks at Home—,"* quoted in Asprey, *At Belleau Wood*, p. 123.

[27] Cowing and Cooper, *"Dear Folks at Home—,"* quoted in Asprey, *At Belleau Wood*, p. 123.

[28] Cowing and Cooper, *"Dear Folks at Home—,"* quoted in Asprey, *At Belleau Wood*, p. 124.

[29] Catlin, *"With the Help of God and a Few Marines,"* pp. 93–94.

[30] Catlin, *"With the Help of God and a Few Marines,"* p. 96.

[31] Catlin, *"With the Help of God and a Few Marines,"* p. 97.

CHAPTER 7: TEUFELHUNDEN

[1] Suskind, *The Battle of Belleau Wood*, p. 28.

[2] Hamilton and Corbin, *Echoes from Over There*, quoted in Asprey, *At Belleau Wood*, pp. 125–26.

[3] Hamilton and Corbin, *Echoes from Over There*, quoted in Asprey, *At Belleau Wood*, p. 126.

[4] Hamilton and Corbin, *Echoes from Over There*, quoted in Asprey, *At Belleau Wood*, p. 126.

[5] Hamilton and Corbin, *Echoes from Over There*, quoted in Asprey, *At Belleau Wood*, p. 126.

[6] Martin Gus Gulberg, *A War Diary* (Chicago: Drake Press, 1927), quoted in Asprey, *At Belleau Wood*, p. 126; Catlin, *"With the Help of God and a Few Marines,"* p. 86.

[7] Spaulding and Wright, *The Second Division American Expeditionary Force in France*, quoted in Asprey, *At Belleau Wood*, pp. 126–27.

[8] William R. Mathews, "Official Report to Headquarters, U.S. Marine Corps, September 28, 1921," quoted in Asprey, *At Belleau Wood*, p. 128.

[9] Mathews, "Official Report," quoted in Asprey, *At Belleau Wood*, pp. 128–29.

[10]Paul H. Clark to John J. Pershing, June 2, 1918, Papers of Paul Hedrick Clark, Library of Congress, quoted in Asprey, *At Belleau Wood*, p. 130.

[11]E. N. McClellan, "Capture of Hill 142, Battle of Belleau Wood, and Capture of Bouresches," *Marine Corps Gazette*, (September 1920), p. 278

[12]Catlin, *"With the Help of God and a Few Marines,"* pp. 103–4.

CHAPTER 8: HILL 142

[1] Suskind, *The Battle of Belleau Wood*, p. 28.

[2] Suskind, *The Battle of Belleau Wood*, p. 30.

[3] Mattfeldt, *Records of the Second Division*, 9, quoted in Asprey, *At Belleau Wood*, p. 142.

[4] Mattfeldt, *Records of the Second Division*, 3, quoted in Asprey, *At Belleau Wood*, pp. 142–43.

[5] Matfeldt, *Records of the Second Division*, 5, quoted in Asprey, *At Belleau Wood*, p. 144.

[6] John W. Thomason, *Fix Bayonets!* (New York: Charles Scribner's Sons, 1970), pp. 9–10.

[7] Thomason, *Fix Bayonets!* p. 10.

[8] Thomason, *Fix Bayonets!* p. 10.

[9] Thomason, *Fix Bayonets!* p. 12.

[10]Thomason, *Fix Bayonets!* p. 12.

[11]Thomason, *Fix Bayonets!* p. 12.

[12]Thomason, *Fix Bayonets!* p. 12.

[13]Thomason, *Fix Bayonets!* p. 13.

[14]Thomason, *Fix Bayonets!* p. 13.

[15]Thomason, *Fix Bayonets!* p. 12.

[16]Cowing and Cooper, *"Dear Folks at Home—,"* quoted in Asprey, *At Belleau Wood*, p. 145.

[17]Cowing and Cooper, *"Dear Folks at Home—,"* quoted in Asprey, *At Belleau Wood*, p. 146.

[18]Cowing and Cooper, *"Dear Folks at Home—,"* quoted in Asprey, *At Belleau Wood*, p. 146.

[19]Thomason, *Fix Bayonets!* p. 13.

[20]Thomason, *Fix Bayonets!* p. 15.

[21]Thomason, *Fix Bayonets!* p. 15.

[22]Thomason, *Fix Bayonets!* p. 15.

[23] Thomason, *Fix Bayonets!* p. 15.

[24] Cowing and Cooper, *"Dear Folks at Home—,"* quoted in Asprey, *At Belleau Wood,* p. 147.

[25] Mattfledt, *Records of the Second Division,* 5, quoted in Asprey, *At Belleau Wood,* p. 148.

[26] Mattfledt, *Records of the Second Division,* 5, quoted in Asprey, *At Belleau Wood,* p. 149.

[27] Mattfeldt, *Records of the Second Division,* 6, quoted in Asprey, *At Belleau Wood,* p. 149.

[28] Mattfledt, *Records of the Second Division,* 5, quoted in Asprey, *At Belleau Wood,* p. 150.

[29] James G. Harbord to Wendell Neville, June 6, 1918, Personal War Letters, Washington, DC, Library of Congress, quoted in Asprey, *At Belleau Wood,* pp. 151–52.

[30] Mattfeldt, *Records of the Second Division,* 5, quoted in Asprey, *At Belleau Wood,* p. 152.

[31] Mattfeldt, *Records of the Second Division,* 5, quoted in Asprey, *At Belleau Wood,* pp. 152–53 (my italics).

[32] Mattfeldt, *Records of the Second Division,* 5, quoted in Asprey, *At Belleau Wood,* p. 153.

[33] Mattfeldt, *Records of the Second Division,* 5, quoted in Asprey, *At Belleau Wood,* p. 153.

[34] Thomason, *Fix Bayonets!* p. 10.

[35] Thomason, *Fix Bayonets!* p. 22.

Chapter 9: A Dark, Sullen Mystery

[1] Thomason, *Fix Bayonets!* p. 19.

[2] Catlin, *"With the Help of God and a Few Marines,"* p. 103.

[3] Duke of Wellington to Thomas Creevey, June 19, 1815, in John Gore, ed., *Creevey: Selected and Re-edited from "The Creevey Papers" and "Creevey's Life and Times"* (London: Murray, 1948), p. 150.

[4] Harbord, *The American Army in France,* p. 289.

[5] Ernst Otto, "The Battles for the Possession of Belleau Woods, June 1918," *U.S. Naval Institute Proceedings* (November 1928), quoted in Asprey, *At Belleau Wood,* p. 161.

[6] Catlin, *"With the Help of God and a Few Marines,"* pp. 104, 106, 106–7.

[7] Mattfeldt, *Records of the Second Division,* 4, quoted in Asprey, *At Belleau Wood,* p. 162; Mattfeldt, *Records of the Second Division,* 6, quoted in Asprey, *At Belleau Wood,* p. 162.

[8] Mattfeldt, *Records of the Second Division,* 6, quoted in Asprey, *At Belleau Wood,* p. 161; Catlin, *"With the Help of God and a Few Marines,"* p. 112.

[9] Catlin, *"With the Help of God and a Few Marines,"* pp. 112, 108.

[10] Catlin, *"With the Help of God and a Few Marines,"* p. 108.

11 Catlin, *"With the Help of God and a Few Marines,"* p. 108.

12 Catlin, *"With the Help of God and a Few Marines,"* p. 109.

13 Catlin, *"With the Help of God and a Few Marines,"* p. 110.

14 Catlin, *"With the Help of God and a Few Marines,"* p. 111.

15 Catlin, *"With the Help of God and a Few Marines,"* p. 112.

16 Gibbons, *"And They Thought We Wouldn't Fight,"* p. 307.

17 Gibbons, *"And They Thought We Wouldn't Fight,"* p. 307.

18 Gibbons, *"And They Thought We Wouldn't Fight,"* p. 307; Catlin, *"With the Help of God and a Few Marines,"* p. 111; Gibbons, *"And They Thought We Wouldn't Fight,"* pp. 307–8.

19 Gibbons, *"And They Thought We Wouldn't Fight,"* p. 308.

20 Gibbons, *"And They Thought We Wouldn't Fight,"* p. 308.

21 Gibbons, *"And They Thought We Wouldn't Fight,"* p. 309.

22 Catlin, *"With the Help of God and a Few Marines,"* p. 112; Gibbons, *"And They Thought We Wouldn't Fight,"* p. 298; Catlin, *"With the Help of God and a Few Marines,"* p. 113.

23 Catlin, *"With the Help of God and a Few Marines,"* p. 114.

24 Mackin, *Suddenly We Didn't Want to Die*, p. 83.

Chapter 10: "Do You Want to Live Forever?"

1 Catlin, *"With the Help of God and a Few Marines,"* p. 114.

2 Catlin, *"With the Help of God and a Few Marines,"* p. 114.

3 Gibbons, *"And They Thought We Wouldn't Fight,"* p. 303.

4 Gibbons, *"And They Thought We Wouldn't Fight,"* pp. 303–4.

5 Marine Corps Legacy Museum, "Sergeant Major Daniel J. Daly, USMC," http://www.mclm.com/tohonor/ddaly.html. Accessed January 25, 2007.

6 Medal of Honor, "Double Congressional Medal of Honor Recipient Sergeant Major Daniel Joseph Daly," http://www.medalofhonor.com/DanDaly.htm. Accessed January 25, 2007.

7 Catlin, *"With the Help of God and a Few Marines,"* p. 126.

8 Catlin, *"With the Help of God and a Few Marines,"* p. 114; Mattfeldt, *Records of the Second Division*, 5, quoted in Asprey, *At Belleau Wood*, p. 172; Catlin, *"With the Help of God and a Few Marines,"* p. 114.

9 Gibbons, *"And They Thought We Wouldn't Fight,"* pp. 310–11.

[10] Gibbons, *"And They Thought We Wouldn't Fight,"* pp. 310–11.

[11] Gibbons, *"And They Thought We Wouldn't Fight,"* pp. 311–12.

[12] Gibbons, *"And They Thought We Wouldn't Fight,"* p. 312.

[13] Gibbons, *"And They Thought We Wouldn't Fight,"* p. 312.

[14] Gibbons, *"And They Thought We Wouldn't Fight,"* p. 313.

[15] Gibbons, *"And They Thought We Wouldn't Fight,"* pp. 313–14.

[16] Gibbons, *"And They Thought We Wouldn't Fight,"* p. 314.

[17] Gibbons, *"And They Thought We Wouldn't Fight,"* p. 314.

[18] George V. Gordon, *Leathernecks and Doughboys* (Chicago: privately printed, 1927), cited in Asprey, *At Belleau Wood,* p. 173.

[19] Catlin, *"With the Help of God and a Few Marines,"* p. 115.

[20] Catlin, *"With the Help of God and a Few Marines,"* p. 115.

[21] *Leatherneck,* "Oldest Marine Found Living in Syracuse, NY," http://www.leatherneck.com/forums/showthread.php?t=10334. Accessed January 25, 2007.

[22] Catlin, *"With the Help of God and a Few Marines,"* pp. 115–16.

[23] Catlin, *"With the Help of God and a Few Marines,"* p. 116.

[24] Catlin, *"With the Help of God and a Few Marines,"* p. 117.

[25] Catlin, *"With the Help of God and a Few Marines,"* pp. 117–18.

[26] Catlin, *"With the Help of God and a Few Marines,"* p. 119.

[27] Catlin, *"With the Help of God and a Few Marines,"* p. 119.

[28] Catlin, *"With the Help of God and a Few Marines,"* p. 119.

[29] Catlin, *"With the Help of God and a Few Marines,"* pp. 120–21.

[30] Catlin, *"With the Help of God and a Few Marines,"* p. 121.

[31] Louis F. Timmerman, *War Diary, 1917–1919* (unpublished manuscript in private collection), quoted in Asprey, *At Belleau Wood,* p. 179.

[32] Timmerman, *War Diary,* quoted in Asprey, *At Belleau Wood,* p. 179.

[33] Timmerman, *War Diary,* quoted in Asprey, *At Belleau Wood,* pp. 179–80.

[34] Timmerman, *War Diary,* quoted in Asprey, *At Belleau Wood,* p. 180.

[35] Timmerman, *War Diary,* quoted in Asprey, *At Belleau Wood,* p. 181.

Chapter 11: Taking Bouresches

[1] Catlin, *"With the Help of God and a Few Marines,"* p. 123.

2 General Graves B. Erskine, USMC (ret.), letter to Asprey, quoted in Asprey, *At Belleau Wood*, p. 182.

3 André Maurois, *Semper Fidelis* (New York: Marine Corps League of New York, n.d.), quoted in Asprey, *At Belleau Wood*, p. 183.

4 Mr. and Mrs. William Wyly, letter to Asprey, quoted in Asprey, *At Belleau Wood*, p. 183.

5 Wyly to Asprey, quoted in Asprey, *At Belleau Wood*, p. 184.

6 Wyly to Asprey, quoted in Asprey, *At Belleau Wood*, p. 184.

7 Wyly to Asprey, quoted in Asprey, *At Belleau Wood*, p. 184.

8 Wyly to Asprey, quoted in Asprey, *At Belleau Wood*, p. 184.

9 Wyly to Asprey, quoted in Asprey, *At Belleau Wood*, p. 184.

10 Wyly to Asprey, quoted in Asprey, *At Belleau Wood*, p. 185.

11 Catlin, "*With the Help of God and a Few Marines*," p. 133.

12 Catlin, "*With the Help of God and a Few Marines*," p. 133.

13 Catlin, "*With the Help of God and a Few Marines*," p. 134.

14 Mackin, *Suddenly We Didn't Want to Die*, p. 68.

15 Mackin, *Suddenly We Didn't Want to Die*, p. 69.

16 Mackin, *Suddenly We Didn't Want to Die*, p. 69.

17 Catlin, "*With the Help of God and a Few Marines*," pp. 126, 128.

18 Catlin, "*With the Help of God and a Few Marines*," pp. 128–29.

19 Mattfeldt, *Records of the Second Division*, 6, quoted in Asprey, *At Belleau Wood*, p. 191.

20 Mattfeldt, *Records of the Second Division*, 5, quoted in Asprey, *At Belleau Wood*, p. 188; Mattfeldt, *Records of the Second Division*, 6, quoted in Asprey, *At Belleau Wood*, p. 189.

CHAPTER 12: ARMIES OF THE NIGHT

1 Mattfeldt, *Records of the Second Division*, 6, quoted in Asprey, *At Belleau Wood*, pp. 193–94.

2 Suskind, *The Battle of Belleau Wood*, p. 47.

3 Mattfeldt, *Records of the Second Division*, 6, quoted in Asprey, *At Belleau Wood*, p. 196.

4 Cooke, "*We Can Take It*," quoted in Asprey, *At Belleau Wood*, p. 197.

5 Wise and Frost, *A Marine Tells It to You*, p. 239.

6 Wise and Frost, *A Marine Tells It to You*, p. 239.

7 Wise and Frost, *A Marine Tells It to You*, p. 239.

[8] Wise and Frost, *A Marine Tells It to You*, p. 240.

[9] Interview with Shepherd, Asprey, *At Belleau Wood*, p. 199.

[10] Interview with Shepherd, Asprey, *At Belleau Wood*, p. 199.

[11] Cooke, "We Can Take It," quoted in Asprey, *At Belleau Wood*, p. 199.

[12] Cooke, "We Can Take It," quoted in Asprey, *At Belleau Wood*, p. 199.

[13] Hamilton and Corbin, *Echoes from Over There*, quoted in Asprey, *At Belleau Wood*, p. 200.

[14] Interview with Shepherd, Asprey, *At Belleau Wood*, p. 200.

[15] Cooke, "We Can Take It," quoted in Asprey, *At Belleau Wood*, p. 201.

[16] Cooke, "We Can Take It," quoted in Asprey, *At Belleau Wood*, p. 201.

[17] Cooke, "We Can Take It," quoted in Asprey, *At Belleau Wood*, p. 201.

[18] Cooke, "We Can Take It," quoted in Asprey, *At Belleau Wood*, p. 201.

[19] Cooke, "We Can Take It," quoted in Asprey, *At Belleau Wood*, p. 201.

[20] Mattfeldt, *Records of the Second Division*, 6, quoted in Asprey, *At Belleau Wood*, pp. 203–4.

[21] Mattfeldt, *Records of the Second Division*, 6, quoted in Asprey, *At Belleau Wood*, pp. 203–4.

[22] *Chicago Daily Tribune*, June 6 and 7, 1918, p. 1; *New York Times*, June 9, 1918, p. 2.

[23] Robert Lee Bullard, *Personalities and Reminiscences of the War* (Garden City, NY: Doubleday, Page, 1925), pp. 208–9.

[24] Bullard, *Personalities and Reminiscences of the War*, p. 209.

[25] Bullard, *Personalities and Reminiscences of the War*, p. 209.

[26] *New York Times*, June 9, 1918, p. 18.

CHAPTER 13: "CHEAP SUCCESSES"

[1] *New York Times*, June 7, 1918, p. 1; Lee Meriwether, *The War Diary of a Diplomat* (New York: Dodd, Mead, 1919), quoted in Asprey, *At Belleau Wood*, p. 219.

[2] Suskind, *The Battle of Belleau Wood*, p. 49.

[3] Suskind, *The Battle of Belleau Wood*, p. 50.

[4] Suskind, *The Battle of Belleau Wood*, p. 50.

[5] Gordon, *Leathernecks and Doughboys*, quoted in Asprey, *At Belleau Wood*, pp. 204–5.

[6] Catlin, *"With the Help of God and a Few Marines,"* p. 150.

[7] Catlin, *"With the Help of God and a Few Marines,"* p. 150.

[8] "Medical Department" records quoted in Asprey, *At Belleau Wood*, p. 207.

[9] Mattfeldt, *Records of the Second Division*, 6, quoted in Asprey, *At Belleau Wood*, p. 207; Cooke, "We Can Take It," quoted in Asprey, *At Belleau Wood*, p. 208.

[10] Cooke, "We Can Take It," quoted in Asprey, *At Belleau Wood*, pp. 208–9.

[11] Interview with Louis F. Timmerman, Asprey, *At Belleau Wood*, p. 211.

[12] Catlin, *"With the Help of God and a Few Marines,"* pp. 124–25.

[13] Interview with Timmerman, Asprey, *At Belleau Wood*, p. 212.

[14] Mattfeldt, *Records of the Second Division*, 5, quoted in Asprey, *At Belleau Wood*, pp. 212–13.

[15] Mattfeldt, *Records of the Second Division*, 6, quoted in Asprey, *At Belleau Wood*, p. 213.

[16] Mattfeldt, *Records of the Second Division*, 6, quoted in Asprey, *At Belleau Wood*, p. 213.

[17] Interview with Timmerman, Asprey, *At Belleau Wood*, p. 238.

[18] Mattfeldt, *Records of the Second Division*, 6, quoted in Asprey, *At Belleau Wood*, p. 243.

[19] Cooke, "We Can Take It," quoted in Asprey, *At Belleau Wood*, p. 252.

[20] Cooke, "We Can Take It," quoted in Asprey, *At Belleau Wood*, p. 252.

[21] Cowing and Cooper, *"Dear Folks at Home—,"* quoted in Asprey, *At Belleau Wood*, pp. 252–53.

[22] The following is from an interview with General Gerald C. Thomas, USMC (ret.), Asprey, *At Belleau Wood*, p. 253.

[23] Cooke, "We Can Take It," quoted in Asprey, *At Belleau Wood*, p. 255.

[24] Cooke, "We Can Take It," quoted in Asprey, *At Belleau Wood*, p. 255.

[25] Cooke, "We Can Take It," quoted in Asprey, *At Belleau Wood*, p. 255.

[26] Cooke, "We Can Take It," quoted in Asprey, *At Belleau Wood*, p. 256.

[27] Cooke, "We Can Take It," quoted in Asprey, *At Belleau Wood*, p. 256.

[28] Mattfeldt, *Records of the Second Division*, 6, quoted in Asprey, *At Belleau Wood*, p. 257.

[29] Mattfeldt, *Records of the Second Division*, 6, quoted in Asprey, *At Belleau Wood*, pp. 258, 259.

[30] Harbord, *Leaves from a War Diary*, p. 297.

[31] Harbord, *Leaves from a War Diary*, pp. 297–99.

[32] Mattfeldt, *Records of the Second Division*, 4, quoted in Asprey, *At Belleau Wood*, p. 259.

Chapter 14: A Mad Lust

[1] Harbord, *Leaves from a War Diary*, p. 298.

[2] Harbord, *Leaves from a War Diary*, p. 298.

[3] Suskind, *The Battle of Belleau Wood*, pp. 54, 55; George S. Patton Jr., *War as I Knew It* (1947; repr., Boston: Houghton Mifflin, 1995), p. 339; Suskind, *The Battle of Belleau Wood*, pp. 55–56.

[4] Mattfeldt, *Records of the Second Division*, 6, quoted in Asprey, *At Belleau Wood*, p. 259.

[5] Mattfeldt, *Records of the Second Division*, 6, quoted in Asprey, *At Belleau Wood*, p. 261.

[6] Mathews, "Official Report," quoted in Asprey, *At Belleau Wood*, p. 262.

[7] Mathews, "Official Report," quoted in Asprey, *At Belleau Wood*, p. 262.

[8] Mathews, "Official Report," quoted in Asprey, *At Belleau Wood*, p. 262.

[9] Mathews, "Official Report," quoted in Asprey, *At Belleau Wood*, p. 262.

[10] Mathews, "Official Report," quoted in Asprey, *At Belleau Wood*, p. 262.

[11] Mattfeldt, *Records of the Second Division*, 6, quoted in Asprey, *At Belleau Wood*, p. 262.

[12] Mathews, "Official Report," quoted in Asprey, *At Belleau Wood*, p. 263.

[13] Mathews, "Official Report," quoted in Asprey, *At Belleau Wood*, pp. 263–64.

[14] *New York Times*, June 12, 1918, p. 1.

[15] Mattfeldt, *Records of the Second Division*, 6, quoted in Asprey, *At Belleau Wood*, p. 270.

[16] Mattfeldt, *Records of the Second Division*, 6, quoted in Asprey, *At Belleau Wood*, p. 270; Suskind, *The Battle of Belleau Wood*, p. 57.

[17] Wise and Frost, *A Marine Tells It to You*, p. 239.

[18] Wise and Frost, *A Marine Tells It to You*, p. 239.

[19] Wise and Frost, *A Marine Tells It to You*, p. 240.

[20] Wise and Frost, *A Marine Tells It to You*, p. 241.

[21] Mattfeldt, *Records of the Second Division*, 6, cited in Asprey, *At Belleau Wood*, p. 273.

[22] Cooke, "We Can Take It," quoted in Asprey, *At Belleau Wood*, p. 274.

[23] Cooke, "We Can Take It," quoted in Asprey, *At Belleau Wood*, p. 275.

[24] Cooke, "We Can Take It," quoted in Asprey, *At Belleau Wood*, pp. 276–77.

[25] Mattfeldt, *Records of the Second Division*, 5, quoted in Asprey, *At Belleau Wood*, p. 281.

CHAPTER 15: BOIS DE LA BRIGADE DE MARINE

[1] Wise and Frost, *A Marine Tells It to You*, p. 245.

[2] Wise and Frost, *A Marine Tells It to You*, p. 245.

[3] General Clifton B. Cates, USMC (ret.), letter to his family, June 18, 1918, quoted in Asprey, *At Belleau Wood*, pp. 289–90.

[4] Cates, letter to his family, June 18, 1918, quoted in Asprey, *At Belleau Wood*, p. 290.

[5] Suskind, *The Battle of Belleau Wood*, p. 66; Mattfeldt, *Records of the Second Division*, 6, quoted in Asprey, *At Belleau Wood*, pp. 291–92.

[6] Mattfeldt, *Records of the Second Division*, 6, quoted in Asprey, *At Belleau Wood*, p. 292.

[7] E. N. McClellan, "Capture of Hill 142, Battle of Belleau Wood, and Capture of Bouresches," *Marine Corps Gazette* (September 1920), p. 278.

[8] McClellan, "Capture of Hill 142," p. 278.

[9] Wise and Frost, *A Marine Tells It to You*, p. 241.

[10] Cooke, "We Can Take It," quoted in Asprey, *At Belleau Wood*, pp. 297–98; Suskind, *The Battle of Belleau Wood*, p. 67; Wise and Frost, *A Marine Tells It to You*, p. 244.

[11] Suskind, *The Battle of Belleau Wood*, p. 67.

[12] Cates, letter to his family, June 18, 1918, quoted in Asprey, *At Belleau Wood*, p. 299.

[13] Mattfeldt, *Records of the Second Division*, 6, quoted in Asprey, *At Belleau Wood*, p. 296.

[14] Cates, letter to his family, June 18, 1918, quoted in Asprey, *At Belleau Wood*, pp. 306–7.

[15] Mattfeldt, *Records of the Second Division*, 6, quoted in Asprey, *At Belleau Wood*, p. 313.

[16] Laurence Stallings, *The Doughboys* (1963; reprint ed., New York: Popular Library, 1964), p. 128.

[17] Mattfeldt, *Records of the Second Division*, 5, quoted in Asprey, *At Belleau Wood*, p. 316.

[18] Catlin, *"With the Help of God and a Few Marines,"* p. 125.

[19] Mattfeldt, *Records of the Second Division*, 6, quoted in Asprey, *At Belleau Wood*, p. 322.

[20] Mattfeldt, *Records of the Second Division*, 6, quoted in Asprey, *At Belleau Wood*, p. 345.

[21] Harbord, *Leaves from a War Diary*, pp. 294–95.

[22] Bliss and Ridgway quoted in Suskind, *The Battle of Belleau Wood*, p. 75; Robert Lee Bullard, quoted in Anne Cipriano Venzon, ed., *The United States in the First World War: An Encyclopedia* (New York: Garland, 1995), p. 77.

▪ Index ▪

June 4

June 4

June 14

June 5 –

June 15 –

July 10 (a.m.)

Ais.
Ar.
Cen

Les Mares
Farm

CHAMPILLON

MARIGNY

LUCY-LE-BOCAGE

Paris Farm

▲ TO PARIS

COMPRU

2ND DIVISION OPERATIONS JUNE 4–JULY 10, 1918 • (7